THE HERITAGE STATE

THE HERITAGE STATE

RELIGION AND PRESERVATION
IN CONTEMPORARY QATAR

TRINIDAD RICO

CORNELL UNIVERSITY PRESS
Ithaca and London

First published 2025 by Cornell University Press

Library of Congress Cataloging-in-Publication Data

Names: Rico, Trinidad, author.
Title: The heritage state : religion and preservation in contemporary Qatar / Trinidad Rico.
Description: Ithaca : Cornell University Press, 2025. | Includes bibliographical references and index
Identifiers: LCCN 2024029629 (print) | LCCN 2024029630 (ebook) | ISBN 9781501781216 (hardcover) | ISBN 9781501781223 (epub) | ISBN 9781501781230 (pdf)
Subjects: LCSH: Cultural property—Protection—Qatar. | Cultural property—Protection—Religious aspects—Islam. | World Heritage areas—Qatar.
Classification: LCC DS247.Q33 R53 2025 (print) | LCC DS247.Q33 (ebook) | DDC 363.6/9095363—dc23/eng/20241112
LC record available at https://lccn.loc.gov/2024029629
LC ebook record available at https://lccn.loc.gov/2024029630

To Ailin, Kenza, Liyam, Juli, and Nadia

Contents

Acknowledgments

I had the opportunity to live and work in Doha for five years, first, as faculty member at the (now-disbanded) University College London Qatar (UCL Qatar) and, later, at the (soon-to-be-disbanded) Texas A&M University at Qatar, where I taught heritage and anthropology at graduate and undergraduate levels. My fieldwork and research during this time were supported by these institutions and two interdisciplinary grants from the Qatar National Research Foundation's National Priorities Research Program from 2013 to 2017. These involved heritage ethnography in Qatar, as well as archival research in Qatar, the United Arab Emirates, France, Switzerland, and the United Kingdom. Shorter field trips after I emigrated from Qatar to the United States were supported by my current institution, Rutgers University, and a generous Senior Visiting Fellowship at UCL Qatar in 2019. The final stages of research, writing, and projecting the direction of this volume were supported by a Burkhardt Residential Fellowship for Recently Tenured Scholars from the American Council of Learned Societies (ACLS), a residential fellowship at the Center for Advanced Study in the Behavioral Sciences (CASBS) of Stanford University; a very supportive visiting scholar position at the Institute for Research in the Social Sciences (IRISS) at Stanford University; an affiliate visiting scholar position at the Abbasi Program in Islamic Studies at Stanford University; and a visiting faculty position at the Center for Philanthropy and Civil Society, also at Stanford University. This monograph was possible thanks to all of these institutional programs and their supportive leadership.

This research project in Qatar was infused with a profound and transformative attachment to locality. Ethnographic heritage fieldwork involves personal and sensorial interactions that, in my case, included becoming a lecturer and a parent for the first time while living in the field. Yet affective interactions in the literature of heritage studies are focused mostly on the experience of heritage by its legitimate stakeholders and stewards, not necessarily on the experience of the researchers who are documenting and translating these relationships and conversations. Therefore, I am profoundly indebted to all those who accompanied me so patiently in this strange, uncomfortable, and at times intoxicating journey of infatuation with one's field site. A long and diverse list of colleagues who provided comments and platforms for discussing much earlier versions of my work at their seminars and events hail from the fields of anthropology, archaeology, architecture, art history, Egyptology, history, Islamic studies, Middle East studies, political science, religious studies, and history of science. They include David Morgan, Gertjan Pletz, Hassan Bashir, Kishwar Rizvi, Lynn Meskell, Mirjam Brusius, Nora Barakat, Rob Reich, Roberto Fabbri, Rodney Harrison, and Sultan Sooud Al Qassemi. For providing additional input and encouragement however small, I thank Aliasger Madraswala, Andrew Bauer, Anna Bigelow, Elizabeth Roberts, Giulia El Dardiry, James Delbourgo, Jörg Matthias Determann, Kristin O'Brassil-Kulfan, Maria de los Ángeles Picone, Mudit Trivedi, Nancy Um, Natalie Koch, Omür Harmanşah, Rachel Ama Asaa Engmann, Rachel Douglas-Jones, Robert Carter, Okasha El Daly, Remah Gharib, Shanon Fitzpatrick, Sharon Block, Suzie Kilshaw, Tanya Kane, and Todd Reisz. Other valuable friends and acquaintances, particularly in Qatar, cannot be listed in full, but I hope that they can identify themselves in this brief list: Ahmad, Alaa, Alice, Anya, Aziz, Ben, Farouq, Fran, Khadija, Mariam, Michael, Nour, Sebastian, and Simone. A special thanks goes to Alexandre Coutelle at the UNESCO Archives in Paris, the archivists at the Research Library and Archives of the National Gallery of Australia, and Ibrahim Jaidah and his team.

List of Abbreviations

ALECSO	Arab League Educational, Cultural, and Scientific Organization
COP	United Nations Climate Change Conference of the Parties
GCC	Gulf Cooperation Council
GSAS	Global Sustainability Assessment System
ICESCO	Islamic World Educational Scientific and Cultural Organization (formerly ISESCO)
ICOMOS	International Council on Monuments and Sites
IUCN	International Union for Conservation of Nature
MAC	Msheireb Arts Center
MIA	Museum of Islamic Art
MME	Ministry of Municipality and Environment
NMQ	National Museum of Qatar
ODQ	Origins of Doha and Qatar
OIC	Organization of the Islamic Conference
PEO	Private Emir Office
QBG	Quranic Botanic Garden
QDF	Qatar Development Fund
QGBC	Qatar Green Building Council
QMA	Qatar Museums Authority (now Qatar Museums, QM)
QNL	Qatar National Library
QNV	Qatar National Vision 2030
QUIP	Qatar Unified Imaging Project
UNESCO	United Nations Educational, Scientific, and Cultural Organization

Introduction

Heritage (Cult)ure

In December 2001, specialists in Muslim law and religion, as well as cultural heritage experts, convened in Doha for the Doha Symposium of 'Ulamâ on Cultural Heritage.[1] Through the involvement of 'ulama' (Muslim scholars), the meeting was organized to formulate the point of view of Islam regarding the preservation of cultural heritage. Earlier that year, in February 2001, the Taliban leadership of the Islamic emirate of Afghanistan had completely and theatrically destroyed the sixth- and seventh-century Buddhist statues at the valley of Bamiyan. Despite international and institutional outcry, the leader of the Taliban, Mullah Muhammad Omar, issued a religious edict that condemned non-Islamic statues and sanctuaries across Afghanistan. Observers and critics called it a jihad, an oversimplification of a "holy war," while the Taliban argued that the 'ulama' "had not advanced any convincing religious arguments against the destruction of the statues."[2] Against this backdrop, attendees of the Doha Symposium drafted the Doha Statement, a consequential document laying out principles for preserving cultural heritage. The foreword of this statement declared, "Muslims can neither approve nor sanction the intentional destruction of any part of human heritage."[3] It also called for strengthening the Muslim religion's tolerance of pre- and non-Islamic heritage.

The recommendations contained in the Doha Statement joined other doctrinal and advisory documents on matters of cultural protection and understanding under the United Nations Educational, Scientific, and Cultural Organization (UNESCO). Contrary to widely circulated documents such as the Hague Convention for the Protection of Cultural Property in the Event of Armed Conflict (1954), the Doha Statement is a lesser-known but historically significant collaboration between UNESCO and key regional organizations that represent the Muslim world: the Organization of the Islamic Conference (OIC), the Islamic World Educational Scientific and Cultural Organization (ISESCO, now ICESCO) and the Arab League Educational, Cultural, and Scientific Organization (ALECSO). While these are long-standing institutions in the political culture of the Muslim and Arab world, this kind of diplomatic intervention on global cultural heritage debates was unprecedented. Until then, representation of Muslim voices—in terms of both expertise and authority—had been very limited in the history of UNESCO's culture sector, restrained by a global heritage tradition that favored Western and secular interpretations of heritage value.[4]

The December 2001 meeting partly built on this tradition. It was chaired by His Highness Sheikh Hamad bin Khalifa al-Thani, then emir of the State of Qatar, and supported by key diplomatic figures, including Afghan and Syrian ambassadors, the French ambassador to Iran and Pakistan, the permanent delegate of Qatar to UNESCO, and high-ranking officials from ICESCO, ALECSO, and various cultural sectors of UNESCO. What was unique was having advocates representing the rich geographical and cultural diversity within the Muslim world come together in Doha to articulate a specifically Islamic vision for the future preservation of cultural heritage. Nevertheless, this vision contained within it an unresolved tension: the mobilization of secularist ideas of preservation to strengthen national identity while strategically centering traditional religious identities and structures of authority in heritage discourse and governance at local, regional, and global scales.

The meeting in Doha marked a time when the Muslim world was gaining visibility and authority in matters of heritage preservation by expertly engaging with UNESCO's global discourse, while also growing their own brand of heritage advocacy. At the same time, the bolstering of Islamic heritage as a target of heritage safeguarding, which had been sidelined in more Eurocentric preservation efforts, was on the rise in the construction of national identities. A leading player in these strategic mobilizations, Qatar has since launched one of the fastest-growing national heritage industries in the Middle East region, while crafting a privileged place for itself in global heritage debates. Charting the growth of Qatar's heritage preservation culture, therefore, offers crucial insights into the evolving roles of religious value and forms of authority involved in how heritage is conceptualized by myriad institutions and publics that are created and brought into interaction through preservation and its governance.

While Qatar's efforts at creating an influential heritage sector go back to the earliest days of the nation in the 1970s, its stature in this field grew by an order of magnitude following the turn of the new millennium. Qatar's role in the negotiations that aimed to overturn the Taliban's decision to destroy the Bamiyan Buddhas had more of an impact than the mere hosting of a thematic meeting. In the preceding months, the Qatari ambassador to UNESCO, His Eminence Ali Zainal, became instrumental in facilitating negotiations with the Taliban that had aimed to preserve the statues.[5] Early in the crisis, it had become apparent that other diplomatic figures, such as Ambassador Pierre Lafrance in Pakistan (the special envoy for UNESCO in Afghanistan), would not be appropriate brokers for a conflict that had been articulated from the beginning through a crisis of religious principles. Mounir Bouchenaki, director general for the International Study of the Preservation and Restoration of Cultural Property (ICCROM), relied on Zainal's support to liaise with the eminent Sheikh Yusuf al-Qaradawi in Doha, described as one of the most respected religious leaders of the Arab world at the time.[6] Here, al-Qaradawi was persuaded to go to Afghanistan on UNESCO's behest. Traveling on an aircraft provided to UNESCO by Emir Sheikh Hamad bin Khalifa al-Thani, a religious delegation of fifteen personalities met with the Taliban's minister of religious affairs and the Afghan minister of foreign affairs. Alas, they were unable to meet Mullah Omar, nor were they able to convince the religious authorities there to renounce the application of the decree toward the demolition of the monuments, and the two Buddhas were destroyed at the close of the Islamic festival of Eid al-Adha of that year. Qatar then volunteered to host the meeting of religious leaders that resulted in the Doha Statement.

Qatar's 2001 involvement in global heritage governance during a crisis of this magnitude was unprecedented in more than one way. Its actions put a Muslim-majority nation at the center of a debate over an act of iconoclasm, which it portrayed as a concern of and for Islam writ large. This happened at a time when discussions about cultural heritage taking place in the Muslim world had been predominantly, if not exclusively, marked by seemingly constant controversy, stuck into "structures of representation" that produced damaging stereotypes about the way in which the *umma* (community of Muslims) relates to the non-Muslim world.[7] In the predominantly secular contexts for global heritage advocacy historically dominated by the Anglo-American world, cultural heritage preservation narratives associated with Islam overwhelmingly occupy two themes: iconoclasm and uneducated neglect. In fact, the Taliban's actions were not an isolated incident in global heritage governance involving the Muslim world. It was followed by the destruction of fifteenth-century shrines in the Malian city of Timbuktu by the al-Qaeda-affiliated Islamist group Ansar Dine in 2012, and the theatrical erasure of ancient and historic sites by the Islamic State of Iraq and the Levant (ISIL) in both Syria and Iraq starting in 2015. These incidents were accompanied by countless reports in popular and academic circles on the looting, bombing, erasing, and terrorizing of archaeological sites and museums across the region. The trope of Islam being intrinsically opposed to or incapable of protecting what many see as universally significant cultural heritage sites has been especially accentuated in reporting strategies about the region since the first Gulf War in 1991, and intensified in the aftermath of the September 11 terrorist attacks in the United States in 2001 and then, again, in 2011 during the Arab Spring. Qatar's advocacy for aligning with a global heritage culture at the 2001 meeting contradicted these representations.

Another way in which Qatar's efforts were unprecedented was in proposing a solution that foregrounded Islamic tradition, teachings, and expertise. Historically, the emergence of global or universal heritage preservation culture as primarily Eurocentric and post-Enlightenment projects had resulted in an unapologetic marginalization of religious traditions in ideas about heritage, including religious forms of knowledge, expertise, and teachings.[8] Instead, the preservation of cultural heritage on a global scale has operated as a secularist ideology that recognizes, but does not necessarily allow participation in, religious traditions and those who practice them. At best, this stance overrides any existing uses and interpretations of heritage value by religious believer-communities and their authorities. At worst, it severs the connection between a people and their places of significance. Functionally, this can result in the expropriation of sites from communities that have traditionally lived near or used places in the name of a benefit to humanity—in strict alignment with their use as sites of global heritage value, as has been dictated in this field and practice by a predominantly secular Global North. Therefore, Qatar's initiative prior to and during the Doha Statement tested the authority and relevance of a powerful global culture of heritage preservation that has notoriously been dismissive of living religious traditions in general. Engaging the global platform, instruments, and publics of UNESCO itself to architect what could have been a historic move in heritage diplomacy, Qatar centered Islamic vernacular realities and futures, including its own, in the mobilization of heritage value.[9]

In one sweeping move, Qatar's vision of a global and local tradition of heritage preservation consolidated. Simultaneously, the nation embarked on an expansive program to build a heritage industry to serve a growing nation profoundly influenced by Islam. These efforts included training a new generation of scholars and experts, as well as intensifying the development, management, and interpretation of cultural heritage and its public at home. Contributing to global heritage and investing in local heritage are efforts that are difficult to coordinate, as they involve the creation and stimulation of two different cultures of heritage: a global secular heritage culture historically obstructive of religious authority, and a local religious heritage culture invested in vernacular traditions that serve and promote an openly religious civil society. The experts involved in these overlying cultural projects, nonetheless, have often been the same, as are the historical resources and built environments mobilized in support of both heritage industries. Qatar's interventions disturbed these distinctions, proposing to usher in an era of openly religious debate in the work of heritage preservation.

Through the case study of Qatar, this book identifies and analyzes a postsecular heritage awakening that recognizes that "religion maintains a public influence and relevance" and, therefore, influences the way in which heritage preservation traditions or cultures are established, circulated, and understood.[10] There is no single way of constructing heritage resources and narratives, despite what the universalizing discourse of heritage preservation might propose. In fact, heritage preservation practices and agendas are set by powerful interlocutors as part of broader political economies that attend to social and historical processes. While it has been recognized that these processes mobilize global, local, institutional and diplomatic forces, it is now possible to centralize the influence of religious forces, including religious nationalism, in the operations of different heritage traditions. This book asks how Islam can be mobilized in support of heritage preservation objectives and, in turn, how Muslim publics are mobilized in support of heritage agendas. Throughout the chapters that follow, I discuss the configurations of heritage value that permit religious tradition and authority to be coded into curatorial practices that produce heritage places, discourses, performances, and publics within Qatar, and sometimes through Qatari diplomatic channels, at regional and global scales. Through the examination of historical sources, ethnographic accounts, and contemporary archaeology, this book foregrounds Qatar not simply as a place where unique heritage debates happen, but as a regional actor that *makes* unique heritage debates happen. More specifically, in its efforts to navigate the historical gulf between institutionalized preservation ideologies and lived Muslim identities and traditions, Qatar has been leading efforts to assemble a culture of heritage that can and should be altered by religious beliefs and practices. This reassembly is important because of its impacts on preservation practices not only within Qatar, the Gulf, and the wider Muslim world, but also for how heritage culture and its experts, institutions, and publics care for the past and the future on a global scale.

The Fundamentalism of Preservation and the "Heritage Cult"

Qatar's interventions in heritage preservation discourse have continually engaged with a Eurocentric global heritage industry organized around an unstated dogma of secularism. Here, secularism is a coherent ideology that excludes, but does not negate the existence of, religious experiences and authorities in doctrine, institutions, and bodies involved in the sphere of cultural heritage. The exclusion of faith as epistemology does not erase sacrality in heritage value; rather, it subdues sacred narratives and authorities in heritage preservation discourses and practices. This results in a defining tension in the history of global heritage between the clear recognition of religious thought as a constituent force behind the places and traditions that form part of the assemblage of global heritage industries and the discomfort with religious thought and decision-making in contemporary interpretations and uses of heritage. Therefore, we might productively highlight the fundamentalist character of global heritage's commitment to secularism by characterizing it as a "heritage cult" in and of itself. In addition to flipping the script on what and who are considered ideological or extreme in heritage discourse, this framing provides a way of understanding the existing normative assumptions and hierarchies of value and power that defined the global heritage field in which Qatar has increasingly engaged—and sought to reconfigure in key ways—over the last half century.

To appreciate the extent to which the idea of global heritage and its concerns and circulation of expertise have advanced a predominantly antireligious stance, one needs to take a closer look at the foundational principles and driving forces of the era of heritage internationalism that defined the second half of the twentieth century. The emergence of international and intergovernmental agencies, starting with UNESCO, was born of a philosophy for cultural development following the end of World War II that practitioners characterized as "universalist." When the idea of global heritage was conceptualized as one of the corner-stones of UNESCO's philosophy for international cooperation, it came attached to technocratic, materialist, and secularizing projects and ideologies.[11] The early years of UNESCO's work reveals the extent to which secularism was the preferred doctrine for the advancement of universal heritage value. In the young intergovernmental organization, whose motto was "peace in the minds of men," religion was framed as a potentially contentious truth pitted against rational truth and, as such, one of the contributing factors to the disruption of peace. This view was instigated by a legacy of increasing secularism across Europe that can be dated to various national cultural politics since the sixteenth century.[12] The result was an influential leadership of UNESCO that recog-nized the existence and value of religious traditions for humankind but restricted religious ways of seeing and being in their efforts to define new paradigms for culture, education, and science. This influenced the institutionalization of cultural heritage standards across the globe.

Institutionally, a deep-seated concern with siding with any one religion of the world was evident in the foundational documents and ideologies circulated within UNESCO at the time, as well as between UNESCO and its growing membership.[13] These presented religion—as well as politics—as the antithesis of the work of this intergovernmental agency that sought to construct peace through intellectual and moral solidar-ity. The outcome was a mandate that could not "base itself exclusively on any essentially sectarian philosophy or restricted outlook, whether existentialism, or élan vital, rationalism or spiritualism, an economic-determinist or a cyclical theory of human history."[14] Instead, it was pro-posed that the pursuit of objective truth could circumvent these divisive traditions and practices.

Scientific world humanism, the favored philosophy, would have irreparable effects on modern global heritage preservation, especially in the context of profoundly religious societies. As early as 1945, the nascent UNESCO was confronted with the challenge of codifying regionalism within universalizing aspirations. Correspondence between state party representatives of the Arab States and the Preparatory Commission to UNESCO during 1945–1946 makes evident the different ways in which the drafting of the organization would fail to serve the Arab region's cultural interests and aspirations for inclusion. Most notably, a 1945 letter to the president of the commission from Naji al-Asil, head of the Iraq delegation, calls attention to the lack of members from Arabic-speaking countries in the formation of a new Executive Committee for the organization, despite the eligibility of five delegations that were present at the time (Iraq, Egypt, Syria, Lebanon, and Saudi Arabia). In addition, he writes, the fact "that none of these States was elected to represent the views and hopes of the Moslem World in the deliberations of the Executive Committee would naturally impede the effective cooperation between the Middle Eastern States and the European and the American nations represented in UNESCO, a condition which is not in harmony with the spirit of universal cooperation in the realms of the mind and the spirit, which was in fact the desires nobly expressed by all the delegates in the session of the Conference."[15]

It has been convincingly argued in the more recent literature on heritage studies that global heritage preservation institutions and approaches evolved to be better equipped to prioritize the preservation of secular engagements with heritage over religious and spiritual ones.[16] This has been exceptionally damaging for supporting a true heritage of religion in particular, because religious use is often expected to acquiesce to the uses and rules of access of a heritage audience conditioned by secularism. For almost a century, therefore, a *culture of heritage* that has favored global over regional or local uses of heritage, including religious uses, has ironically operated as a sort of secularist cult that recognizes the existence of religious traditions but holds the first right of refusal of religious authority. This is especially true in instances in which religious practices and beliefs run contrary to the key tenets of global preservation ideology.

Examples abound of canonical practices and policies in global heritage preservation that radically undermine local religious use, leading to the opposite of peaceful relations. For example, in Mali in 2006, a riot broke out in response to the Aga Khan Trust for Culture's restoration work on the Great Mosque of Djenné, when the actions of conservation experts came into conflict with vernacular practices of maintaining the architectural integrity of this building.[17] Not only did the restoration team fail to communicate their intentions to local stakeholders and stewards of this mosque, but the proposed restoration also involved the removal of one hundred years of mud additions that had been applied to its surfaces, generation after generation, through the annual tradition of *créppisage* (remudding). It was also in Mali that the militant Islamic group Ansar Dine purposely challenged the validity of UNESCO's governance after their intentional destruction of the Cheick Sidi Mahmud Tomb in Timbuktu in 2012 with the adversarial declaration: "UNESCO is what?"[18] It is clear that, despite attempts to keep religious traditions out of the work of preservation, religious agendas wrapped in political and diplomatic tensions remain entangled with the fate of cultural heritage and must be addressed.

When religious traditions are given a place and presence in global heritage preservation narratives, it is with some caveats. The history of safeguarding tangible and immovable material culture has included the successful preservation of a significant number of monumental temple architectural structures, such as the Pharaonic temples built by Ramesses II in Abu Simbel, Egypt, which had been slated to disappear in the process of constructing the High Aswan Dam on the river Nile. Monumental architecture such as this, whose communities of believers and practitioners were long gone, enjoys a relatively uncomplicated life history as World Heritage Sites. However, for sites and architecture bestowed with heritage value that are also linked to contemporary communities of believers, the narrative proffered by preservationists representing secular norms and institutions often centers on actual or anticipated conflict. Religious voices are more frequently featured as perpetrators of the destruction and neglect of heritage places than as creators and stewards of value, as in the destruction of the Bamiyan Buddhas in Afghanistan. Such a focus leaves little room for rapprochement with the community voices in the valley of Bamiyan. It is the frequency with which destruction has been associated with heritage practices across the Muslim world that has sustained the view of religious voices as irreconcilable with heritage preservation goals, resulting in a forceful separation of places of religious significance from the religious authorities and communities of believers that give their use meaning. This separation constitutes a form of destruction at the hands of the very same ideologues who historically condemned damage to a heritage and its people.

This is why I conceptualize the normatively secular heritage cult(ure) that purports to advance universalist values as a cult of heritage preservation.[19] This heritage cult advances over secularized sites to demand that all other values and uses fold into those of preservation, promoting nothing short of a set of beliefs in preservation as a civilizing and modernizing reality. This, I argue, is itself a form of fundamentalism, but one that has not typically been recognized and theorized as such within the professional heritage preservation community. Reframing secular heritage culture as a fundamentalist heritage cult opens new possibilities for critique of the overarching project, while also helping to demonstrate the significance of interventions from the Muslim world into this structure, such as those led by Qatar.

What has been excluded in this global heritage discourse is a space for religious tradition to be recognized as an active contributor to dynamic and contemporary practices surrounding heritage and its making, stewardship, and preservation. The intentional separation and even erasure of religious legacies in the growth of global heritage culture limit the possibility of any reconsideration of the place of religious authority in preservation care practices today. Throughout the 1990s, debates about the place of religion and belief in heritage preservation culture were a driving force behind a permanent division among preservation professionals and institutions in the cultural heritage field. These early but foundational debates revolved around sites across Asia, as well as in the settler-colonial contexts of Australia and Canada. A recognition of the diverse and alternative heritage values in these contexts resulted in a proliferation of institutional statements, initiatives, and doctrinal documents that aimed to authorize new heritage typologies and voices that once had been obscured or made peripheral to global heritage discourse. The reconfigurations of forms of authority that define what many have referred to as the "critical turn" in heritage studies offered an opportunity to normalize religious practices, values, and stewards in the work of heritage preservation in earnest.

Accordingly, the recognition of communities of believers, including pilgrims and religious leaders, as stewards and custodians of heritage has been gradually reflected in some legal and philanthropic regimes, alongside a greater endorsement of nonacademic experts in heritage and preservation practice and policy overall.[20] The turn of the new millennium not only marked a growing interest in the spheres of religion for the study and management of heritage resources; it was also defined by two types of disruption of the dominant understanding of global heritage value and its management as secular endeavors. The first was a complete disenchantment of the utopian expectation that heritage preservationism, summoned as a universal truth, could neutralize both political and religious discord. The destruction of the Bamiyan Buddhas in Afghanistan in 2001 was not the only crisis that demonstrated the inutility of preservation ideology as a conflict-broker in a religious-led iconoclasm.[21] More recently, in 2020, a presidential decree in Turkey ended the eighty-year history of Hagia Sophia as a secular museum, challenging the World Heritage Site status awarded by UNESCO in 1985. Hagia Sophia, originally an Eastern Orthodox church and then a mosque, had already been secularized before its designation as World Heritage, lending itself to be circulated as a powerful symbol of harmony and coexistence of multiple religious traditions. The violently negative reaction of UNESCO and its supporters to the return of its functions as a mosque, presented as a kind of destruction of its heritage value, is another example of the mythologized role of heritage expertise as a neutral observer and mediator and shows a lack of self-awareness of the biases inherent in global heritage ideology.

Hagia Sophia is also an example of the second, less explored disruption of the hegemony of global heritage culture: the ways in which heritage expertise itself—through secularizing and depoliticizing discourses and practices—is responsible for creating or exacerbating existing and potential tensions in sites of religious significance and use. While heritage experts and institutions have centered narratives of conflict on antipreservation perpetrators, the actions of heritage experts and institutions themselves as instigators of conflict have not been examined. In focusing on their role as monitors rather than agents in religious conflicts, or conflicts between religious and secular uses, heritage elites have failed to recognize their own specters of secularism and how heritage discourse can alter the conditions of coexistence. The religious studies scholar Aike Rots has argued that the specific ways in which sites of religious significance are incorporated into the more inflexible and indivisible discourse of World Heritage have serious consequences for worshipping practices. These consequences are diverse and contextual, but they fall into recurrent patterns.[22] First, he argues, such a shift of status deprivatizes religious sites and practices by enabling or strengthening the control of secular authorities over them. In addition, acquiring a status such as World Heritage secularizes sites by diminishing the agency of private religious or other belief systems and attaching them instead to narratives centering on identities and collectives associated with post-Enlightenment liberal modernity, such as the origins of the nation, collective identity, and others.

These explicit reclassifications serve the strategic purpose of establishing government control over ritual practices. In his study of popular religion and heritage, the archaeologist Denis Byrne makes specific reference to the way in which secularist heritage preservation discourses and practices not only disregarded belief systems but also in fact were used to intentionally target belief systems by governments, religious hierarchies, and reform-minded elites as part of antisuperstition campaigns.[23] Heritage discourse, in this sense, partakes in a form of destruction that is not necessarily visible through physical erasure (although it can eventually lead to it); rather, this destruction entails a discursive transformation that reduces the religiosity of sites and places through secularization. Finally, Rots's analysis considers the rise in tourist visitation that is associated with World Heritage designation as a powerful force of transformation that manifests alongside the reascription of sites as secular public property in the public imagination, or even in legal terms. The concern with the rigid categories that are imposed on sites of religious significance, in this case, is not that devotional elements or religious actors disappear, but that religious actors must compromise and negotiate with the demands of secular authorities, nongovernmental organizations (NGOs), and entrepreneurs, engaging in what Rots calls "discursive secularization."[24]

Efforts to secularize global heritage sites as a mechanism to neutralize conflict constitute a self-fulfilling prophecy in the history of global heritage governance. Conveniently, maintaining a concern with conflict and iconoclasm remains part of the "symbolic capital" on which preservation agencies and experts rely on for gaining access to sites but without paying attention to the ways in which heritage preservation as a social field encompasses sacred spaces and "constitute those places, that is, relate to, and impact upon, the rituals which take place within them."[25] Any conciliatory mechanisms that global heritage discourse may be supposed to possess are attached to ideologies that center on objectification, rationalism, and secularism, making heritage preservation inherently ill fitted to manage its own conflict with religious practices. Meanwhile, heritage preservation practices and institutions have nominated themselves as mediators in the project of disarming structures of misrepresentation, often ignoring the ways in which heritage itself is mobilized as "artifacts of ideological discourse."[26] It is because of the legacies of what I have termed the "heritage cult" that "we cannot just add a living and popular religious heritage discourse to the institutionalized heritage discourse," as Anna Karlström argues.[27]

Despite significant reconfigurations brought about by the critical turn in heritage studies and its concern with alterity, efforts at closing the gap between materialist and spiritual preservation philosophies have not challenged the marginalization of living, spiritual traditions substantially or impactfully, nor have they offered a vision for the amelioration of conflicts emerging from these sites of tension.[28] This is because recognizing the existence of religious stakeholders and empowering religious stewards to take the lead in practices of caretaking of uniquely localized cultural heritage are different commitments.

While it was framed by the distinctive focus of iconoclasm, conflict, and destruction, the platform of the Doha Statement signaled a turn and an opportunity for an expansive and diverse Muslim world to carve a productive space out of the history of global heritage that resists the trajectories of secularism. At a time when profoundly religious nations are quickly becoming top investors in global heritage governance, the stage has been set for productive examinations of Islamic instruments and Muslim figures of authority in heritage preservation ideologies at the local, regional, and global levels. The state of Qatar on the Arabian Peninsula has quickly become a leading force in fomenting change in this area, as evidenced in the Doha Statement and myriad initiatives that preceded and followed this key moment of engagement with and intervention in the secularizing cult of heritage. However, to support and promote global heritage values in the ways that Qatar has expertly done is also to support a certain sidelining of particular elements of religious tradition in the development of culture past, present, and future, at home and abroad.

After the Doha Statement: Qatari Visions for a Culture of Heritage

Despite falling under the umbrella of UNESCO's advocacy for universal cultural heritage safeguarding, the recommendations contained in the Doha Statement, indicative of Qatar's broader trajectory, boldly contradicted the global heritage preservation dogma that is nurtured by this United Nations (UN) agency. First, it proposed that the preservation of non-Islamic heritage in the context of contemporary Muslim societies is permissible, so long as its intended use is adapted to the Islamic sensitivities of its contemporary Muslim stewards.[29] A unanimous concern with the practice of idolatry posited that heritage stewardship must orient itself to its Muslim environs rather than the universal and more inflexible standards imposed by international conventions, charters, and recommendations of various organizations. Second, the Doha Statement deprivileged original use—that is, the idealization of original authorship and form—as the benchmark for establishing authenticity. Debates about authenticity are as old and unresolved as the discipline itself, with modern conservation theory proposing a range of positions vis-à-vis original use and intention. In the case of the Doha Statement, Muslim experts argued that the use of a heritage place or object must align, first and foremost, with Muslim practice. Overall, the Doha Symposium did the dual work of confronting a legacy of misrepresentation about Islamic agency and recentering Muslim voices of authority as authors and creators of heritage values and narratives, not destroyers of them. Qatar's project to give a platform to Muslim expertise, therefore, pushes back on decades of rhetoric and imagery of a Muslim world hostile to heritage value as it is reenacted over and over in visual and textual archives that conform with heritage history and training.[30] Qatar's own experience with growing a national heritage culture negotiates this viewpoint and offers a redirection.

Within Qatar, disciplinary engagements with heritage resources have stood practically disconnected from histories of modern conflict or even direct colonial oppression.[31] Qatar was a British protectorate until its peaceful independence on 3 September 1971. Nevertheless, as archaeologists across the Middle East have argued for decades, "ongoing conflicts play a substantial part in shaping the conditions in which knowledge about archaeology of the region is produced and used."[32] Coupled with the extremism inherent in disciplinary framings of heritage preservation agendas in Muslim communities, the misrepresentation and decontextualization of the intentions and aspirations of a diverse region have had a marked effect on Qatari territory.[33] As in museum exhibitions across Europe, the Qatari cultural sector has had to be mindful of the ways in which the representation of Islamic art under a rhetoric of tolerance has often reinforced "a contrast between contemporary Islam (stagnant and intolerant) and early Islam (advanced and tolerant), which informs much of global politics."[34] Likewise, across institutional safeguarding initiatives, the Arab world is often represented as containing "an extraordinary wealth of monuments and archaeological sites and collection from the human past . . . [but] a lack of trained and qualified staff and inadequate public support of the work of official heritage institutions."[35] The contrast in this representation between competent sophistication in the past and incompetent apathy in the present brings to center stage the significance of the study of expertise for understanding the pathways through which religious traditions are enabled or disabled in the growth of heritage preservation traditions in Qatar, starting with their growing leadership in the sphere of global heritage advocacy.

Ten years after hosting the historic meeting of 'ulamā', Qatar took the spotlight again as a key supporter of global heritage governance. This occurred during a period of heightened tension around Middle Eastern affairs in the United Nations. In October 2011, the United States suspended their financial contributions to UNESCO after the Palestinian Authority was recognized and accepted as a member-state. Federal legislation in the United States bans the use of funds to any specialized agency that recognizes the statehood of the Palestine Liberation Organization. At the time, the United States contributed 22 percent of UNESCO's annual budget, so their withdrawal brought about the "worst ever financial situation."[36] Director-General Irina Bokova was forced to launch an emergency fundraiser to compensate for this shortfall of $69 million. The Arab states stepped up. Qatar, as well as Saudi Arabia, contributed the equivalent of $20 million each to the cause, while other Muslim-majority countries like Turkey, Indonesia, and Algeria made smaller contributions. Although the actual impact of these donations was arguably low, the gesture nonetheless ushered in a new era in the politics and leadership possibilities of World Heritage governance, which was marked by a possible shift in the channels of influence that sustain the organization.[37]

In the immediate aftermath of this institutional crisis, a new center of gravity for global heritage traditions drew attention to the significance of the Arab world in the future of heritage and preservation debates and management. At the 18th General Assembly of States Parties to the World Heritage Convention in UNESCO headquarters in Paris, on 7–9 November 2011, Qatar was voted into the twenty-one-member World Heritage Committee, together with eight other new members (joining Algeria, Colombia, Germany, India, Japan, Malaysia, Senegal, and Serbia). With no properties on the World Heritage List at the time, Qatar proposed to host the World Heritage Committee in 2013, signaling its intention to take further leadership roles in the work of the organization. In 2013, they were voted as the chair of the World Heritage Committee at its 37th Session in Phnom Penh, Cambodia.[38]

It was a first for Qatar and a rare occurrence for the Arabian Peninsula; the only other member-state on the Arabian Peninsula to ever hold one of the key leadership positions in the history of the World Heritage Committee was Bahrain in 2001.[39]

During Qatar's tenure on the committee, they successfully inscribed the first Qatari site to the World Heritage List in 2013, al-Zubarah Archaeological Site, following the submission of their first Tentative List in 2008 and an initial deferral for al-Zubarah in 2012.[40] Their influence as hosts on the outputs of the 38th Session of the World Heritage Committee in Doha in 2014 was undeniable and unapologetic. For starters, the chair of the World Heritage Committee, Sheikha al-Mayassa bint Hamad bin Khalifa al-Thani, broke protocol during heated debates surrounding the proposal to add the Palestinian site of Battir to the List of World Heritage in Danger. An observer, the anthropologist Lynn Meskell, called it an "unusual state of affairs and suspension of presumptive neutrality" when al-Thani addressed the evaluator from the International Council on Monuments and Sites (ICOMOS) with her own views directly and rhetorically: "So you are saying that the state of Palestine is not an emergency?"[41] The property, titled "Palestine: Land of Olives and Vines—Cultural Landscape of Southern Jerusalem, Battir," was inscribed to the List of World Heritage in Danger at this gathering.

This period, which coincided with the aftermath of the Arab Spring, was a ripe time for raising heritage-safeguarding concerns across the Muslim world. Accordingly, during 2013–2014, the UNESCO Director-General called specific attention to the intentional damage done to the Museum of Islamic Art in Cairo, the mausoleums in Timbuktu (and their manuscripts, an item specifically highlighted by the Qatari delegation), and, relatedly, the design competition to build the new Bamiyan Cultural Centre in Afghanistan.[42]

At a regional level, Qatari heritage leadership and advocacy were similarly consolidated, complementing its influence on international platforms. In 2013, Director-General Irina Bokova appointed Anna Paolini from Italy to the post of director of the UNESCO office in Doha and UNESCO representative to Bahrain, Kuwait, Oman, Qatar, Saudi Arabia, United Arab Emirates, and Yemen. During this mandate, the work of UNESCO in the region focused significantly on the Yemeni civil war. For example, the "Connect 2 Socotra" campaign, in collaboration with the Friends of Socotra Association (2019), raised awareness of the rich and distinct natural and cultural heritage of the Yemeni island of Socotra (a UNESCO Natural World Heritage Property) in relation to climate change. The program involved major museums, botanical gardens, and academic institutes around the world.

In line with this emphasis, during the opening ceremonies of the World Heritage Convention in Doha, the prime minister of Qatar, Sheikh Abdullah bin Nasser bin Khalifa al-Thani, pledged a $10 million donation to a new fund intended to protect World Heritage Sites affected by conflicts or natural disasters.[43] Following this offer, in her opening address, Chairperson Sheikha al-Mayassa called on "all of the States of the big World Heritage family" to support Qatar's initiative by "contributing to this newly created fund."[44] Accordingly, in December 2015, the Qatar Development Fund (QDF) and UNESCO signed their first Memorandum of Understanding to support the implementation of a program aimed at protecting cultural and natural heritage in emergency situations[45]—UNESCO's Heritage Emergency Fund—with a focus on tackling the threats of climate change and war. Signed at the UNESCO headquarters in Paris, the agreement came as the 38th Session of the General Conference of UNESCO adopted a comprehensive strategy for the protection and promotion of culture and pluralism in times of war. While it holds a global scope, the Heritage Emergency Fund is another vehicle for addressing regional requests for immediate interventions in the aftermath of conflict and disaster. For example, it supported the Rapid Assessment Mission to Palmyra on April 2016 in line with the Executive Board's decision to safeguard and preserve Palmyra and other Syrian World Heritage Sites at their 199th session.[46] In March 2017, the fund sponsored a meeting in Beirut to bring together Syrian stakeholders and international experts to evaluate the damage to historic monuments and to strategize Aleppo's recovery.[47] With a Donors' Advisory Group, under the joint leadership of the Qatari diplomat Hamad bin Abdulaziz al-Kuwari and the UNESCO assistant director-general for culture Ernesto Ottone, the Heritage Emergency Fund is intimately tied to Qatari leadership, while also enjoying the support of the Government of Canada, the Qatar Fund for Development, the Kingdom of Norway, the Government of Canada, ANA Holdings Inc., the Principality of Monaco, the Republic of Estonia, the Kingdom of the Netherlands, the Grand Duchy of Luxembourg, the Slovak Republic, and the Principality of Andorra.[48]

Qatari ambitions to lead heritage governance took another step forward in 2017. After accumulating an unpaid balance of $600 million, the United States finally announced their withdrawal from UNESCO, to take effect at the end of 2018. The day after the US withdrawal announcement, the UNESCO executive board elected Audrey Azoulay from France to replace Director-General Bokova at the end of her term. Azoulay bested Hamad bin Abdulaziz al-Kuwari, the delegate from Qatar, in "an unusually heated election that was overshadowed by Middle East tensions."[49] Failure to have an Arab state gain the leading seat at UNESCO may have also been caused by other factors. Jewish groups decried al-Kuwari's preface to a 2013 Arabic book called *Jerusalem in the Eyes of the Poets* for containing anti-Semitic rhetoric. In addition, in the months leading up to the election, Egypt and three other Arab nations were engaged in a boycott of Qatar ("the blockade") over alleged ties to extremist groups. The rise of Qatar in UNESCO seemed to have reached its zenith. However, in 2021, Qatar was elected to the World Heritage Committee for another term of five years, suggesting that the nation had gained a sustainable and recurrent role as an influential player in global heritage matters.

Despite their unique contribution to a key debate that pitted heritage preservation and religious integrity in the Doha Statement of 2001, none of the initiatives under Qatari leadership touched directly on the topic of religion in cultural heritage preservation advocacy. In 2014, Sheikha al-Mayassa, acting as chair of the board of trustees of the Qatar Museums Authority, defined heritage and art as a "system of reference to culture, society, politics and religion in our time" in Qatar's debut article for UNESCO's World Heritage magazine.[50] While highly aspirational, this statement came out at a time when global heritage initiatives appeared to be more inclusive of religion in general. The launch of thematic initiatives across many organizations recognized the significance and complexity of sacrality as a constituent part of heritage places, at least discursively.[51] Notably, a 2005 resolution at the General Assembly of ICOMOS launched a thematic program and set the focus of the International Day for Monuments and Sites in 2008 as "Religious heritage and sacred places." A task force on the cultural and spiritual value of protected areas propelled a collaboration between UNESCO's Man and the Biosphere Programme and the International Union for Conservation of Nature (IUCN), which resulted in the 2008 UNESCO guidelines for the conservation and management of sacred natural sites.[52] The concern with sacrality was reiterated at the 2011 ICOMOS General Assembly, and also at the launch of the UNESCO Initiative on Heritage of Religious Interest, which included the Kyiv Statement on the Protection of Religious Properties within the Framework of the World Heritage Convention.[53]

Despite the alignment of agendas supporting a better examination of heritage and religion and Qatar's efforts, the absence of a committed engagement with religious traditions continued. In the dynamics of World Heritage governance, the growth of a unique, Muslim-oriented heritage preservation culture was obscured by the logics of heritage diplomacy. The funding sources that powerhouses such as Qatar offered to the organization were welcome and celebrated in the shaping of the intergovernmental agency, but not necessarily transformative of the agency's practices and priorities. One independent UNESCO observer, in confidence, referred to this selective influence as "pimping the Gulf," referring to the inclusion of Qatar in the inner circles of governance in UNESCO's heritage as an act of tokenism, whereby Paris could instrumentalize Qatar without needing to incorporate actual Muslim viewpoints into the world of global heritage.

Nevertheless, the state of Qatar actively resisted this tokenization, developing a pervasive influence on heritage resources within and beyond its borders. Accompanying the growth of its domestic heritage assemblage, comprised of archaeological, historical, and natural Qatari resources through the establishment of Qatar Museums in 2005, the Qatar Foundation sponsored broader regional and transregional research, through the Qatar National Research Fund's National Priorities Research Program and the opening of University College London Qatar (UCL Qatar) in 2011, to focus almost exclusively on heritage and conservation capacity-building. The latter provided an institutional framework and base for the launch of archaeological projects in al-Ain, in the United Arab Emirates, and Morocco, as well as the more high-profile Qatar-Sudan Archaeological Project (QSAP), endorsed by UNESCO as an integral part of the management strategy of Gebel Barkal and the Sites of the Napatan Region.[54] QSAP served as an umbrella for forty-two scientific missions hailing from twenty-five institutions from eleven countries. Weaving itself into the long history of global (but mostly Western) interventions in the Arab region, "Qatar Museum's funding for QSAP represents the most extensive, targeted initiative by a single institution worldwide since UNESCO's International Nubia Campaign (1960–80)."[55]

Such an integrated engagement with national, pan-Arab, and pan-Islamic objectives orchestrated the growth of a heritage preservation culture in Qatar. Under the umbrella of the Qatar Foundation, advocacy for Islam-attuned cultural development projects expanded Qatari cultural agendas beyond the country's borders through other modes of urban rehabilitation. For example, through their Reach Out to Asia (ROTA) office, the Qatar Foundation partnered with the Titian

Foundation in Indonesia to rebuild a learning center in the Acehnese village of Lamreh following its massive destruction caused by the 2004 Indian Ocean tsunami. They also launched the Bayat Schools Reconstruction Project to rebuild schools and libraries, as well as support the teaching and management capacity in the region of Klaten, in Java. At one of these schools, they supported training in traditional ceramic and batik techniques, reinforcing the significance of tradition and heritage as languages and avenues of cultural and economic development.[56]

Since the issuing of the Doha Statement, it has been clear that Qatar has created the resources, infrastructure, and agendas targeted at strengthening the preservation of traditional heritage practices that are seen to support cultural and economic well-being abroad and at home. As a catalyst for and driver of the most intense and multilayered project of heritage construction, Qatar has established the roots of an Islamic or postsecular culture of heritage. Capacious in its ambitions, this culture of heritage underpins everything from projects of urbanization and reurbanization to the establishment of museums, strategies for the management of biodiversity, and humanities and social-science programs in institutions of higher learning, as well as structures of governance of state and nonstate institutions.

The Heritage State: Cultural Spheres, Choreography, and Collaboration

Building on five years of ethnographic research as a resident, lecturer, and heritage expert in Qatar, from 2012 to 2017, followed by four more years of ethnographic fieldwork and archival research in France, the United Kingdom, Switzerland, and the Gulf, this book traces Qatar's culture of heritage preservation and its influences on the role of religion in global heritage governance. Understanding Qatar's culture of heritage preservation involves considering not only formalized preservation agendas, but also the rules of experts that are a constituent part of political, social, and diplomatic institutions that together conform this culture. This was a formative time for Qatar's heritage industry in the lead-up to hosting the FIFA World Cup in late 2022. This period also laid especially bare the limitations and possibilities of cultural heritage advocacy, bracketed by two diplomatic crises: I began my residence in Qatar in mid-2011, at the heels of the Arab Spring, and left just before the infamous *al-hisar*, the diplomatic crisis of June 2017 that saw Saudi Arabia, the United Arab Emirates, Bahrain, and Egypt sever diplomatic relations and enforce a widespread blockade on Qatar until January 2021.

My concerns with Qatari influence on world cultural affairs had begun years earlier, over seven thousand kilometers away, in the aforementioned town of Bayat, Indonesia, where I was researching post-tsunami interventions. A short and accidental visit to Bayat coincided with preparations for a visit by Sheikha Moza bint Nasser al-Missned, chair of the Qatar Foundation. Schoolteachers at Bayat explained that the Qatar Foundation had arrived in the region with an offer to donate trees. Instead, they settled on building a trade school and providing patronage for living heritage in their support for traditional arts and crafts. Henceforth, I approached Qatar as a site of entanglements of different temporal and geographical scales and forms of agency. Embarking on a study of Qatar as an influential philanthropist and advocate for heritage in Southeast Asia also offered me an opportunity to document the emergence of a culture of heritage preservation beyond the representational trap of the Middle East and the Muslim world as hostile territories.

In Qatar, my role in the burgeoning ecosystem of heritage expertise was that of a participant observer wearing many hats. I was considered a heritage expert, and often a translator of heritage policy to foreign visitors conducting their own research who were hard pressed to gain access to official Qatari spokespeople. I was also an instructor in the fields of heritage studies, museums, archaeology, and anthropology in institutions of higher education where the next generation of local experts was trained. At the same time, I was a researcher contributing to the growth of a small academic network of social scientists on the ground. The latter included becoming a member of the Social and Behavioral Institutional Review Board in Qatar, the regulatory body for research involving human subjects, based in the Georgetown School of Foreign Service at Qatar. And yet I was also a tourist and bystander who discovered the cultural and natural heritage of Qatar as a new arrival.

As my research on Qatar demonstrates, the culture of heritage that grows and strengthens heritage preservation ideologies and traditions produces heritage subjects in objects, places, and performances along identifiable processes of nation-building agendas that support and invent traditions. In a nation frequently described by Qatari and non-Qatari bystanders (but not by the official state discourse) as a modern state without a past in a rapidly changing landscape, examining the cultivation of individuals, communities, and organizations is as critical as the mapping of the cultural resources themselves. These subjects are acculturated to become stakeholders, stewards, and knowledge-brokers in the operationalization of practices of preservation, making this a heritage ethnography concerned with people more than simply resources. Simultaneously, this book examines how the Qatari state, its national agencies, UNESCO, and other intergovernmental agencies, as well as disciplinary experts, practitioners, and observers from Qatar, the region, and beyond, are giving shape to their idea of an engaged public and an engaging heritage product. Choreographing these actors and goals in Qatar is not seamless: channels of stewardship are tied to a complex social landscape of cosmopolitanism and stratified access to citizenship, while legitimizing curatorial practices of heritage resources in one of the richest countries of the world is still filtered through the notion that society favors oral over material traditions.[57] My ethnographic subjects in Qatar, therefore, included Qatari and non-Qatari former students, colleagues, and collaborators in academic and nonacademic institutions, as well as engagements with different migrant communities that are active participants in what could be referred to as an informal and unaccounted-for culture of preservation.

Qatari lifestyle, global interconnectivity, and international agency have shifted dramatically in the last fifty years, despite maintaining the constitutional hereditary monarchy of the al-Thani family, whose primary source of legislation is sharia (Islamic law). But what makes Qatar a good vantage point for the examination of a culture of heritage that navigates its own secularizing ideologies is not its formidable speed of change and adaptation, but the way in which heritage preservation traditions balance global/local and secular/spiritual tensions in strategic and encoded ways. More broadly, the intense heritage preservation activity and advocacy that has taken place in Qatar over the past twenty years offers an opportunity to examine how heritage preservation has aligned with or resisted global processes of heritagization deriving from the aftermath of the September 11 terrorist attacks, the War on Terror, and Western histories of empire.[58] Archival work traces Qatar's imbrications in wider global heritage discourses at institutions that sought to have a stake in the cultural development of the nation. This approach also captured the traces of local and regional expertise in a global history of heritage; that is, the shifts between visibility and invisibility that reflect the spheres of influence of Qatari, Arabian, Middle Eastern, and Muslim actors on the global stage.

Qatar's development of a culture of heritage attentive to Islam has required the participants and stakeholders of this effort to negotiate political, social, and cultural challenges. While some of these challenges, such as the encroachment of urbanization, are nearly universal among preservation efforts everywhere, others are sharper in Qatar. The particular context of Qatar's postcolonial history, development trajectory, ecology, and demographics has resulted in specific manifestations of secular and religious tensions. It is through the negotiations of these tensions, which resonate across broader swaths of the region and the world, that Qatar has built an expansive heritage industry and a thriving international influence on heritage governance.

Each of the chapters in this book identifies a specific cultural sphere in and through which Qatar has navigated tensions between secularism and religion in its development of a national and globally ambitious heritage sector that has been helping to define a Muslim culture of preservation: through its statecraft, while building the apparatus of the state at home and creating a place in international relations; through its development of formal heritage languages related to the built environment, across subsequent waves of modernization; through its approach to resource stewardship, amid growing concerns about sustainability; and through its cultivation of civic participation in heritage, especially via collecting practices, in the face of social conflict structured around an "us versus them" division. Looking at these distinct but overlapping arenas together shows Qatar's multipronged approach to creating a heritage sector that serves the state and has also led to a broader project of developing a Muslim-oriented culture of heritage, which has wider ramifications for how global heritage is conceptualized, practiced, and studied.

Since its earliest manifestations, heritage debates in Qatar have grown in synchronicity with the formalization of the nation, and also under the watchful and influential eye of an international community of interest that sought Qatar's allegiance to predominantly Western and European cultural and diplomatic agendas. Chapter 1 situates Qatar in both contexts. It explores how the postindependence Qatari state formulated an approach to heritage that sought to use foreign norms and expertise to strengthen and legitimize new state institutions that could advance Qatari nationalist projects. In turn, these helped enhance Qatar's power to assert Islamic nationalist political, economic, and cultural ambitions on the world stage. Since the 1970s, Qatar has hosted different forms of expertise, oscillating between local, regional (i.e., Arab), and European agents of knowledge production, resulting in legacy trends that influence heritage preservation institutions today. Significant among these, this chapter shows, was the development of influential state institutions that could serve as platforms for reconciling seemingly opposing worldviews that typically had arranged cultural developments in Qatar, along with the opposing forces of a secular and a Muslim future.

Chapter 2 traces the advent of modernity and the push for modernization in Qatar, which had to be negotiated against the idealization of a modern nation built on traditional knowledge. This chapter examines two main waves of modernization that mobilized heritage languages in different (and perhaps opposing) relationships to their Muslim cultural and religious contexts: the first modernist turn in Qatar that accompanied the accelerated expansion of the country starting in the 1950s, and then a late modern reappraisal of urban spaces and architectural styles that accompanied an intensely global era of cosmopolitanism in the cultural production of the nation. Development of the built environment in the former paid some attention to tradition, but it was a tradition decanted and purified from its religious context. The latter foregrounded a Muslim context in specific ways, including the creation of new visual statements that pay homage to Islamic art, urban interventions that engage with traditional knowledge and uses of space, and regeneration projects that combine and integrate traditional uses, modern materials, and design elements. In this chapter, I illustrate how the creation of heritage languages cements these legacies to reconcile old and new imaginations of a city that is slated to represent traditional and Muslim lifestyles and culture.

In chapter 3, I consider Qatar's strategic alignment of cultural preservation and natural conservation discourses and agendas. Intertwined through the sharing of some history and forms of expertise, cultural heritage and environmentalism in Qatar have been promoted as key nation-building strategies in the new millennium. The aim has been to connect Qatar's heritage renaissance sustainably to local cultural and environmental contexts, whose preservation can make various kinds of resources more available to future generations. This has involved an Islamicization of the objectives and practices of sustainability. Drawing on traditions that Islamic law outlines for communal stewardship over waqf (endowments), Qatar has sought to preserve intangible forms of performed heritage (such as religious worship in historical mosques), while also participating in various "greening" initiatives, which have had to be adapted to local ecological circumstances.

Finally, chapter 4 considers the mechanisms through which a concerned civil society is generated and empowered in support of a culture of heritage preservation in Qatar, including the active circulation of art as a form of generating new Qatari heritage traditions. As Qatari institutions find new and innovative ways of encouraging a public that is invested in the heritage renaissance of Qatar, the temporality of heritage value poses certain challenges, driving heritage users and audiences beyond a manicured chronology that is invoked in the more art-historical periodicity of an "Islamic heritage." The rigidity of heritage discourse and action means that in this case, *being traditional* may imply choosing between observing the cult of heritage or observing religious traditions, with few opportunities for hybridity.

The chapters in this book suggest that the choreographed efforts across institutions in Qatar often resist the anticlerical tendencies that make the global heritage movement an effective advocate for secularism. This resistance rests on an occasional involvement of *Awqāf* (the Ministry of Endowments) and a tentative civil society that occasionally vocalizes their own ideals, while also being thrust into the center and cross-fire of debates on conflict and postconflict heritage that have defined a heritage preservation tradition across the regions of the Levant, North Africa, and Central Asia. Participation in local and global heritage governance then requires a certain asymmetrical collaboration and acquiescence into both global and local agendas. This suggests that an alignment of Muslim-majority states with UNESCO's work comes at a cost, while also providing a foothold to enact changes and transformations. This book examines exactly what was lost, and gained, in these exchanges.

Chapter 1

Institutions and Expertise
Statecrafting National and Global Heritage

Hosting the Doha Symposium of *'Ulamâ* on Cultural Heritage in December 2001 was not the first time that Qatar stepped up to propose a game-changing transformation in global heritage preservation culture. In fact, Qatar had been contributing to international heritage institutions since its first days as an independent state in the early 1970s, when it was also laying the groundwork for a network of institutions at home that would strengthen national identity. Across both the domestic and international realms, the Qatari state navigated tensions and ambiguities in the role that religion might play in building a culture of heritage that acknowledged its Muslim context and could also advance the goals of the nation in the overlapping arenas of national development and international diplomacy. Both spheres for cultural development, however, were territories heavily dominated by outside actors and agendas, an influence that left a legacy on the rules of expertise that operate in the cultural sector of Qatar.

During the early decades of heritage internationalism, starting in the late 1940s, representation of stewardship from Muslim-majority countries in the work of the United Nations Educational, Scientific, and Cultural Organization (UNESCO) was weak and highly circumscribed, with relations between UNESCO and the Arab States region in particular becoming especially vexed. Externally, these tensions were driven by the persistence of colonial and neocolonial policies by states whose representatives held powerful sway in international governance and institutions. Political developments in the Middle East region starting in 1948 had an especially dramatic impact: during this critical period, the United Nations Partition Plan for Palestine had shaken the trust in the United Nations.[1] Internally, the productive coordination of cultural heritage preservation efforts between Muslim-majority states and UNESCO was impaired by the particular framing of religion within its instruments. The global scene, therefore, did not present inviting grounds for the development of the type of regional and thematic leadership that Qatar would eventually achieve in the early 2000s.

Qatar was not part of these early negotiations for regional recognition within the United Nations (UN) intergovernmental system. The 1940s was a period of transformation for the sheikhdoms of the Arabian Peninsula. Before oil was found, these economies relied on the pearling industry, which was in a state of precarity that only worsened between the two world wars, when the introduction of Japanese cultured pearls forced the region into starvation. After the discovery of oil, the domestic scene in Qatar was heavily influenced by legacies of colonialism that infused the politics of the protectorate under Great Britain. This ensured that national development often went hand-in-hand with reliance on importing or collaborating with foreign institutions and expertise, including in the cultural and educational sectors. In 1974, the British ambassador to Qatar, Edward Henderson, wrote that "Qatar in 1950 was living in the austere and limited atmosphere of Islam of the 9th century," adding that "already by 1969 the physical development of the country (services, hospitals, buildings) as well as the intellectual (education, culture) were impressive, and they had sprung from nothing."[2] In this report to James Callaghan, the foreign secretary of the United Kingdom, he concluded that "perhaps the only regrettable aspect of the part we played is that we did so without leaving more signs of our own culture in Qatar." In one sweeping move, this statement exemplifies the three ways in which locality in Qatar was historically conceptualized and also undermined, as a legitimate force, by outside parties: one, the notion that the territory of Qatar was practically empty in terms of material and cultural riches prior to the discovery of fossil fuel reservoirs; two, the rapid modernization of the country over the second half of the twentieth century as compared to (one would assume) European history; and three, the colonial narrative proposing that this development was possible thanks to the stewardship of the

British during their protectorate over the region, including the Trucial States (now the United Arab Emirates) and Qatar, against Ottoman expansionism from 1916 to 1971.[3]

Interrelated developments on global, regional, and national scales shaped Qatar's growth of a national heritage culture attentive to Islam, which would eventually be translated into uniquely effective forms of leadership in the international arena of heritage governance. From its origins in the post–World War II era, this arena cohered around Western conceptualizations of heritage and expertise; yet Arab states eventually developed strategic forms of regional internationalism based on shared priorities, creating heritage institutions that reflected the religious and cultural values of established and new Muslim-majority nations. Still deeply influenced by the history of British control but also shaped by Arab nationalist discourses and the rise of Islamic political leadership, postindependence Qatari statecraft prioritized the production of cultural heritage, which served in turn as an arena for further domestic and diplomatic state-making efforts. Aligning on the global stage with regional neighbors and Muslim-centered causes, and yet adopting international heritage agendas as well as Eurocentric modes of expertise to develop its national heritage culture at home, the Qatari state did more than navigate a complex, politicized landscape of heritage production. Swelling state resources and the nation's growing stature facilitated the Qatarization of heritage culture at home and the eventual advancing of Qatari leadership in shaping discourses and institutions of heritage culture internationally.

Global Heritage Governance Meets Regional Internationalism

The building of Qatar's heritage sector and the institutions that would emerge from this process were shaped by historical and contemporary trends in the global field of heritage. Once UNESCO was up and running, the recognition and support of regionalism in global heritage governance fell under the remit of Special Regional Centers of UNESCO. In the early years of UNESCO, delegates at the Second General Conference in Mexico City suggested creating an operational group within the organization that would serve the Muslim and Arab worlds. However, this idea was met with resistance from the UNESCO Secretariat in Paris. This resistance reflected solidifying philosophical disagreements over the organization's official stance on religion, as well as fears of competition and possible secession. These disagreements were inextricably imbricated with international tensions over the enduring influence of European and American imperialism and related regional alliances and nationalist movements transpiring across the Muslim world at this time.

In 1946, progress reports on the "Program of UNESCO" responded indirectly to the letter from the Iraqi delegate, Naji al-Asil, to the Preparatory Commission to UNESCO calling for a better representation of the Muslim world. In these documents, the Letters and Philosophy Committee expressed concern about "siding with any one of the various religions existing in the world," appearing to put to rest the question of religion.[4] Shortly after, the drafting of an official philosophy of UNESCO formalized this view, stating that the organization "cannot base its outlook on one of the competing religions of the world as against the others. . . . The general philosophy of UNESCO should, it seems, be a scientific world humanism, global in extent and evolutionary in background."[5] The Arab states were aware of the European outlook that underpinned UNESCO's Culture Sector as a successor to the International Institute for Intellectual Cooperation at the League of Nations. They quickly forged alliances to consolidate and safeguard what they saw as their shared values and interests.

The letter from al-Asil was followed by a proposal circulated by the Ministry of Education of Egypt in support of the establishment of a permanent center of UNESCO in Cairo. What was initially called the "Near and Middle-East Cultural Centre" initiative, accepted under resolution 4.3.3 at the Second General Conference in Mexico City in 1947, marks a short but intense period of negotiations (1947–1949) aimed at increasing representation of the Arab States in the organization.[6] For UNESCO, the Near and Middle East became a strategic region to address two key concerns of the executive board: the question of representation of UNESCO in the main cultural areas of the world; and the associated efforts to address tensions affecting international understanding. However, calls for regional representation of Arab States were perceived to be too autonomous by the Secretariat of UNESCO. Concerned that such a center would compete with UNESCO, the Secretariat counteroffered to establish themselves a center for cultural exchange in the Near East, coordinated by representatives of UNESCO.[7] Simultaneously, a survey was launched to measure regional support for the organization and to ensure that the people of the region "gain consciousness of their authentic cultural patrimony

. . . in views of the birth of a universal culture."[8] With this focus on tute-
lage, the search for regional experts and leaders loyal to the mission of
UNESCO was a key objective in Director-General Julian Huxley's tour
of the Middle East in early 1948.

Discussions within the executive board of UNESCO through 1948
reflect institutional anxiety surrounding the unilateral search for UNESCO
to be the official arbiter of heritage patrimony and preservation in the
main cultural areas of the world, which included the Middle East. In
other words, UNESCO expressed a concern with establishing their influence on regions in non-European and non-Anglophone parts of the
world that they saw as being rich in human heritage resources, but they
appeared to discourage the influence of these same regions in the workings and agendas of the organization.

Citing financial constraints, impracticalities, and the need for a "modest
beginning," UNESCO first projected a center that clustered Arab, Turkish, and Iranian interests.[9] Debates about its physical location reflected
a concern with preventing "purely nationalist motives from exerting an
effect, and to guard against cultural imperialism or what may be called
'regional nationalism' in the cultural field."[10] As Project 4.3.3, as it was
sometimes called, was stalled through various bureaucratic channels,
it oscillated between different visions and strategies: an experimental
versus a definitive project,[11] a regional versus a Parisian center,[12] and a
cost-sharing versus a budgetary responsibility that was too ambitious
and burdensome on UNESCO.[13] Throughout these negotiations, the
aspirations of the Arab States to regionalize in the eyes of UNESCO were
carefully monitored by the UNESCO Secretariat. This was not the only
region that felt restrained by the dynamics of the organization.

In 1952, the UN General Assembly was warned of an eventual withdrawal from the organization of Asian and African nations, which
rejected the polarizing and destructive ideology of the Cold War. By
April 1955, these regions had gathered at the Bandung Conference in
Indonesia, where Asian and African states voiced their opposition to
colonialism and neocolonialism, propelling the formation of the Non-
Aligned Movement against major power blocs. After Bandung, what
was clearly an increasingly influential non-European membership
called on UNESCO to improve the mutual appreciation between Eastern and Western cultural values among member states.[14] UNESCO then
launched an Advisory Committee on Mutual Appreciation of Eastern
and Western Cultural Values and an initiative called the East-West
Major Project (1957–1966), which revealed the civilizational conflict

that underpinned rapid decolonization and the assertion of UNESCO's views.[15] Laura Wong argues that this conflict echoed Director-General Huxley's polarizing idea of a clash between East and West as one of the main threats to UNESCO's work.[16]

Important for shaping UNESCO's advocacy for heritage preservation through the following decades, the views consolidated by the East-West Major Project held that Eastern cultural values were primarily defined by their spiritual, not material, riches. This assertion disconnected living religious practices and their communities from the archaeological and historical resources that were cherished and acknowledged by the organization. Such a conceptual distinction between tangible and intangible dimensions of culture would persist in rise of global heritage and consolidate through the 1972 Convention Concerning the Protection of the World Cultural and Natural Heritage (commonly known as the 1972 Convention). This document formalized the ordering and governing instrument for heritage stewardship known as the World Heritage List, favoring monumental, architectural and art historical, and ancient historical sources that left a restricted space for the possibilities of religious, and particularly Muslim, stewardship of cultural heritage resources.

Now encompassing institutional categories at UNESCO that included "the East," "Arabs," and "Islam," Arab and Muslim states amplified their efforts to regionalize in order to address cultural progress on their own terms. Supporting the region was especially urgent in the face of increasing hostility against their historical and cultural resources during and after the acts of vandalism on the al-Aqsa Mosque in Jerusalem, where on 21 August 1969, the Australian kibbutz volunteer Denis Rohan started a fire, nearly igniting a regional war. At the peak of the Arab nationalist movement led by the Egyptian president Gamal Abdel Nasser, the Arab state parties ratified the Arab Cultural Unity Charter, establishing the Arab League Educational, Cultural, and Scientific Organization (ALECSO) with their base in Tunis, Tunisia. Reflecting a certain symmetry with UNESCO's organizational chart, ALECSO's Culture Department was charged with promoting culture and protecting and safeguarding heritage across the Arab world, with special attention to the city of al-Quds in Jerusalem and other occupied Palestinian and Arab territories. Previously existing efforts to promote heritage awareness and strengthen inter-Arab cooperation through periodic conferences were brought under the coordination of ALECSO,[17] who communicated to UNESCO its intention to act as stewards to the region's cultural resources.[18] By 1976, UNESCO announced the creation of an Advisory Committee for Arab Culture in cooperation with ALECSO,[19] partly achieving the goals of Project 4.3.3 in matters of cultural heritage.[20]

In a similar turn, the Islamic World Educational, Scientific and Cultural Organization (ISESCO, now ICESCO), under the Organization of Islamic Cooperation, launched in 1979 the Islamic World Heritage Committee to fulfill a similar role as UNESCO's list but with a focus on Islamic heritage. In 1984, UNESCO and ICESCO signed an agreement to enforce the cooperation between the two organizations. UNESCO, ALECSO, and ICESCO have since often partnered to support heritage safeguarding agendas for the region, as they did for the Doha Symposium. This partnership, which Qatar would eventually engage with and build on, reflects the fruits of a decades-long strategy among Muslim and Arab nations to build strength through regional alliances and solidarities. Forging discourses and approaches to heritage sensitive to Islamic values was one of the potential outcomes enabled by these alliances.

Regional Expertise

The late 1960s was a formative period for the involvement of the Arab states in UNESCO's cultural agenda and the creation of parallel initiatives that served the region and its *umma*. These regional initiatives and their alignment and collaboration with the work of UNESCO resulted in increasing recognition of Arab and Muslim leadership and stewardship in the work of global heritage preservation in such a way that a different possibility for the growth and use of heritage expertise was envisioned. In the earlier years of UNESCO, member-states within and beyond the Arab region requested the support of foreign expertise through UNESCO.[21] Notably, the International Campaign to Save the Monuments of Nubia, which saw the relocation of twenty-two monuments in southern Egypt and northern Sudan, invoked an international coalition of experts and funding that were coordinated by UNESCO from 1960 to 1980. In this way, UNESCO-backed expertise raised awareness of specific resources and challenges that illustrated regional interests along discreet issues. However, this model was bound to be challenged by those seeking deeper acknowledgment of religious authority as a constituent aspect of expertise. In 1980, a UNESCO-supported international symposium on the conservation of Islamic heritage in Lahore, Pakistan, brought together Muslim experts who alerted UNESCO to the need to consult "Islamic scholars and specialists."[22] The preservation of this type of regional heritage, they argued, was primarily "the general duty of Muslims . . . in order to understand their due place in God's creation," rather than a universal responsibility bestowed on an international community.[23] Such antiuniversalist undertones were not popular in UNESCO and touched on the very concerns about regionalism that UNESCO had already expressed, so Muslim-centered initiatives such as this one were few and far between in the organization's official programming.

Muslim-majority states made an impact on the organization in other, more gradual, ways. Qatar is exemplary for its rise to the ranks of regional experts and leaders throughout the growth of global and regional heritage traditions even prior to joining UNESCO as an associate member in November 1962.[24] Still under British mandate, Qatar was reported to have made contributions to the iconic international campaigns for the safeguarding of the Nubia monuments in 1964 and Indonesia's Borobudur in 1972.[25] In addition, the small protectorate was a subject of interest for UNESCO's efforts to grow their influence in the region through what can be described as a project of resource mapping and alignment of cultural agendas. In 1968, the Indian archaeologist and former director general of the Archaeological Survey of India, Amalananda Ghosh, completed an expert mission to Qatar as a UNESCO consultant to various territories of the Arabian Peninsula.[26] His visit was followed by other UNESCO missions intended to assess library and documentation resources and to project the future development of the University of Qatar in 1978.

Ghosh's visit and report, in particular, provide a snapshot of the pre-independence cultural landscape of Qatar and the ways that the nation was already being fashioned in dialogue with heritage discourses and practices. His visit was intended to assess existing caretaking strategies for the development of cultural heritage and museums, as well as to identify existing and potential archaeological resources across the peninsula. His observations reveal the fragmented landscape of cultural production of Qatar at the time: archaeological material had already been collected by the Danish Archaeological Expedition (1956–1974) and taken to Denmark. The potential of different ruins to be developed as archaeological or heritage sites remained unclear, leading to pessimistic projections from Ghosh that proved to be comically inaccurate. Ghosh dismissed any cultural future for the coastal towns of Khor and Wakhrah, now prominent reconstructed heritage villages.

Of what would later become the World Heritage site of al-Zubarah, he wrote, rather hopelessly, that "the ruins have now been leveled down by bulldozers for building-material." In addition, he observed that "medieval remains in Qatar are surprisingly few. I could not find a single mosque which is more than just a few years old; this is perhaps due to the practice of demolishing old mosques to make room for new ones with better amenities."[27] This expert assessment reflects the priorities and interpretive lens of UNESCO more than the actual potential of Qatari cultural landscapes. Ghosh was trained by the British archaeologist Mortimer Wheeler and, at the time, led an institution born out of a tradition of antiquarianism promoted by British administration in South Asia. Despite his point of origin and established leadership in the Indian subcontinent, his judgment shows a strong influence of European ideas on the value of monuments, the authority of material authenticity, and a preference for temporal and aesthetic homogeneity in the determination and projection of heritage as a viable resource. His assessment, therefore, represented the existing landscape of expertise that Qatar would respond to as it navigated independence and the creation of a national strategy for heritage production.

Through Ghosh's and other UNESCO expert missions during this period, the development of culture and the arts for Qatar and its institutions grew around and through internationalist agendas that aligned with certain Eurocentric expectations. Shortly after gaining independence, Qatar joined UNESCO as a member-state in 1972, along with Bahrain and Oman. Throughout the 1970s and 1980s, they formalized their allegiance to the organization through the acceptance of the 1954 Convention for the Protection of Cultural Property in the Event of Armed Conflict (in 1973), the 1970 Convention on the Means of Prohibiting and Preventing the Illicit Import, Export, and Transfer of Ownership of Cultural Property (in 1977), and the 1972 Convention (in 1984). During these early years of formal involvement as a state party, Qatar not only worked toward growing their own infrastructure for heritage and preservation but also took a position of leadership in regional efforts to support of the growth of a heritage preservation sensibility across the Arabian Peninsula. The UNESCO Doha Office was set up in 1976 to serve as a cluster office for Bahrain, Kuwait, Oman, Qatar, Saudi Arabia, and the United Arab Emirates, while the Arab Gulf States Folklore Centre was established in 1981 in Doha with a mission to collect, record, study, and disseminate the folklore of the Arab Gulf States as an integral part of the heritage of the region.[28] The emerging nation

of Qatar also took advantage of this global network to plan an investment into its own cultural and natural heritage industry. For example,
in 1981, the assistant head of the Archaeology Section of the Ministry of Information in Doha, Jassem Saleh al-Reyes, sought assistance
from UNESCO to gain more knowledge of preservation and protection
of Islamic monuments through a study trip to Spain and Morocco.[29]
Conversely, in 1989, Qatar proposed to host a Training Workshop on
the Conservation and Management of Natural Heritage in the Arab
Region.[30] Jointly sponsored by UNESCO's Man and the Biosphere Programme and the Qatar National Commission for Education, Culture
and Science, it would be the first workshop of its kind in the region.

For their strong alignment with UNESCO's agendas for natural and
cultural projects, Qatar received praise from the organization's execu-
tives. The UNESCO Director-General Amadou-Mahtar M'Bow attended
the opening of the new campus for Qatar University in 1985 and pledged
further efforts to preserve the cultural and religious heritage of Jerusalem, a cause dear to Qatar.[31] He also praised the significant financial
support for the bureau coming from Qatar and the Arab States. Mere
months before this official visit, the United States had withdrawn from
UNESCO, so every opportunity to mobilize regional causes to garner
future voluntary financial contributions from the region was taken.
Qatar continued to make financial contributions to UNESCO's safeguarding projects through the 1990s and used their growing influence
in support of deliberations of the World Heritage Committee on issues
within and beyond the Muslim world at the turn of the new millennium,
for example, commenting on heritage safeguarding in Hampi (India),
Panama, and Jerusalem.[32] Qatar's expertise and leadership on this stage
often revolved around financial rather than intellectual contributions,
suggesting that Qatar, along with other Arab states, was assigned a very
specific role in the workings of the organization.

Qatar's leadership role was dictated by the state's ambition as much
as it was primed by UNESCO itself, which clearly saw in Qatar a strong
partner to align the interests of a politically volatile region with those of
UNESCO.[33] Across the region, the opportunity to rise within the ranks
of UNESCO was met by nascent heritage industries and new national
visions that defined the guiding principles of nations as much as their
relationship to their partners and neighbors. Accordingly, their visibility in the operations of ICESCO increased dramatically starting in the
late 1980s. In 1989 and thereafter, the reports on sessions of the Executive Council of ICESCO record an active presence by Qatar through

their involvement in key committees and their voice on the direction of the organization, advocating for the concerns of the Gulf region and key sectors of interest.[34] These included support for an education strategy for the Islamic world (the Qatar Symposium on the subject had been held in 1988) and the setting up of an Islamic satellite television channel specializing in the issues relating to Islam, Muslims, and Islamic civilization in modern languages.[35] Qatar also raised important contemporary issues for the organization—namely, the events of September 11 that "had cast dark shadows on the Islamic world epitomized in suspicion and allegations concocted against Islamic countries and Muslims, revealing thereby a deeply-seated ignorance of the image and real causes of Arabs and Muslims."[36] After this, the organization articulated a duty to sensitize the world about true Islamic religion and causes as a key concern of the Third Islamic Conference of Culture Ministers in Doha on 29–31 December 2001. This sentiment that was undoubtedly driving the drafting of the Doha Statement at this gathering, and its attempts to mediate and translate the aftermath of the Taliban's actions in Afghanistan. Meanwhile, at home, the growth of local and locally serving cultural expertise that was almost entirely derived from a Eurocentric perspective stood in stark contrast to their international alignment with Arab and Muslim-centered causes.

Qatarization of the Cultural Landscape

It is undeniable that the 1960s and 1970s were transformative decades for the development of cultural industries in Qatar and the region. By the 1960s, oil-rich states like Qatar were sending their brightest citizens to study geology, petroleum engineering, and management at leading Western universities. This quickly gave rise to a new generation of Arab technocrats who challenged the power exercised by foreign oil companies, marking "the end of the era of the Western oil barons and the beginning of the age of the Arab oil shaykhs."[37] Qatar joined the Organization of Petroleum Exporting Countries (OPEC) in 1961, and, by 1977, their own home-grown but British-educated Qatari, Ali Jaidah, became the secretary general of the intergovernmental organization after obtaining a BS in economics and an MS in petroleum economics from London University,[38] with a stint at Oxford University.[39] While it became common for Qataris to use British education to achieve globally recognized credentials that legitimized their economic and political leadership in the eyes of figures such as the British ambassador, Britain had missed its chance to exert even more influence over education and culture in Qatar. In Ambassador Henderson's view, the project of ensuring that English became the second language of Qatar and that London remained the first resort for Qataris for medicine, entertainment, and leisure was in jeopardy due to the growing influence of other foreign powers. By 1984, the French Cultural Center had opened in Doha, the American Mission had established a cultural center, and the West Germans had promised to increase their input into education and culture in Qatar.[40] Meanwhile, programs supported by UNESCO and the United Nations Development Programme (UNDP) were largely carried out by Arab experts from Egypt, Syria, and Jordan.

No sooner had Qatar gained independence in 1971, than the British Council was finding ways to retain British influence on Qatari cultural and commercial affairs through the establishment of permanent representation in the country. A week after the declaration of independence, J. G. Hanson, the British Council representative in Bahrain, wrote to the director of the Office of Emir Sheikh Ahmad bin Ali al-Thani (r. 1960–1972) to propose an expansion of the activities of the British Council. Opening a British Council center in Doha, he explained, would ensure better support for English-language training, increase access to educational opportunities in the United Kingdom for qualified Qatari citizens, and generally facilitate the exchange of expertise.[41] A target for immediate support by the council was the Teacher Training College in Doha, which was predominantly run by Egyptian nationals, likely as a result of the overwhelming majority of Egyptians in the Department of Education at the time.

The interests of the following emir, Sheikh Khalifa bin Hamad al-Thani (r. 1972–1995), in securing British support lay elsewhere. Early in the conversations between the British Council and the emir's cabinet, it became evident that the monarch had his eyes set on the founding of the first university in Qatar. At this time, Henderson reported to London that the emir was under political pressure to prevent the Kuwaitis from gaining ground in the educational sphere.[42] However, it seems from this correspondence that the United Kingdom and Qatar had a common adversary in matters of cultural influence: the Egyptians. In a visit to the region, Robert Bertram Serjeant from the University of Cambridge described the University of Kuwait as "almost an Egyptian monopoly."[43] In Doha, representatives from Durham University had become involved in early assessments toward the setting up of a university in Qatar. Reporting on their mission in 1971, Sir James

Cook from the Inter-University Council for Higher Education Overseas and Howard Bowen-Jones from Durham University discovered, upon arrival in Doha, that a UNESCO team of three Egyptians had already produced a report.[44]

However, the window of opportunity for intensifying British influence in the cultural scene was clear and evident in parallel and sometimes coordinated efforts. In 1974, the Director-General of the British Council, John Llewellyn, reported that "[the emir] was not at all happy about the choice his own people were making in undergraduate studies. Too many were choosing the arts particularly sociology and he wanted doctors, engineers and technical experts to build his country and to avoid relying on expatriates."[45] In early 1974, Llewellyn proposed the involvement of a university like Loughborough in the United Kingdom, modern and particularly slanted toward technical subjects and science in response to the emir's concerns.[46] Meanwhile, a representative from the Polytechnic of Central London (now the University of Westminster) arrived in Doha to explore collaborations in May 1974. In 1975, the Qatari government requested assistance for the establishment of an Institute of Marine Studies, to be based on the proposed University of the Gulf. The British Council then held discussions with the Department of Oceanography at Southampton University.[47]

Amid the ongoing search for partnerships with foreign (and preferably British) institutions, Qatar announced that the Teacher Training College that had been launched in 1973, with the assistance of UNDP,[48] would become an actual university, "to open by 1976 and to be managed by Egyptians."[49] Following similar projects in other Arab countries, Qatar insisted that all teaching staff hold PhD degrees.[50] At this point, American institutions were reportedly closing in with offers to furnish the type of qualifications sought after by the Qataris. Very quickly, the project to build a university gained momentum with plans to construct a university complex for up to three thousand students. The institution was projected to have faculties of education, science, engineering, and economics/administration.

Qatar University opened in June 1977, proclaiming itself "an Arab university which will be concerned with all aspects of university learning and scientific research, preparation of specialized manpower and expert promotion of science, literature and arts, together with the progress of Qatar *and the Islamic heritage in general.*"[51] This educational landscape was a significant shift from earlier descriptions of Qatar before the 1950s, when Islamic institutions (e.g., madrasas) were charged with teaching "religious science and Arabic arts."[52] The UNESCO regional office for education in the Arab States, established in 1960, strongly encouraged the Arabian Gulf region to project their educational strategy on the basis of new educational methods instead of traditional methods. The push to sideline Islamic-centered education was clear and aligned well with the influence of Western expertise, as well as specific developmental goals of the state.

This shift was also reflected in the development of the built landscape and the eventual emergence of a heritage industry. The age of prosperity that Qatar enjoyed through the 1970s, and especially after the oil embargo of 1973–1974, opened the possibility for new and ambitious public expenditure programs. The personnel required to meet the needs of the rapidly expanding infrastructure and services projected across Qatar forced the recruitment of foreign labor. In some of these industries, labor was sought from other Arab countries to such a degree that it resulted in a "new Arab social order," marked by the exchange of labor and capital between oil-rich and oil-poor states.[53] For other industries, the expertise that was sought after was almost exclusively Western or Western-infused. For the new university project, for example, UNESCO recommended the Paris-based Egyptian architect Ahmed El Kafrawi, who in turn arranged for the appointment of Ove Arup & Partners in London (the structural engineers behind the renowned Sydney Opera House) to become consulting engineers for the project.[54] Arup & Partners had a reputation and interest in expanding their work in this region. In 1970, Sir Ove Arup reflected on the principles and experiences of conducting his work around the world during a speech to his partners in England: "Thank God that we have not been invited to do a job in Timbuctoo—think of all the trouble we are avoiding"—he added—"It's different with the work we do in Saudi Arabia, Tehran and Kuwait. There we are invited in at the top, working with good architects, doing exciting work."[55] At *the top* was a good deal of British support through the Overseas Department and their concerns with "competition hotting up" in Qatar.[56] By these accounts, the culture of expertise throughout the decade of the 1970s was defined by a choreographed interaction of British and Egyptian know-how and agendas, setting the stage for an interesting cultural, linguistic, and religious dichotomy that anticipated, and perhaps reflected, a competitive West versus East dynamic in the way that experts were sought and circulated in Qatar.

Heritage agendas and the corresponding languages in Qatar were developed since the early 1970s through what was then a newly formed

Ministry of Information. This institution took on the function of propagandizing the role of the new state regionally and internationally starting in 1971. The French consultant Anie Montigny described the incorporation of *turāth* (heritage) as a key responsibility of this ministry's work.[57] The process of cultural heritage-making in Qatar, she argued, should be understood as stemming from three interrelated agendas: an emphasis on remembrance independent of any preservation of traces of the past, a deprivileging of the specifics of history while maintaining the symbols and metaphors of past times, and a valorization of the present as a moment of well-being and progress. Importantly, all these agendas were implicated in the process of erasing the remains of what can be considered a "negative" past that undermined the nation-building project. Strategies included avoiding the specificities of genealogy and focusing on the benevolence of the state. Montigny described the thematic characteristics involved in this process of heritage production as consisting of two types of heritage that were presented by the state as complementary: *al-turāth al-arabī*, the heritage of the desert Bedouin; and *al-turāth al-baḥr*, the heritage of maritime traditions. A harmonious combination of these—*al-turāth al-shaʿbī*—then comprised the popular, and unified, tradition of the nation, a product optimized to avoid conflict and to prioritize memory over the construction of history.

A crucial point that Montigny makes in her assessment as a heritage expert in Qatar in the 1970s is that Islam was never considered to be a viable basis for the construction of a national heritage. While *turāth* allowed the emphasis to lie on the construction of a national sentiment, Islam constituted the ideological foundations and values on which society was built but was and is not equipped in this context to confer on members of this society an individuality shaped by a unitary identity.[58] This early assessment of the emergence of heritage objectives and policies in Qatar suggests that the development of heritage preservation traditions was destined to gloss over the significance of their Muslim context on the basis of strategy rather than redundancy. The showpiece for things to come in the emergence of a heritage industry in Qatar was the construction of the first National Museum and Marine Museum and Aquarium, a project that spanned from 1972 to 1977 under Sheikh Khalifa. It was envisioned as an institution that could contain evidence of Qatar's history and the traditional ways of life of its people. Michael Rice & Company, the London-based planner and designer of this project, boasted that the resulting cultural institution "maintains, both in its physical structure and in the material which it presents, the essential duality of the Qatari experience, the perpetual counterpoint of land and sea, water and desert, regulated by the deep-rooted beliefs and precepts of Islam."[59] Exactly how "precepts of Islam" were preserved through this work of restoration and expansion was not further articulated. The interior design featured a nine-panel mural by Barry Evans that illustrated Qatar's history in the "Islamic era," while the design for the museum received praise and recognition through an Aga Khan Award for Architecture in its inaugural cycle in 1980.[60]

This validation of new development as a modern extension of so-called Islamic art and architecture at the close of the 1970s aligned with a revaluation of legacy heritage languages and their utility for the construction of a future national identity in Qatar. At this time, the movement and rhetoric of Arab nationalism and its leaders were challenged by Islamic political leadership across the Arab world. This shift was reflected in the way in which locality became articulated by cultural stewards and observers across cultural projects in Qatar. For example, the opening of the new campus of Qatar University in February 1985 coincided with the celebrations organized to mark the thirteenth anniversary of the accession of the emir of Qatar, Shcikh Khalifa. On this occasion, the emir praised this project for catching up with scientific progress while also mobilizing rhetorically the significance of the Arab nation and Islamic traditions. In internal communications, British officials who were following these developments closely pointed out "the absurdity of imposing Western architecture" in El Kafrawi's architectural vision for the campus. According to British Council representatives, the perceived contradiction indicated "a growing degree of self-assertion and distancing from the West by the Qataris, a tendency to turn to inter-Arab resources, or at least put up an Arab front behind which foreign contractors and companies provide the consultancy services, expertise and execute the work."[61] One of these representatives, William Beniston, referred here to the intergovernmental Arab Satellite Communications Organization (Arabsat), founded in 1976, as indicative of these patterns.

In 1985, Beniston reported to London the difficulty of promoting educational and technical cooperation between Britain and Qatar in the context of an Islamic awakening, attaching an undated, but presumably contemporary, newspaper clipping of an article about the "Qatari Cultural Season," an event organized by the Qatari Ministry of Education.[62] In it, Dr. Yusuf al-Qaradawi, then dean of Islamic Shariah at Qatar University, called on an Islamic awakening that steers "on the straight way without deviating to the left or the right," bringing the period of intellectual slavery to the West to an end.[63] Beniston dismissed these as statements intended "for local consumption and to reassure the fanatics across the water." Yet a British Council policy paper circulated just before, in 1984, recognized religion as the chief regulator of national life that was being disrupted by "contact with Western society, the import into the country of Western equipment and hardware" that turned the country into a modern state with strains within society that were difficult to absorb within a traditional Muslim framework.[64] The context for early cultural heritage production in Qatar was therefore multifaceted and rapidly shifting, torn between a desire to anchor the nation in traditional values and institutions (aided by culturally like-minded partners in the region), and a desire to fast-track different cultural projects through an alignment with established Western institutions and forms of expertise.

Heritage Institutionalization

These tensions were not the only factor defining and constricting the development of a heritage assemblage and industry in Qatar. Chronological and typological categories for identifying, describing, and managing heritage resources were determined by the same channels of expertise that struggled to accompany Qatar through its different cultural and political orientations. Just as Ghosh had proposed areas for future expansion for the institutionalization of cultural resources in 1968, a different UNESCO consultant report in 1976 proposed a plan for the preservation and presentation of sites and monuments.[65] This time, the Pakistani archaeologist F. A. Khan, director of the department of archaeology at the Ministry of Education of Pakistan, provided a survey of archaeological and architectural resources by period (Stone Age, prehistory, history, Islamic) to identify problems and needs for the preservation of sites and monuments and the expansion of a museum service. In Qatar, "the Islamic sites are common," he wrote in reference to Murwab, al-Huwailah, and even Doha Palace.[66] One of the urgent "great gaps" in the historical record of Qatar, according to his review, is the period preceding the advent of Islam, while the Islamic period itself needs stimulating. The stagnation that he refers to is due to "the whims of the previous archaeologists who attached greater importance to the pre-Islamic research work. It appears that Islamic sites lie buried under the debris and sand deposits."[67] The Danish Archaeological Expedition

to the Arabian Gulf (1956-1974), led by the British archaeologist Geof-
frey Bibby and the Danish archaeologist Peter Vilhelm Glob under the
patronage of Qatar Petroleum Company, focused on mapping what is
now known to be Neolithic sites across the peninsula.[68] While most of
this work focused on pre-Islamic settlements and remains, the survey
included the documentation of the early Islamic fort and settlement
at Murwab.[69] In 1973-1974, Emir Khalifa al-Thani invited a British
archaeological expedition in Qatar to support the development of the
new National Museum of Qatar that would "give meaning and coher-
ence to Qatar's past."[70] The 1978 report for this project provided a broad
chronological framework and marginally located Qatar in the Islamic
era through brief mentions of traditional cultural features from the sev-
enth to the eighteenth centuries.[71] Other research projects that followed
surveyed and excavated prehistoric sites in the peninsula more broadly,
such as the Mission Archéologique Française à Qatar (1976-1982),[72]
and the 1986-1991 Japanese Archaeological Mission to the Persian Gulf
from Rikkyo University.[73] The French team tackled the Islamic period
much more explicitly and deliberately at Murwab, Huwailah, and al-
Khor using both archaeological and ethnographic techniques.[74]

The hierarchization of different periods of significance in the history
of Qatar is formalized in the first legal definition of "antiquity." By 1980,
the administration of tourism and antiquity at the Ministry of Information, in consultation with the *shūrā* council (one of the two branches of
Qatar's legislative body), issued Law No. 2 of 1980 on antiquities. Article
1 of this legislation described antiquities as "all monuments of civiliza-
tions, ruins of past generations and movable or immovable discoveries
related to arts, science, ethics, morals doctrines, daily life, and public
incidents or otherwise, with a history of forty years or more, provided
that such monuments are of artistic or historical value."[75] Therefore,
"antiquity," and, by association, heritage potential were defined along
strict chronological and typological boundaries that nevertheless failed
to explain the relative exclusion of an Islamic archaeology and heritage
until that point, contradicting a long-held notion that Muslims have
qualms with pre-Islamic remains.[76] An incremental attention to the significance of Islamic chronologies and materiality in the construction of
a Qatari past followed this period. This shift is visible in the literature,
in funding strategies supported by the Qatar National Research Fund,
and in the growth of the higher education section in Qatar over the
years under the umbrella of a more all-encompassing cultural strategy
for the nation.

Starting in 1995, this cultural strategy was spearheaded by the Qatar Foundation for Education, Science, and Community Development (Qatar Foundation). It was founded as a platform for reconciling the two worldviews that had, on occasion, arranged cultural developments in Qatar along the opposing forces of a secular and a Muslim future. Founded by Emir Khalifa and his wife, Sheikha Moza bint Nasser, Qatar Foundation was envisioned as a unique ecosystem that proposed to serve the dual purpose of fostering uniquely local traditions and displaying global ambitions. In 2003, Qatar Foundation's Education City, a multi-institutional campus, was inaugurated to act as a cosmopolitan hub for higher education, with cosmopolitanism reflected in their curricula and design languages alike. Under the umbrella of Education City, built on the Japanese architect Arata Isozaki's master plan, the institutions Virginia Commonwealth University, Cornell University, Northwestern, and Texas A&M University in the United States established satellite campuses in Qatar to teach arts, medicine, information technology and communications, and engineering. They were housed in landmark buildings designed by the Argentine-American Cesar Pelli, the Dutch-man Rem Koolhaas, the Mexican Ricardo Legoretta, and the American Antoine Predock.[77] University College London (UCL) joined this ecosystem later as the only British satellite campus in Qatar. The collection of foreign institutions was complemented by a uniquely grown Qatar Faculty of Islamic Studies in 2007, designed to enhance thinking, research, and discussion related to Islamic culture. It was later incorporated, in 2010, into Hamad bin Khalifa University, a homegrown institution, as the College of Islamic Studies.[78]

Under new institutions and partnerships with foreign experts, Islamic archaeology was featured more prominently in archaeological surveys and excavations through the 2000s, despite the difficulties involved with locating Qatar in historical sources for the Islamic era.[79] The Qatar Islamic Archaeology and Heritage Project (QIAH) was launched as a collaboration between Qatar Museums Authority (now Qatar Museums, established 2005) and the Institute for Cross-Cultural and Regional Studies at the University of Copenhagen during 2008–2012, working extensively in the Zubarah area and mapping early and late Islamic archaeological sites. The Wales Qatar Archaeological Project, launched in 2010 as a collaboration between the University of Wales Trinity Saint David, QIAH and the Qatar Museums, also focused on excavating Islamic sites in northern Qatar, including Ruwayda and Rubayqa. From 2012 to 2018, the Origins of Doha and Qatar (ODQ) project, run by a team based at

UCL Qatar, focused on a study of Doha, Bidda', and Fuwairit, among other sites, while the South Qatar Survey Project (SQSP) was an interdisciplinary cooperation between the German Archaeological Institute and Qatar Museums from 2012 to 2016 to conduct surveys and excavations of prehistoric and historic cultural landscapes in the southern half of Qatar, ranging from the Neolithic era to the twentieth century. Finally, the Crowded Desert Project, a joint venture between UCL Qatar and Qatar Museums from 2015 to 2016, established a historical narrative of nomadic occupation in northwestern Qatar and documented Muslim funerary structures and sacred spaces.[80]

The investment in Islamic material culture and legacies in archaeological research agendas was not matched in the growth of a heritage industry. In this sphere of cultural production, Qatar Foundation focused instead on engineering an attachment to the more recent nation-building histories of Qatar over any other period, a move that seemed to abandon a traditionally "Islamic" era altogether or, at the very least, invited a reinterpretation of what it meant to be modern *and* traditional.[81]

Statecrafting Heritage in the New Millennium

From the 1970s to the 2010s, rapid and profound changes in Qatar, as well as changes in the al-Thani leadership from Sheikh Khalifa to Sheikh Hamad, left a mark on the heritage terrain. In her in-depth analysis of changes in Qatari society during this period, Montigny characterizes this time as an oscillation between an openness to technological modernization and the recomposition of the conservative values of society.[82] Since 1972, Sheikh Khalifa bin Hamad al-Thani's major project of cultural reconfiguration involved the reduction of traditional features of Qatari culture such as tribalism. Instead, modernization gave way to a new relationship between individuals and the state surrounding the notion of citizenship. The changes to the urban fabric initiated under Emir Khalifa in the early 1970s were seen to progress toward an improvement of the living conditions and lifestyles of Qataris. But Montigny argues that subsequent changes under Sheikh Hamad after the soft coup d'état of 1995 were perceived to be even more dramatic and dissociated from Qatari self-interest. Under Sheikh Hamad, this new round of changes affected a predominantly urban society based in Doha, which was anxious about the erasure of familiar landscapes and the influx of large numbers of migrant workers. Accompanying these changes, then, concern with anchoring Qatari history along genealogical lines was reflected in archaeological research priorities, heritage agendas, and the documentation and celebration of contemporary and oral traditions. This trajectory accelerated in the new millennium. In 2008, for example, Qatar National Day was moved to 18 December, the date when Sheikh Jassim bin Mohammed al-Thani, the founder of the state of Qatar, came to power in 1876. Previously, Qatar National Day had been celebrated on 22 February under Sheikh Khalifa, and on 27 June under Sheikh Hamad, commemorating the dates when each of these leaders had ascended to power.

While the state pursued Qatarization of the cultural landscape at home, it grew its ambitions in the sphere of internationalism. In 2006, Qatar hosted the 15th Asian Games, constituting the first time that an Arab and Middle Eastern country hosted such an international event. It motivated a new wave of intense development in the name of modernization that included heritage preservation projects and initiatives across Doha. In April 2009, Qatar announced the largest expansionary budget in the country's history, resulting in ambitious infrastructure projects: a new bridge between Bahrain and Qatar, a new airport, and plans for a subway system, the Doha Metro.[83]

In the cultural and educational spheres, and backed by Qatar Foundation, the government announced the opening of the Museum of Islamic Art in 2008 and the Qatar Technology Park in April 2009. The first Doha Tribeca Film Festival was held in November 2009, and Doha became the Arab Capital of Culture for 2010. Not long after, Qatar orchestrated another regional milestone: a winning bid in 2010 to host the 2022 FIFA World Cup. However impressive, these massive cultural and infrastructural projects were not well received by the Qatari population, Montigny argues, as "the date of completion [seemed] distant, when the project [was] not associated, in the minds of the inhabitants, with the monstrous construction sites spread all over the center of the capital."[84] Yet from the perspective of the state, they constituted strategic statecrafting of the cultural landscape that consolidated Qatar's reputation as an international power, making distinctive contributions to global culture.

Ending the first decade of the millennium, Qatar closed a period of dramatic metamorphosis in the urban and cultural landscape that can hardly invoke a heritage sensibility in the strict sense. Providing a backbone for the development of heritage and tradition within the framework of rapid modernization, and following the ratification of Qatar's Permanent Constitution in 2004, Qatar National Vision 2030 (QNV) was launched in 2008.[85] This document sought to address five major challenges, including "modernization and preservation of tradition," among other areas of economic, social, and environmental growth and management.

The representation of Qatar as part of the *umma* (i.e., as an "Islamic" nation) is clearly articulated throughout the objectives of this document. In the preface of the QNV, then-heir apparent Sheikh Tamim bin Hamad al-Thani wrote that "Qatar National Vision 2030 builds a bridge between the present and the future. It envisages a vibrant and prosperous country in which there is economic and social justice for all, and in which nature and man are in harmony. We need to galvanize our collective energies and direct them toward these aspirations. Strong Islamic and family values will provide our moral and ethical compass."

The text of QNV posits that, despite rapid economic, political, and social changes, "Qatar has maintained its cultural and traditional values as an Arab and Islamic nation that considers the family to be the main pillar of society."[86] The promise of social development is anchored in ideas of tolerance, benevolence, and constructive dialogue toward other cultures, echoing the key contributions that Doha made while brokering the Doha Statement, through "effective public institutions and strong and active civil society organizations that . . . preserve Qatar's national heritage and enhance Arab and Islamic values and identity."[87] Accordingly, QNV specifically commits to "enhance its important and constructive regional role, especially within the framework of the Gulf Cooperation Council (GCC), the Arab League and the Organization of Islamic Conference."[88] Since the launch of QNV, key cultural and educational institutions and initiatives in Qatar aligned their missions to support the goals of this document. This includes the establishment of the Ministry of Culture, Arts, and Heritage in 2008 (with deep roots in the original Ministry of Information founded in 1966); and two institutions charged with heritage preservation work: the Private Engineering Office, established in 2004 by Emiri Decree No. 64 and operating directly under the emir, and Qatar Museums, established in 2005 under Qatar Foundation and arranging its work around three themes: Qatari heritage, Qatari environment, and contemporary Qatar. Through these institutions, the pressure to archive and legitimize—to *discipline*—Qatar through the instruments of preservation resulted in seemingly endless projects of documentation and cataloguing of heritage resources. Since the early 2000s, systematic and thematic surveys to document archaeological, architectural, and archival resources created a template for locating Islam on the cultural map of Qatar. Headed by foreign partners, these included the QIAH (University of Copenhagen), the SQSP (German Archaeological Institute), and the Qatar National Historic Environment Record Project (University of Birmingham and Qatar Museums Authority).[89]

Qatar Foundation's Qatar Unified Imaging Project (QUIP) promoted a transnational identification of primary resources in Qatar, the United Kingdom, India, Denmark, and France through a collaboration between Virginia Commonwealth University Qatar, Exeter University, the Ministry of Culture Arts and Heritage, and the Qatar Museums.[90] It was followed closely by the efforts of the new Qatar National Library (QNL), an institution that became a hub of cultural heritage preservation resources, events, and expertise from the time of its opening in late 2017. Here, the photographic archive of Arab and Islamic worlds, Qatar, the Arabian Gulf, and the Arabian Peninsula, complemented by the work of the early Orientalist photographers Paul Nadar, Francis Firth, Francis Bedford, Pascal Sébah, Félix Bonfils, and Felice Beato, constitute a comprehensive record of local history, traditional practices, the discovery and early production of oil, and urban development until the 1980s. Its sphere of influence further expanded through their partnership with the British Library in the United Kingdom, which holds the second-largest collection of archives on the Arabian Gulf after India, and a partnership with Liverpool University for the Gulf Architecture Project, resulting in a center of gravity for the mapping and formalizing of heritage assemblages across Qatar.

This array of collaborative and multisited mapping projects successfully outlined Qatari culture in disciplinary and institutional terms that aligned with, and translated to, global discourses and forms of mastering heritage. At the same time, each of these initiatives was part of a larger network of projects of cultural and educational development that worked to support the growth of a specific instrument of heritage that could find a home in an international setting. For example, the rise to prominence of QNL as a repository and platform for heritage resources and expertise in matters of archiving was accompanied by the inauguration of UCL Qatar's graduate degree in library and information studies, and also fulfilled UNESCO's vision to establish a documentation and bibliographic center, exactly as it had been recommended by UNESCO observers in the 1970s.

However, this process also left behind cultural and historical resources that did not align with the disciplinary and legal scopes used to formalize heritage preservation initiatives at this time. Cultural resources left out of the spotlight, therefore, enjoyed a certain freedom to evolve in different directions. Without the burden of representation imposed by globalizing ideas of heritage that often focused excessively on serving an idea of the past, aspects of the built landscape could adapt to modern ideas of the state. In these liminal spaces, modern and traditional stewards and stakeholders of national identity could negotiate aesthetics and languages for heritage in ways that archaeological excavation, colonial archiving, and intergovernmental cultural brokering could not.

One of the instruments that allowed this experimentation was Law No. 2, passed in 1980, which defined the era of antiquity in Qatar up to the year 1940. While the law protected traditional (premodern) architecture, it turned its back on the more recent and dramatic decades of expansion and production of art and architecture that took place in Qatar after 1940, despite the critical role that this period played in the construction of modern Qatar. In this way, state policies and instruments placed the architectural remains of the second half of the twentieth century beyond official and institutional heritage preservation agendas in Qatar. Outside the purview of these expectations, different identities—such as the idea of a modern Islamic city—could be more freely reflected and experimented with across the built fabric and eventual stewardship strategies.

CHAPTER 2

Modernism versus Modernization

Constructing Heritage Languages and Landscapes

An iconic image of the urban landscape of Qatar circulated among residents after the Eid al-Fitr religious holiday of 2013: against the characteristic dusty sunset of Doha was a silhouette of two laborers talking after what must have been a hard day of work under the scorching sun. Temperatures in August of that year averaged 96° Fahrenheit and reached a maximum of 111° (35.5° and 43.8° Celsius, respectively). The image was framed by two resting Caterpillar excavators, with their hydraulic arms pointed at the ground, and a row of streetlights in the near distance. This could be depicting any intersection of Doha at dusk were it not for the unusual protagonists: in the foreground, a statue of two oryxes—*maha*, the national animal of Qatar—was propped on top of a double helix pedestal at the center of the aptly named Oryx Roundabout on the Corniche (figure 2.1). Shortly after this image was released, the oryxes and their impressive pedestal disappeared from the urban fabric of Doha as the roundabout was replaced by a multilane intersection.

The oryx statue on the roundabout was not the only public art-cum-monument to be decommissioned during the reconfiguration of the scenic waterfront throughway. Construction along the Corniche and the concentric street Majlis al Taawon resulted in the erasure of all roundabouts, including their striking (and sometimes puzzling)

FIGURE 2.1.   Removal of the Oryx Roundabout, 2013. Marvin Fernandez for Getty Images.

sculptural art that had become iconic across the cities of the Arabian Peninsula. It was these sculptures that had given each intersection their eponymous labels: "Oryx Roundabout" on the Corniche; "Sports Roundabout" in Al Rayyan; "Arch Roundabout," removed to make way for the Lusail Expressway; and Qatar's iconic clock tower in Umm Ghuwaylīnah Roundabout, the gateway to the old Doha International Airport. Roundabout art had become such a distinctive feature of the modern Gulf city that it had been widely documented and commented on by foreign visitors, often disparagingly. As one such visitor to Doha described in the 1970s, "Every city has its eccentricity, Doha's is quite indisputably from the sugar-pink and white-and-blue clock tower on the roundabout in front of the divan. It looks decidedly Alice-in-Wonderlandish, as if a white rabbit were at any moment to appear and stare at it."[1] This classic expatriate trope was used to document the modernization of Doha in such a way that its authenticity as a Qatari, Arab, or "Islamic city" could be put into question. Yet the widespread circulation of the 2013 photograph among both Qataris and non-Qataris and the accompanying commentary on social media indicated that these now-defunct monuments evoked genuine nostalgia among residents.

Throughout its reign as a distinctive landmark up to its removal, the Oryx Roundabout had been the centerpiece of diverse narratives that speak to the challenges inherent in different waves of modernization in Qatar. Its relative immutability as a wayside feature had been disrupted by episodes of structural transformation marked by controversy over their place in a Muslim society. The oryxes' removal in 2013 propelled a rumor that South Asian migrant workers had been seen praying to the oryx due to the animal's likeness to cows, a sacred animal esteemed by Hindus.[2] It was an unlikely but sensational story that spread like wildfire, fueled by protracted tensions between South Asian migrant workers and citizens in cosmopolitan Doha. In fact, the pair of oryxes had apparently been removed before following a similar rationale. As conversations about disappearing landmarks escalated in social media, blurry images of this very same roundabout resurfaced depicting a time when the pedestal featured an oversized globe instead of the pair of antelopes. This time, rumors surrounding the removal of the oryxes sustained that an influential citizen of Qatar had deemed the depiction of the animals inappropriate for an "Islamic city," whose identity was perhaps better—or at least less controversially represented—by a depiction of our planet. The evolving narratives over the disappearance of this landmark, then, offer insights into the ways in which different periods of modernization made and remade Qatar's heritage landscape in the public sphere. In these peripheral arenas, away from official and institutionalized heritage at the hands of the state, innovative and dynamic ideas of culture and tradition could be expressed and negotiated through heritage languages reflected in urban architecture, planning, and design.

Elsewhere in Doha, remnants of this modern turn had fared equally poorly or been tolerated ambivalently. The built landscape of the 1950s through the 1980s, itself reflecting modernization, was being ravaged by another wave of modernization taking place throughout the first and second decades of the new millennium. The institutionalization of heritage preservation agencies and agendas in the 1980s was not equipped to support the preservation of historical resources that fell broadly under the era of modernism. The Law of 1980, written with the aim of supporting the preservation of pre-oil traditional architectural styles dating up to 1940, put in jeopardy the visibility and viability of the urban fabric built thereafter. Yet the impact of decades of large-scale expansion across Qatar—the modernist turn—was unmistakable and significant: the prominence of the iconic pyramidal Sheraton Hotel,

FIGURE 2.2. *Qatar Post*, designed by Twist and Whitley Architects and completed in 1982, Doha, 2018. Photo by author.

a 1982 modernist landmark designed by the firm William L. Pereira & Associates from Los Angeles, USA, has defined the skyline and the waterfront landscape of the capital city since its inauguration.

The architecture of the Corniche itself tells an exciting modernist story of Qatar through a coordinated display of state institutions whose structures remain today (figure 2.2): from north to south, the Qatar Post, the Qatar National Theater, the Ministry of Interior, and the Emiri Diwan (the seat of the Qatari government) were arranged in a semicircle along the Corniche. Boasting designs from a range of international architects and designers (Triad Cico, Twist and Whitley Architects, and ComConsult), this assemblage of landmarks stood the test of time despite the ever-changing landscape and cityscape behind them. Jumanah Abbas summarizes this persistence as being driven by a modernization project that also represented the government's investment in the preservation of Gulf architecture.[3] At the southernmost end of the promenade from the Sheraton, however, the remains of a modernist city were systematically dismantled through the second decade of the 2000s, with few exceptions. In this area, a different wave of modernization was in full swing through revitalization projects such as Msheireb

Downtown Doha, where modernism was all but erased and replaced by a new heritage language.

There could be multiple reasons for this erasure. Some have argued that the core idea of modernization as heritage in Qatar and across the Gulf Cooperation Council (GCC) pitted the traditional culture of pearling (a positive value) against that of petroleum exploitation (a negative value), in the context of mounting concerns with pollution, environmental degradation, and unsustainable consumption in Qatar.[4] In this view, the modernist era of Qatar and post-oil livelihoods and economies that this era ushered in were put at odds with modern discourses of sustainable progress. Later on, in alignment with new social and environmental values, political histories of resource exploitation, and human-environment interactions of the new millennium, cultural references to the traditions associated with natural pearls and pearl-diving thrived in heritage languages. An appreciation of a heritage of fossil fuels—what would be largely represented chronologically in a heritage of modernism—made a comeback only in discreet ways (e.g., curated in the narrative structure of the National Museum and in the core subject matter of the Company House museum in Msheireb). Here, the advent of industrialization as a heritage of citizens, not of foreign interests and migrant workers, is narrativized primarily through oral history. But nevertheless, the disappearance of the modernist city in Qatar ruptured a historical continuity between a traditional preindustrial and a modern industrial nation and livelihood.

The influence of a culture of preservationism imported from Euro-American heritage preservation traditions since the 1970s was reflected in this rupture in various ways. Primarily, this philosophy has traditionally prioritized older periods and styles and idealized distinct local and regional identities over the documentation of global and cosmopolitan trajectories, minimizing hybridity and assimilation. In this sense, the advent of preservation instruments served well the project of construction of national identities in the Middle East, which sought to "erase recent colonial and imperial pasts and narrate a new history based on indigenous forms and ideals."[5] Commenting on this kind of process, the Turkish architectural historian Doğan Kuban argued that, in the Muslim world as in other non-Western countries, modern preservationism imported from the West allowed the destruction of select historical environments as a sacrificial rite in the modern world.[6] The modernist era was sacrificial on other accounts, too. It made its mark in the urban landscapes of Qatar in earnest through the decades that fall "after the demise of late 19th century Muslim peril propaganda and before the rise of modern post-Cold War Islamophobia," when Islam is "still largely viewed as a quaint remnant of a traditional way of life that it was assumed would disappear in the ongoing modernization of the world."[7] As an expression representing the advent of technology and urbanization in Qatar, it was further endangered by its apparent ability to threaten not only tradition and social life, but also religion. The project of modernization in Qatar that brought about all the comforts of modern living (air conditioning, running water, and electricity, among others) was also a project that promoted secularization and homogenization.[8] On the surface, this transitional landscape was not encouraging for the preservation of any aspects of traditional life. The British self-proclaimed chronicler of Arabian life, Helga Graham, described hyperbolically the cityscape of Doha in the 1970s, where "the construction cranes outnumber the mosque towers in the ratio of at least four to one."[9] Could the modernizing city maintain the centrality of Islam in the livelihoods of Qatar—the essentializing myth of the "Islamic city"?[10] Naturally, everything about the new city was anathema to traditional lifestyles and values and unprecedented in historical Arab-Islamic epochs, but behind the rising skyscrapers of the modern world lay ancient tribal practices and Islamic customs that were still very much alive. Still, modernism thrived for a period of time, despite its claim to "being utterly and totally rational, a claim that, if true, would make modernism altogether incompatible with the qualities of sacred, or religious, space."[11] Modernism, it could be said, was a force that could absorb and reduce the influence of both Islam and tradition through its predominantly secular homogeneity. Yet the iconicity of modernist structures in Qatar and the importance of modernization processes to shaping its trajectory as a nation have had a significant influence on the development of heritage languages in architecture, design, and planning, leading projects of "revival" that invoke an era before the Muslim world became "contaminated" by the West.[12]

Islamicizing Modernization

The sense of alienation of local values, including religion, in the different bouts of modernization of Qatar was not just prompted by aesthetics. It was also associated with the type of expertise that was selected to put these projects into operation. The rush to build in Qatar, starting as early as the late 1960s, resulted in tight schedules and an intricate process of development that included specific types of consultants and systems of foreign collaboration.[13] Roberto Fabbri and Iain Jackson point out that, from the mid-1970s onward, European firms that catered to rulers and private investors were gradually replaced by large corporate firms and state-led agencies hailing from countries located at opposite sides of the political spectrum. The remaking of Doha included firms like Energoprojekt, Miastoprojekt, and Bulgarconsult from the Soviet bloc,[14] as well as the British architecture and planning firms Llewelyn-Davies, Weeks, Forestier-Walker, and Bor, and the American architecture and urbanism firm William L. Pereira & Associates.[15] In this landscape of specialists, the emergence and consolidation of local expertise across the region were made more difficult, although eventually, the emergence of the Arab expert, al-muhandis,[16] reflects socioeconomic exchanges between the Gulf and the Levant in the context of an Arab renaissance during the first oil boom, between the 1950s and the 1970s.[17]

Major players brought in to lead the urban and architectural renewal of Qatar advised and worked under local institutions. For example, Michael Rice & Company's project to craft the first National Museum in 1977 was carried out under the direction of the Ministry of Information, while the construction of structures was charged to the Ministry of Public Works.[18] In addition, the project included the Design Construction Group as the architects for the grounds, Ahmad Assad al-Ansari, who was head of the Maintenance Section, as the restoration supervisor, and the Engineering Services Department of the Ministry of Public Works. The task of localizing this new institution involved strategic site selection and curatorial decisions. The museum was built on and around the ruined remains of a small palace complex first occupied by Sheikh Abdullah bin Qassim al-Thani in the early 1900s. This site was chosen in part due to a shortage of other old town structures that could be repurposed for this initiative, but also due to its role as the seat of power for the governor until this was moved to central Doha by the 1920s, and then deteriorated by the 1970s.[19] Works of reconstruction to turn this structure into the museum used the remaining architectural and artistic features and supplemented them by oral and visual sources, thus engaging Qatari citizens and residents in the project of reincorporating this structure into the civic landscape of Qatar. The resulting complex was a cluster of nine buildings intended to represent the domestic and official quarters of one ruling Qatari family, accompanied by a purpose-built pavilion to house the Museum of the State, the Marine Museum and Aquarium, and a lagoon where traditional vessels could be put on display.[20]

The National Museum restoration project received the Aga Khan Award for Architecture in its inaugural cycle in 1980 due to its ingenuous utilization of the old 1918 Emiri Palace and the addition of a new three-level structure whose facade echoed the older building. Supporting documentation for this award shows that, south of the Little Majlis on the eastern corner of the courtyard, the remains of a destroyed mosque still stood at the start of the restoration project.[21] This mosque was not incorporated into the redevelopment of the structure and its surroundings, where instead, "landscaping and a network of paths . . . transformed the compound into a lush garden, welcome in the inhospitable climate."[22] An aerial photograph of the Old Palace taken by the Royal Air Force in 1934 shows a compound without a mosque, perhaps suggesting that colonial sources were used over contemporary remains to guide the works of restoration. The uneventful disappearance of the mosque represented the more sophisticated ways in which the Islamic was to be celebrated in the modernization of architecture and design of Doha and across the region.

The jury of the Aga Khan Award highlighted the challenge of infilling the relatively long period of abandonment that had taken a toll on this complex in their assessment of the project, writing that "in a period of rapid social and economic change, when the widespread and indiscriminate destruction of the architectural heritage has broken all continuity with the past, the preservation, enhancement and adaptation to a new public use of this important group is a noteworthy achievement."[23] At the launch of the first cycle of Awards in Architecture in 1980, His Highness the Aga Khan reflected on "whether the awarded projects truly correspond to the great traditions of Islamic architecture. There are no mosques among them, no madrasas, no palaces, no gardens, no mausoleums, hardly any monuments that are visited by millions of tourists, cherished by those who live near them, and utilized by historians to define the Muslims' past." However, he clarified that

> [these] are only part of the built environment of the past . . . the recognition of a human scale, of local decisions (even if they required outside expertise), of local needs and concerns is, I believe, a profoundly Muslim requirement. It is the expression of that societal requirement, that consideration of thousands of separate communities within the whole *umma*, that is so uniquely a central part of the Muslim message. . . . Through architecture, we are recognizing the quality of life within the Muslim World today. And, by recognizing a medical center or housing project developed by a whole community, we are preserving for all time the memory of this quality of life.[24]

The Aga Khan's particular ideology and leadership in the articulation of heritage value and its preservation in the context of development
was an ideal endorsement of the ways in which heritage construction
was expanding in Qatar in uniquely Muslim ways as part of the efforts
to localize the built landscape. Commenting on the balance between
preservation and destruction within the framework of the Aga Khan
Award, Doğan Kuban added that the "unfortunate destruction of our
older buildings is more apt to be justified on the basis of cultural and
economic obsolescence. Ordinarily, for example, we do not destroy
mosques; instead, we make them comfortable by adding heating systems. We preserve the minarets and install loudspeakers for the greater
comfort of the muezzins. We are also able to maintain and even use the
old palaces, the old khans, the old madrasas; we simply redefine their
functions."[25] Such an approach to prioritizing the reuse and adaptation
of historical resources over original form in Qatar would become a subject of significant debate over the following four decades, with different
philosophies of authenticity pitted against each other to legitimize (or
delegitimize) Qatari know-how in the face of rapid development.

Since the earliest days of the newly established nation, cultural institutions in Qatar were charged with the task of reconciling the aims
of progress and the well-being and sustainability of traditional values
that included a nod to its Muslim cultural, social, and political contexts, without much of a blueprint to maintain an intimate connection
between modernization and traditional, including Islamic, aesthetics.
The intended audience for the National Museum was primarily Qatari,
but the projection of its paneling in both Arabic and English suggested
that a wider audience was contemplated. In fact, Michael Rice explains
that the museum, while imparting a historical and cultural consciousness onto Qataris, would also convey to foreigners "the nature of Qatar's
history and the flavor of its traditions."[26] Confronting a lack of readily
accessible published material about Qatar at the time, a research program was put in place to provide the academic and scholarly foundations that each section of the museum would require. For this purpose,
distinguished scholars, Arab and non-Arab, were recruited to imple-
ment a specially designed research program to provide the information
base needed for the establishment of the museum.

The National Museum project, then, created as much as it represented
a coherent Qatari identity. Rice wrote that "it is safe to say that the very
calling into existence of the Qatar National Museum has resulted in the
horizons of knowledge about Qatar and its immediate surroundings

being significantly extended."[27] The collections that furnished the National Museum were assembled from various locations. The Danish Archaeological Expedition to the Arabian Gulf (1956–1974) had already sent all its finds to Aarhus in Denmark for conservation and study, citing a lack of museum facilities in Qatar in the 1950s and 1960s, but some of these were returned to Doha to be part of the first permanent archaeological exhibition in the museum.[28] Such a process of archival repatriation lasted several decades.[29]

Jonathan Raban, the author of the reductive chronicle of the region titled *Arabia through the Looking Glass*, visited the museum in the late 1970s and described a gallery devoted to the oil industry and, outside, restored antique dhows that floated in an ornamental pool, flanked by two 1940s Cadillacs—one of which was labeled "the First Cadillac on Qatar."[30] The dhow, a traditional lateen-rigged ship of the Indian Ocean, and the classic American car bracketed two key cultural periods that now coexisted in the representation of the history of Qatar: a traditional and a modern (and in some cases, explicitly imported and generic Western) livelihood. While the process of Qatarization was already underway at the time of his visit, Raban observed in his writings about various institutions and government offices that none of the actual custodians of this past seemed to be Qataris. Ministers were Qataris, he clarified, but directors were nearly all from northern Arabia; the Qataris had commissioned foreign experts to keep their own memories intact.[31]

A similar pattern of expertise was followed throughout the expansion of projects of infrastructure across the nation. Starting in the 1970s, standardization and prefabrication of building materials that sought to negotiate locality through decorative finishes resulted in a modern architecture that "has a seemingly contrarian approach of 'starting again' whilst also 'flirting' with so-called traditional (and sometimes fabricated, imagined or appropriated) elements of locality, such as geometrical motifs, shapes, textures or colour palette."[32] What Fabbri and Jackson call "an expression of the Orientalist fantasy of the Middle East" was accompanied, they argue, by the liberal grafting of decoration, patterns, and ornamentation over forms and arrangements "more generally associated with a more austere modernist agenda."[33] Raban's descriptions suggest that this could be due to a popular perception of Qatar as a "tabula rasa" of enormous tracts of sand, marsh, and sea, an interpretation of the terrain that ignored a rich, preexisting, built, and symbolic landscape.[34] Accordingly, architectural design processes during this decade leaned on the idea of being able to start again, to remake, reimagine, and remodernize.[35] Such a view sustained the perception that Qatar was comprised of historical fabrics that stretched back mere decades. In this view, modernization could only bring gains.

Those who proposed it argued that the integrity of the radial pattern of the *fareej* (neighborhood) system was observed and strengthened through the work of British and American urbanists and planners, celebrating the ways in which modernist urbanism and architecture expanded the existing city and its livelihoods. The reshaping of the natural coastline of Doha into the manicured Corniche as a waterfront park was celebrated for creating new public spaces that could be used recreationally. The opposing view recognized preexisting urban and social heritage histories of Qatar, but this view turned each episode of the modern remaking of the city into a narrative of loss. One such narrative holds that aerial photos since 1947 show a rapid erosion of the organic *fareej* patterns of Doha, driven by new economies. The ring-road system that is characteristic of Doha, as well as its urban expansion of the 1950s to 1970s, were fueled by projects of land reclamation and urbanization that forever changed the natural and built landscapes of the city. This observation pays particular attention to the ways in which an urban shift affected the social bonds of Qatar, shifting from familial and community-based decision-making processes to an anonymous, centralized process of urbanization based on statistics.[36] What kinds of processes negotiated these views and ultimately defined each project of modernization and redevelopment?

Expert Negotiations

The history of the advent of modernism in the built landscape of Qatar used to be on display in the form of publications at the Atlas Bookstore, an establishment located on the ground floor of the iconic Sheraton Hotel. Here, the founder, Fatma al-Sahlawi, curated the history of architecture and urbanism across the Middle East and North Africa.[37] Prominently displayed was the September 6, 1963, issue of *Time*, which marks the opening of a new chapter in the urban modernity of Qatar.[38] On the cover of this issue, headlined "Vistas for the Future," was a portrait of William Pereira, the architect behind the Sheraton Hotel itself. Next to this issue, a January 1979 cover of *Time* featured a photograph of Philip Johnson holding a model of the AT&T corporate headquarters in New York City (completed 1984) for the cover story headlined "U.S. Architects Doing Their Own Thing."[39] Johnson had already won the prestigious AIA Gold Medal and would also win the first Pritzker Architecture Prize later that year.

Together, these two magazine issues bracket a critical time for the development of the first heritage languages in Qatar that were intentionally embedded into modernist design.[40] The way in which these architectural innovations influenced the urban fabric of Doha was not only through commissioned works by "starchitects." The mobilizations of the objectives and tools of modernism also offered a pathway to the continuous production of tradition and heritage to be liberated from ascetic ideals of temporal and aesthetic purity. For example, Johnson advocated for and inspired, among other things, the idea of a "shaped modern," a design marked by glass and mirrored facades that was critiqued for its abstract features "sealed from all memory."[41] Instead, the surfaces reflected the surroundings—a tempting proposition that could simultaneously accommodate the era of air-conditioned interiors while mirroring the traditional facades and landscapes around it.

Since 1972, two different emirs commissioned master plans from four different firms to envision the future of Doha.[42] In the first instance, Sheikh Khalifa hired the architecture and planning firm Llewelyn-Davies with the aim of creating a city that would improve the lives of everyday Qataris. Thus far, the modernization of the city had been supported through loans, land grants, and allowances that encouraged citizens to vacate their ancestral homes in the city in favor of new villas in the outskirts.[43] But the result of this master plan was a crumbling city center devoid of Qatari nationals that became occupied by low-wage migrant renters instead.[44] The Llewelyn-Davies plan for revitalization of the old city was then interrupted by the financial downfall of the 1970s, but it left its mark on the road system of concentric rings, the Corniche, and the planning of West Bay (Dafna), the financial district of Doha located north of Old Doha. The architect Peter Chomowicz describes a plan that called for sweeping social and architectural change to the original tight-knit fabric of Doha, championing public policy, pedestrian passage, and a sensitive balance between old and new.[45]

The following master plan went in a different direction. William Pereira was tasked with imagining a "New Doha" directly north of the existing city instead of rehabilitating the old city. This plan linked the historic center and the new city to the north through an extension of the ring-road system, proposed a series of Western-suburban-style cul-de-sac residential neighborhoods, and completed Llewelyn-Davies's proposal for the waterfront Corniche, complete with the creation of West Bay, where Pereira located his landmark Sheraton Hotel. Chomowicz concludes that the second master plan represents "the moment when Doha decided it no longer needed or wanted a past."[46]

But the Qatari officials saw Pereira's work as one of the moving parts of a city that selectively modernized and retained features of its heritage. Johnson Fain and Pereira's proposal for the New District of Doha was much more expansive than the vision for the new Sheraton Hotel. It also included features such as a Cooperative Marketplace, a commercial core intended to support the new district that also served as the social and cultural complement to the adjacent Jumma mosque and other civic and community facilities. It was designed to include indoor courtyards with arcades roofed under fiberglass tents, in a design that was oriented to "3 major (Islamic) formal prototypes: to the courtyard, to the nomadic tent, and to the traditional souk as a linked sequence of larger and smaller public nodes and passages."[47] The design for the Sheraton Hotel itself was informed by criteria intended to serve the future needs of the country while relating to culture, tradition, and climate. The resulting structure, the architects claimed, resembled a desert tent, consistent with the inward-focused nature of Qatari social life and the need for privacy that is important in Middle Eastern cultures, while displaying finishes and motifs with origins in "Arabic traditions."[48]

Pereira's legacy in the architectural history of Qatar did not end at the singularity of the Sheraton Hotel on the city skyline.[49] The US-trained Jordanian Hisham Qaddumi, the planning and development advisor for the Emiri Diwan (1974–1987), described being fascinated by Pereira's work when it was featured on the cover of *Time* magazine in 1963, prompting an invitation for William L. Pereira & Associates to design the hotel.[50] Raban's descriptions of Doha in the 1970s included a meeting with Qaddumi himself, who described how planning a modern Qatari city might be different from planning other cities: "everything that is workable in the Arab city . . . of course we retain it," and the plan also fit "the best features of the Western city."[51] Under his purview, the Action Plan 1398 for Qatar (1977–1978) involved infrastructure projects such as roadworks, land reclamation, water supplies, and sewage. However, he clarified, "no one's going to take a bulldozer to the souk."[52]

The souk, an archetype of the Arab city, had already become the centerpiece of an emerging conversation about authenticity that has since accompanied the growth of Qatar's heritage industry. Qaddumi explained to Raban that he did not want "a phoney souk either. Put in tiled ceilings and marbled floor and eliminate the dirt—that's a fake, not a souk. You just have to get some of the dirt out. . . . Just as much as is needed to stop it blocking up the air conditioning."[53] Restoration of Souk Waqif was eventually preserved following a modernizing view that supported the reimagination and remixing of the original historical fabric, resulting in a design that challenged more conservative notions of continuous material authenticity.

In hindsight, the development of arts and culture in Qatar during this period seemed to confront a lose-lose scenario. On the one hand, Qatar would surrender the stewardship for their past in favor of moderniza-tion. As Farah El Nakib demonstrates in her study of Kuwait, the past could become a hindrance to the modernist project since reaching for an imagined future required the removal of historical context.[54] In this process, city-making was caught in the tensions and idealizations of the Middle East as "an almost timeless place, a region that stands in distinct and didactic contrast with the disruptive displacement and disillusion-ment that has resulted from its own industrialization."[55] On the other hand, any process of modernization in Qatar that attempted to hybridize local cultural and aesthetic norms with the principles of modernism was going to be ridiculed and deemed inauthentic by its critics. Accordingly, John Harris, the famous master planner of Dubai, declared that "there is something ridiculous about a thirty-story Islamic tower."[56] The second phase of modernization in Qatar would come to challenge that opinion.

This was initiated during the mandate of Sheikh Hamad bin Khalifa al-Thani through the 1990s. Under his leadership, a much-publicized campaign of liberalization promised to embark on "Qatar's own 'route to modernity'"—namely, an intensification of a locally grown heritage industry under the banner of the Qatar Foundation and the Qatar National Vision 2030 (QNV).[57] The systematic reorganization of exist-ing heritage resources and the growth of new ones during this period offered opportunities for rethinking the possibilities of a modern "Islamic city." Critics have argued that this process of modernization was able to mobilize traditional knowledge strategically, but this remained decanted and purified from religious tradition.[58] To qualify the extent of this purification, Rosanna Law and Kevin Underwood synthesize the ways in which new visual statements and designs paid some homage to Islamic art (Museum of Islamic Art), celebrated traditional uses of space (Souk Waqif), and combined and integrated traditional uses, modern materials, and design accommodating both traditional and modern views (Msheireb Downtown Doha). However, the authenticity and depth of some of these urban interventions and processes of regeneration showed superficial engagement with some traditional heritage languages. For example, among the modern towers of West Bay, motifs extracted from across the Arab world were used in ways foreign to their origins. Chomowicz interprets this as showing a desire by foreign designers to appear "local" and knowledgeable about "Islamic" customs, appealing to a broad field of "Islamic architecture."[59] Chomowicz adds that this desire also served local Qatari clients that wished to appear cultured in a way that reflected ideas of cosmopolitanism associated with their role in an increasingly affluent segment of society.

A ubiquitous example of this hybridity is the inclusion of Islamic geometric patterning across the postmodern built landscapes of Qatar. For example, the renowned tower Burj Qatar (2012) was designed by the French architect Jean Nouvel to feature a facade in a star-shaped *mashrabiya* pattern, which according to the design team was inspired by a column in a local mosque of Doha. Falling back on generic Islamic design could also be seen as a failure to capture more local elements of design. It has been argued that most Western designers working in Qatar have used southern Spain, Iran, or ancient Baghdad or Damascus for inspiration for their highly evolved aesthetic innovations rather than the less-spectacular Islamic motifs of Gulf origin.[60] Perhaps most notably, the Chinese-American architect I. M. Pei openly discussed his lack of prior knowledge of Islamic design and an elaborate search for what he called "the essence" of Islamic architecture after he was recruited to build the Museum of Islamic Art by Luis Monreal, now general manager of the Aga Khan Trust for Culture. Pei's search for a pure expression saw him discard iconic structures from the styles of Andaluz (Grand Mosque of Cordoba), Mughal (Fatehpur Sikri), and Umayyad (Grand Mosque in Damascus). It was in Tunisia where he found inspiration in the form of the ribat fortresses at Monastir and Sousse, "where sun brings to life powerful volumes and geometry plays a central role."[61] He finally settled for the Mosque of Ibn Ṭūlūn in Cairo, with its small ablution fountains, double arcades, and an almost cubist expression of geometric progression from the octagon to the square and the square to the circle. Alluding to pan-Islamic heritage is only one of the ways in which this architecture transcends Qatar's borders.[62] In a personal statement where he describes the guiding principle behind this design, Pei describes a structure that can "bring forth in the desert sun of Doha,"[63] an empty landscape that invokes the spirit of a tabula rasa and a timeless essence intended to mediate the global and local.[64]

Localizing his work in the specific context of Qatar is further complicated by the language of architectural descriptions used to celebrate this endeavor in all its sophistication: the final structure was built from cream-colored Magny and Chamesson limestone from France, Jet Mist granite from the United States, and stainless steel from Germany. Indoors, the galleries designed by the French architect Jean-Michel Wilmotte feature dark gray porphyry stone and Brazilian Louro Faya wood.[65] The idealization of a local essence concretized through the hype over the use of luxurious foreign materials added to the challenge of localizing new design in both Qatari and Islamic languages. While *khaliji* architecture reflects cosmopolitan exchanges, the modern discourse about luxury as an imported good appeared to make new design and tradition mutually exclusive.

Architects and developers struggled to fluidly engage with the specifics of locality well into the new millennium. In 2019, the grand opening of the National Museum of Qatar was accompanied by a public discussion on architecture at the National Library, titled "Architecture as a Face of a Nation."[66] The panel moderated by Philip Jodidio, editor in chief of the French art magazine *Connaissance des Arts*, featured renowned architects Rem Koolhaas, Jean Nouvel, Ben van Berkel, Jacques Herzog, and the US-trained Qatari architect Ibrahim Jaidah. In this highly anticipated public celebration, Jodidio's task of coordinating a conversation about the legacies of design for national identity-building in Qatar was met with frustration by some of these architectural icons. They seemed more inclined to celebrate the uniqueness and avant-garde qualities of their legacies than to align their efforts with the project of reinforcing locality for the architectural futures of Qatar. In a sort of rebellion against the aims of the panel, Koolhaas, who has famously argued against preservation movements, eventually proposed that "we drop the face of the nation from this question. We are individuals."[67] Herzog then downplayed the distinctiveness of Muslim architecture for the design future of Qatar, arguing that "there was never a dominant culture dictating where architecture should go, they were always some kind of hybrid," whereby "Muslim architecture has been very much inspired by older architecture."

Nouvel, the designer of the desert rose–shaped National Museum of Qatar, which was being celebrated that night, was asked by Jodidio why he selected a geological element and not a cultural one to represent Qatari identity. "It is a symbol," he responded, and "at the same time, it is an energy." Nouvel's official description of the museum project invokes "the desert, its silent and eternal dimension, but also the spirit of modernity and daring that have come along and shaken up what seemed unshakeable."[68] Later in the panel discussion, Jaidah would scaffold Nouvel's vague response, helping him localize Nouvel's design but also challenging existing characterizations by asking, "Who can say that the desert rose is not our identity?"

As the only Qatari on the panel, it was Jaidah who was asked about the role of Islamic identity in the design for a future era. Despite his known design trajectory, which heavily features elements of Islamic patterning on modern high-rises, he quipped that Islamic identity, more than aesthetics, is a function. His 2000 modern high-rise, Barzan Tower, features glass surfaces and an "Arab street" facade that challenges traditional scale in what Chomowicz calls "a struggle to remain ontologically Islamic against its modern embodiment."[69] Since Jaidah was the sole Qatari on stage, his views carried the weight of bringing legitimacy and diversity to the conversation on nation-building and locality that this panel had promised. He lamented, for example, that "we [Qataris] tend to forget our early modern history," pointing out the preference for some historical periods over others in the development of an architectural language in Qatar. A few years before this event, in a 2016 lecture at the Georgetown School of Foreign Service in Qatar, Jaidah called for a more careful consideration of what it means to think in traditional or vernacular terms, adding that "it doesn't have to be a mud house to become history."[70]

Jaidah's work celebrates a revival of traditional vernacular style in such a way that a contemporary Qatari heritage language becomes, over time, a fusion of multiple worldviews that remains nonetheless locally grown. The regionally and internationally recognized work of Ibrahim Jaidah Architects and Engineers includes the preservation of traditional architectural structures (the 1910 Barzan Towers), the renovation of modernist architecture (the 1982 Fire Station Civil Defense complex), and the design and construction of modern high-rises that often include a nod to traditional aesthetics and far-reaching influences of Islamic art (such as the aforementioned Barzan Tower high-rise). A known supporter of modernism, Jaidah was also behind the exhibit that accompanied the opening of the National Museum, titled "Making Doha, 1950–2030," which featured extensive references to the modernist era among the architectural successes of the country, including the post-oil era.[71] His efforts to visualize a wider range of architectural styles and languages for Qatar, inclusive of Islamic elements, forge more dynamic and inclusive heritage futures.

Localizing Authenticity through Heritage Languages

The struggle to formalize and chart the evolution and future of heritage languages for Qatar is not a zero-sum game in Jaidah's proposition: traditionalism, modernism, and continuous modernization can coexist in the fabric of the modern nation-state, and the incorporation of Islam as an aesthetic and functional element of design can be seen as the linchpin that puts these apparently disparate concerns into conversation. In one of his published works, *Qatari Style*, Jaidah acknowledges hybridity at every historical turn of the cultural development of Qatar, observing that heritage languages for Qatar are grouped into three distinct phases.[72] The first represents the time before the discovery of oil, a period marked by humble decorations in color and style. More intricate facade carvings, decorative ceilings, and wooden features could be observed in elite structures (royal family and important merchants), while simple vernacular designs were shaped by life in the desert: temporary tent settlements were made from camel, sheep, and goat hair, black-and-white textiles for the *bait al-sha'ar*, or colored wool for the *sawd* fabric displaying geometric patterns in their own visual language. In coastal fishing communities, structures were made of limestone and dolomite and displayed pale colors that can now be seen as the basis for the traditional Qatari architectural palette. The next phase in the development of heritage languages in Qatar, he describes, was influenced by eighteenth-century migration across the Middle East and Persia. It resulted in the incorporation of the *najdi* style of the broad Arabian Peninsula region, including building techniques and decorative patterns such as pastoral images. Slave trade also brought with it traditions, songs, and visual languages that became incorporated into aspects of tradition in Qatar.

The discovery of oil in the mid-twentieth century resulted in a third Qatari style, which was influenced by cultures beyond the Arabian Peninsula and the Indian Ocean. This features cross-cultural imports from the Levant, North Africa, India, and the West. In this period, the local vernacular met and incorporated new and luxurious materials and artifacts and can be appreciated in elements of Indian style, vibrant interior design, and even the incorporation of air conditioning technology. In alignment with Jaidah's advocacy for a recognition of cosmopolitanism in the traditional fabrics of Qatar, other figures in preservation in Qatar, such as Mohammed Ali Abdullah, from the Private Emir Office (PEO), have pointed out that local, pre-oil architectural styles in Qatar are a testimony to regional and transoceanic trading networks that brought with them essential building materials: *danshal* (mangrove) wood from the African coast,[73] *nargil* (coconut) fiber from India and Africa, and reef from the Euphrates region in Iraq. Too often, the cosmopolitanism represented in these fabrics has been used to delegitimize the authenticity of a local Qatari architecture. And yet, as Abdullah argues in support of his work across Qatar, both material and design satisfy local climatic and social factors in meaningful cultural ways, such as through the preservation of privacy and the accommodation of Qatari family structures.

An amalgam of earlier architectural styles and modern preservation approaches is reflected in the redeveloped Souk Waqif, the traditional commercial hub of Doha that had been continuously occupied and noticeably adapted to the continuous modernization of Qatar. The souk was redesigned between 2004 and 2007 by the Private Engineering Office of the Emir and shortlisted for the Aga Khan Award for Architecture in the 2008–2010 cycle. The judges for the award celebrated this project as a "unique architectural revival," achieved through a "thorough study of the history of the market and its buildings" that reversed processes of decay and inappropriate alterations and additions.[74]

It was precisely the dramatic attempts at rejuvenation that put the souk at odds with modern conservation philosophy and the public in general: modern buildings and additions were demolished, modern materials on roofing and finishes were replaced by traditional ones, and traditional insulation against extreme heat was reinstated. At the same time, though, many features were reinforced with concrete frames, modern lighting systems were allowed on interior and exterior spaces, and modern heating, ventilation, and air conditioning (HVAC) systems were installed; the latter, in particular, cannot help but be blatantly visible on the rooftops. Nevertheless, at the street level, the souk can be experienced as a coherent and homogeneous heritage fabric that appears quite literally to have been preserved over time. Ironically, the only feature of the entire complex that is visually dissonant now is the original Bismillah Hotel, a modernist structure that remained untouched throughout the various phases of the souk and now operates as a luxury boutique hotel.

Mohamed Ali Abdullah, who was charged with the project of restoration for the souk, developed and used a preservation approach approved by the emir himself across multiple projects in Qatar.[75] Per his own account of the origin of PEO's restoration agendas and approaches, in 2003, then-emir Sheikh Hamad noticed Abdullah's house, designed in the traditional Qatari building style, and was drawn to his efforts toward reviving local architecture, an aesthetic that captured the built landscapes of the emir's youth. Abdullah, a painter and illustrator, was summoned to the Emiri Diwan at the same time that international consultants were presenting a proposal for the rehabilitation of Souk Waqif. Seeking a more authentic and local style, the emir asked Abdullah for a proposal of his own on the spot. After producing a few paintings, Abdullah was asked to start right away. He was then provided with contractors, engineers, and architects to bring his vision to life.

The first thing he did was train contractors to use traditional materials, including "how to treat the plaster with an aging technique."[76] The next challenges were securing ownership rights on the souk's properties and modernizing its infrastructure. His own research suggested that about two thirds of the souk was still in its original condition; that is, made from stone, earth, wood, and gypsum. Some of it was more than two centuries old. The sections of the souk that had been previously demolished by its owners in the 1980s and 1990s were then rebuilt to match the original fabric based on oral histories and aerial photography.

From the standpoint of UNESCO's standards for heritage preservation, the liberal interpretation of authenticity employed by PEO's restoration would expose Qatar's modern heritage industry as fraudulent at worst, unsophisticated at best. Approaching the hosting in Doha of the World Heritage Committee of UNESCO in 2014, a Qatar Museums heritage expert privately expressed concerns about international scrutiny of PEO's own brand of heritage rehabilitation. Other archaeologists working in Qatar shared this concern about PEO's aggressive disassembling of existing urban features to reassemble them in the chosen style of pre-1940s Qatar. "It is all mere 'wall tracing' and a destructive one at that," one senior archaeologist explained alarmingly over the years. "Wall tracing" referred to the practice of demarcating the remaining foundations of original structures through unstructured excavation that pays little to no attention to the location of any finds and their stratigraphic contexts. While it is expected that archaeologists would find this practice reprehensible, PEO's tried and tested methodology was not as improvised or unsubstantiated as it was made out to be in terms of preservation. Neither was it necessarily against UNESCO's modern global principles and standards, which have come to recognize certain forms of reconstruction as legitimate, such as anastylosis (i.e., reassembling original pieces) and the renewal of original fabric with modern materials so long as it follows a traditional, often spiritual practice. What this practice did encourage was the large-scale erasure of post-1940s fabric, such as modernism, and a sentiment against gradual modernization in general.

Abdullah's heritage language, after the restoration of the souk, draws much of its authenticity from the directive of the ruler himself and in this sense cannot be accused of constituting "fake architecture."[77] Critiques of the souk, one of the constituent parts of the imagined "Islamic city" of Doha, for being inauthentic heritage transcend the materiality and aesthetics of these restoration efforts. While this likely represents the most locally grown approach to heritage preservation and heritagization in Qatar, no other project of architectural revitalization across Qatar has received more accusations of inauthenticity, both as an element of national identity and as a suitable platform for the representation and performance of tradition. Flippantly characterized by some as a "Disney version of Qatar's past,"[78] the public and professional critique of the souk's facades and the uses of its spaces as tourist destination received disapproval from both ends of the spectrum. On the one hand, the more conservative segments of society resented the display of scantily clad tourists and hookah cafés that populated the main throughways of the souk. On the other hand, the progressive segments of society resisted such Orientalizing depictions that presented Qatari leisure activities exclusively through local and Middle Eastern traditions. As observed for other public and commercial spaces in Qatar that re-created the intricacies of a traditional village, such as Katara Village, the simulation of traditional public spaces is no assurance of the preservation of traditional livelihoods. So-called family days are instituted to keep spaces free of bachelors (as male migrant workers are often called), but many female informants still refused to be seen in these socially unregulated spaces. Nevertheless, when it was not wrapped in the controversy of proper attire and public smoking, the souk remained invariably traditional on Qatari and Muslim accounts: it was practically deserted on Friday mornings, in observance of the Muslim calendar, and it is also host to Shay Al Shamoos restaurant, the traditional eatery for Qataris where the father emir was often sighted.

Actions and reactions at Souk Waqif suggest that heritage preservation mechanisms in Qatar could not simply accompany gradually changing landscapes, instead resorting to bold reconfigurations through projects of revitalization that matched the impact of sidelining traditionalism. The hybridity that resulted from cultural encounters experienced by the growing nation in the earlier decades of modernization had evidently failed to inspire a local sense of belonging in Qatari and even Muslim ways. As a result, tradition was wiped out, not necessarily through the erasure of a historical fabric, but through decades of failed stewardship and associated abandonment. Located adjacent to the souk and a candidate for the next round of demolitions, the central neighborhood of al-Asmakh has remained a rundown and dense area of town, offering a glimpse of what the traditional streetscapes of Doha looked like before their redevelopment, both architecturally and in terms of occupancy. Here, the archaeologists Gizem Kahraman and Robert Carter recorded an architectural microhistory that helps understand the afterlives of the city long after Qatari stewardship had withdrawn, taking this segment of the city from locally supported and thriving to alien and derelict. The central district of Doha, only sparsely populated before 1950, grew significantly from 1950 to 1959. The involvement of Western urban planners starting in the 1970s redesigned the city to align with a more commercial and high-density residential plan that invited Qatari families to relocate to more spacious and newer parts of the city.[79] The neighborhood has since reflected changing patterns of stewardship and needs-based adaptation of spaces: the installation of air conditioning units and the conversion of traditional *majlis* meeting rooms into bedroom areas, to name a few. The residences and shops in al-Asmakh had long been vacated by their original Qatari owners, instead, housing low-wage migrant workers from countries like Bangladesh, Pakistan, and Nepal. Outside the purview of citizens, the burden of maintaining these traditional spaces that once aligned with Qatari identity and traditional uses, which included religious uses, was presumably over.

The al-Asmakh and the adjacent al-Najada neighborhoods were the focus of Qatar Museums' Mapping Old Doha project, which aimed to preemptively assess the heritage value of the urban fabric of these two areas of the city from 2012 to 2014.[80] Launched by the Restoration Department of Qatar Museums, the emphasis of this initiative appeared to revolve around identifying first and foremost traditional buildings (from the first half of the twentieth century), with a secondary concern with documenting early modern buildings (from the mid-1950s to the 1970s). In a simple survey, this project asked untrained volunteers to visually identify structures belonging to one of four categories: "traditional with inner courtyard without arcades," "traditional with inner courtyard with arcades," "early modern," and "modern." The courtyard house was the centerpiece of identification of traditional lifestyles, associated with the significance of maintaining privacy for the family unit

FIGURE 2.3.   A traditional family residence in al-Sadd encroached by the construction of a mid-rise structure whose windows look over private patios and gardens in Doha, 2019. Photo by author.

and recognizing the needs of different gendered uses of space. As the Qatari population was encouraged to relocate to larger and more luxurious residences along the ring-road system of Doha, the search for privacy that is quintessential to a Muslim-practicing community was assisted by the addition of a new design element: the perimeter wall. Perimeter walls across the villas of Qatar are elaborate and often monumental, with the most stunning examples displaying elements of modernist design and the more functional examples displaying metal, cane, or plastic extensions that add height to the original walls. This is because, in the newest bout of modernization, detached homes from all periods are finding themselves encroached by the demolition and construction of new midrises that infringe on the privacy of their gardens, outdoor spaces, and windows once protected by the perimeter walls (figure 2.3). The limits of the perimeter wall for providing this desired privacy, in this sense, marks the limits of the modernist urban infrastructure of Qatar to adapt to the growth of a society upheld by the vision of a primarily Muslim nation. A modernizing heritage language would have to take these limits into consideration to advance a more sustainable approach to modernity in the making of a future landscape for Qatar.

Reconfiguring Modernity

Efforts at "Qatarizing" modernization in support of Qatari nation-building reached its zenith in a project of redevelopment for Old Doha. Msheireb Downtown Doha foregrounded the Islamicization of a local vernacular that also meets and incorporates new, luxurious, and sustainable materials and technologies. How little the decades of modernist design and construction contributed to what became the architectural history and heritage language of Qatar is evident in the motivations for the establishment of Msheireb Properties, the real estate arm of the Qatar Foundation. At the launch of this initiative, its founder, Sheikha Moza, envisioned a project that addressed a gap in the architectural history of Qatar. Short of calling it the long, modernist era that had been systematically demoted to rubble, the gap was the perceived absence of a cohesive architectural style to bridge traditional architectural heritage and the modern era of Qatar. The first project by and in Msheireb, the aptly named Msheireb Downtown Doha project, participated in its own self-fulfilling prophecy: this large project of redevelopment was largely built over the razing of traditional and modernist architectural and urban fabrics almost indiscriminately, including a rare "Arabian Art Deco" that Jaidah had taken care to document.[81] In this role, this project offered a perfect example of selective marginalization of some historical styles over others in the preservation efforts of Qatar, supporting the idea that some eras contained more cultural potential than others.

The Msheireb development, named after the *wadi* running through that part of town, marks an iconic time in the development of Qatari heritage languages in the 2000s and a dramatic intervention in the heart of the capital city. Also called "Heart of Doha," the project occupies thirty-five hectares adjacent to the Emiri Diwan and once imposed an approximately five-story-deep hole in the ground during the early phases of construction. This dramatic intervention redefined the old city to become the face of the capital of Qatar and of Qatari design itself. However, in line with the history of development in the country, the expertise that supported this development was far from local. Msheireb was launched through an international competition in 2008 that was judged by a prestigious jury of academics and architects. This included scholars from Princeton University, the Harvard Graduate School of Design, Yale University, and the Department of Architecture at the Massachusetts Institute of Technology (MIT). The master plan of Msheireb was created by the American infrastructure firm AECOM and British firms Arup and Allies and Morrison. Through this partnership, a new urban quarter was proposed, with a spatial organization and architectural expressions that spoke to the specific culture and climate of Qatar. Emphasis on the latter made Msheireb the first sustainable downtown regeneration project in a modern metropolis, at a time when "sustainability" was a widely circulated but loosely defined concept. Ironically, the role of Msheireb for reawakening Qatari tradition had had some strange detours: originally, the project was called "Dohaland," while the famous al-Kahraba Street, the spine of the old city that was the first street ever to be electrified, was described in earlier architectural plans as "the Champs-Élysées of Doha." The politics of toponymy and the outsourcing of expertise to Ivy League institutions in the United States made the indigeneity of place-making of this project sometimes difficult to capture.

Like many cultural and infrastructural projects across Qatar in the new millennium, Msheireb materialized many of the goals of QNV 2030, in particular, the goal of balancing the need for heritage preservation against the need for progress, while encouraging economic development and sustainability.[82] Reiterating the idea that there was no preexisting architectural language nor structures of heritage value in urban Doha, as it had been similarly articulated back in the development plans of the 1970s, the starting point in this project was the crafting of a new heritage language and architectural legacy through three years of research on Qatari architecture and regional urban planning. Described as "a reawakening of an architectural heritage that was in danger of extinction," this language promised to result in buildings with a shared DNA, reviving local heritage and culture through a unified architectural idiom.[83] But it was the location of Msheireb—flanked by the Emiri Diwan, Souk Waqif, and the al-Asmakh and al-Najada neighborhoods—that made the quest for a lost language a bit bewildering. The encyclopedia of relevant and authentic design in the life history of Qatar was right at its threshold, with the very structures that represented and reflected so many formative phases in the architectural history and heritage of Qatar: the birth of the nation, the continuously thriving commercial and social hub of the city, and the early residential neighborhood of Doha.

In this context, Msheireb was not simply a process of regeneration, as it had been labeled by its proponents.[84] The influential scholar and critic of architecture and urbanism of the region, Ashraf Salama, questioned the driving philosophy behind the redevelopment project that entailed the full destruction of the old heart of the city and the eradication of a whole neighborhood from top to bottom. He points out that "the same architect who orchestrated this eradication [at Msheireb] is conducting a huge campaign to convince the decision-makers in the country, including the Qatar Museum Authority and the Ministry of Urban Planning, of the importance of preserving the heritage of al-Asmakh area, just across the street from the Heart of Doha (Msheireb Development)."[85] The razing of Msheireb was somewhat offset by the identification and storage of four historical houses that were later dismantled and boxed in storage to be reassembled as a cluster in Msheireb's new grid and provide credibility to the heritage preservation mission for the project. The new Msheireb plan then featured a sector called "Heart of Doha Cultural and Historical Quarter," where knowledge of history and tradition was curated through a number of thematic museums, galleries, and exhibition spaces contained within the remaining historical houses.

These new institutions included Company House, set in the actual headquarters of Qatar's first oil company and holding objects and oral history related to oil discovery and exploitation; Radwani House, once a 1920s residential structure in traditional courtyard style and now restored as a museum presenting a snapshot of traditional Qatari family life before the advent of oil; Mohammed bin Jassim House, built by the son of Jassim bin Mohammed al-Thani, the founder of modern Qatar; and, finally, Bin Jelmood House, the slavery museum that acknowledges the social, cultural, and economic contribution of formerly enslaved people to the development of Qatar. Significantly, Bin Jelmood explores the role that Islam played in "providing guidance for humane treatment of enslaved people, their integration into society and the eventual abolition of slavery."[86] This institution and narrative attempt an important corrective for crafting the modern future of Qatar, where the *kafala* system of immigration and sponsorship of migrant workers still rules. *Kafala*, grounded in Islamic law, codifies the practice of indentured servitude derived from the era of pearling and therefore can claim the protected status of tradition.[87] Less explicitly, the design of Msheireb acknowledged a Muslim-majority culture and society in multiple ways: in toponymy, in the organization of space and finishes, and more straightforwardly, in the inclusion of three mosques and an Eid prayer ground in the new heart of the city (which were actually a replacement for the mosques that were removed during the process of revitalization).

In broad terms, the new language championed by the Msheireb development proposed community living, traditional Qatari heritage and aesthetics, and modern technology that celebrated and encouraged harmony with the environment. In no uncertain terms, the project aimed to bring people *back to their roots*, while simultaneously re-creating said roots within the context of modern comforts and luxuries. Tim Makower, then a principal architect at the British firm Allies and Morrison with an interest in heritage architecture, proposed orchestrating this project by following "the seven steps":

> One, to ensure continuity between the past, the present and the future through *finding* timeless motifs and techniques and using them in new ways that represent time-honored traditions.
>
> Two, to achieve harmony and cohesion in the city by promoting diversity bound together by a common language.
>
> Three, to reflect the character and informality of the traditional "carved city" where buildings are carved as part of an "urban clay" rather than constituted as objects.
>
> Four, to deliver exceptional living environments that offer privacy and security, supporting the spirit of a family and sense of community.
>
> Five, to create a lasting setting for a vibrant and memorable streetscape through the use of spaces, shading, and comfortable pedestrian infrastructure.
>
> Six, to use old and new technology to achieve maximum climatic comfort and minimum energy use.
>
> Seven, to build on Qatari architectural tradition by using a new language, rich in reference and strong in resonance; flexible, to be spoken in many accents but consistent, to be understood by all.[88]

The seven steps involved in the Msheireb Downtown Doha project characterize an iconic moment in the development of Qatar in the 2000s by promising to integrate the spirit and aesthetics of Qatari architecture and to restore the unique quality of Qatar's built environment and strong social ties. Promotional material circulating throughout the formative period of the project emphasized the goal to affirm the strong social ties but, at the same time, the visual language that accompanied many of these projects at the time layered smiling shoppers in Western clothing mingling with women and men dressed in traditional *abayas* and *thoubs*, enjoying beautifully rendered rows of (Western) designer storefronts. Likewise, the various heritage languages in Qatar oscillated between hopeful hybridity and conservative homogeneity, with Islam and Qatariness mobilized strategically in support of either view as needed. In large part, this was the result of diverse and often foreign views involved in different projects of preservation and revitalization, and a by-product of marketing departments creating an aesthetic that had little to do with the actual design process.[89] These openly fabricated visual languages also put Msheireb in a position to be criticized for the degree of influence that foreign consultants had in the determination of heritage languages that later influenced the fate of entire neighborhoods.

However, the lack of attention to locality was not simply a by-product of foreign influence on the history of the urban and architectural development of Qatar. The discourse and practices that surround the promises of new and more traditional cities since the 1970s show the extent to which these visions were, in fact, cocreated by the Qatari state and the consultant culture that it hosts. The architectural language proposed for Msheireb is eerily similar to one proposed by William Pereira when he led an earlier bout of modernization in the region. A project contemporary to the Sheraton Hotel, but in Yanbu, Saudi Arabia, foregrounded Islam much more explicitly than in the promotional material and press releases circulated by Pereira for the Sheraton Hotel project. Yanbu was put forth as a "'city of the future,' designed to be modern, yet accommodating traditional Islamic architecture" and accompanied by what his firm called "Design Principles," itemizing first and foremost "Islam," "Arabian customs," and "privacy," as well as the now-familiar rubrics of "pedestrian," "sun," "wind," "traditional architecture," and "unity and variety."[90] The parallels with the seven steps of Msheireb are uncanny and demonstrate an effective path to localizing architectural design through Islamic and sustainable ideals.

Yet the lifespan of any efforts at preserving local Islamic values and aesthetics in the earliest heritage languages of the region appears to have been short, lost over the decades following the first wave of modernization. A full-page advertisement of the Sheraton Hotel in *Fortune* magazine in 1993 reads, "Stay at a hotel in Qatar inspired by the pyramids" along with a side-by-side image of Pereira's Sheraton Hotel and the ancient Mesoamerican El Castillo pyramid of Chichén Itzá, Mexico, suggesting an exterior design that failed to convey any sense of locality.[91] The modern reconsideration of heritage languages in Qatar, therefore, presented an opportunity to reverse an erasure of Islam from the fabric and uses of the built landscape and bring a more intentional nod to locality, both of which had been endangered by the standardizing effects of modernism despite previous efforts. Yet the centrality of

Islam to the ultramodern city remained abstract. The explicit focus of the new heritage language of the new millennium, instead, was placed primarily on a Qatari architecture defined by proportion, simplicity, space, light, layering, and management of the local climate as ways to reverse a pattern of real estate development in Doha that saw isolated and energy-intensive land use, urban sprawl, and an overreliance on car transportation.

Together, these foci defined the central concern with sustainability that became central to Qatar in the early decades of the 2000s. While the earlier bouts of modernization had been justified through the pressures and perks of a fast-growing nation gaining autonomy and power on the global stage, the justification for further development through the 2000s was predominantly attached to the attainment of sustainability. Urban and infrastructural changes that took place most visibly in the capital city showed the extent to which the value of sustainability became key to justifying these reconfigurations and, also, importantly, to gaining public support. More seasoned heritage languages engineered to revisit "Islamic values" played an important role in supporting this transformation, which included, in no small measure, changes in lifestyle that could be more successfully implemented when they align with what was articulated as a Muslim way of life. Heritage languages that reinterpreted traditional forms and lifestyles along the theme of cultural and natural sustainability provided an avenue for resolving tensions in the alignment of tradition, modernity, and nation-building.

CHAPTER 3

From Mosques to Mangroves

Sustainable "Islamic" Preservation and Conservation

At the turn of the millennium, the rising significance of the environment for the development of a national identity and a heritage industry in Qatar manifested in resource stewardship and nature conservation projects that were strictly aligned with the maintenance of a Qatari heritage and tradition attentive to Islam. The intensification of a heritage industry in Qatar was, in fact, an amalgam of two distinct but interrelated agendas in the nation-building strategies of Qatar. On the one hand, as I have argued, a more-or-less established preservation tradition for cultural heritage resources dated to the earliest days of the nation and, on the other hand, an apparently more recent but fast-growing tradition of conservation of natural resources peaked along relatively new concerns with environmental and sustainable futures. At the intersection of these two paths lay an emerging concern with religious views and authority in matters of resource stewardship for both culture and nature. The question of whether there was a uniquely "Islamic" preservation approach that could be integrated into the foundation of a cultural and natural conservation sensibility in Qatar intensified during this period on both fronts.

For cultural heritage preservation professionals and scholars, the concern with a modus operandi attentive to Islamic contexts constructed a bridge between two expectations for the role of heritage preservation.

One of these views saw heritage practices exclusively concerned with historical resources sanctioned to act as Islamic heritage in the strictest sense, such as mosques. The other, more expansive view proposed the idea that heritage preservation practices surrounding any historical and contemporary resource should be sensitive and reflective of Islamic values in some capacity.[1] Proponents of the latter considered heritage preservation as one of the key lenses through which any aspect of cultural construction and change can be interpreted, experienced, and conveyed as a Muslim. For natural heritage conservation, this shift came at a time when the relevance of faith and belief to questions of climate change began to make an impact on academic literature and institutional initiatives alike. In all instances, a concern with conceptualizing aspects of Islam in practices of care for cultural and natural resources envisioned a Muslim or Muslim-aware expert who could lead close considerations of *ijtihād* (i.e., Islamic teachings and their applications to contemporary issues).[2] In some ways, the mobilization of principles of Islam for ensuring public acquiescence and support into different models of governing resources, including heritage resources, could seem redundant. This is because, across the *umma*, the principles of preservation of resources that are intended to be passed on to and benefit future generations are centuries older than the emergence of the idea of universal and global heritage. An Islamic stewardship for this type of resource is at the core of perceptions and practices of philanthropy in predominantly Muslim societies. It predates Western preservation philosophy, but it is often overshadowed by the majority of contemporary heritage discourses and heritage agendas that accommodate and serve processes of nation-building in alignment with modern institutional characterizations of heritage value.

Badi al-Abed, former dean at the al-Isra University in Jordan, described the field of architectural conservation in 2010 as "a new cultural phenomenon in Western civilization," and, rather accurately, as "an emotional concept."[3] In doing so, he contrasts modern conservation efforts against a much older and rational phenomenon in Islamic civilization governed by Islamic law: waqf (endowment). Historically, such endowments have included buildings that benefit society as a whole, such as a school or hospital. Practices of care for waqf dictate not only technical practices of recording and vocabularies for conservation, but also the management, budgeting, investment, and development of resources in the context of Muslim-majority society. Significantly, under the purview of the institution of *awqāf* (endowments) is a well-oiled ecosystem that oversees the roles of the endower, the appointed trustee, and the custodian. In this way, the upkeep, conservation, and preservation of a historical resource under waqf are ensured to be in alignment with appropriate objectives, channels of expertise, and processes dictated by an Islamic tradition. As for institutional conversations about environmental safeguarding, these foreground Qur'anic teachings that champion a respect for nature, inspired by the rulings of Abu Bakr, as guidance for different initiatives and educational and outreach programs.[4] For example, after Qatar finally ratified the Kyoto protocol in 2005, committing to reduce greenhouse gas emissions, Islamic scholars began to examine whether schemes such as carbon credits and financing protocols established to support climate change initiatives could apply to the particular cultural and religious structures of the country, and, thus, whether these mechanisms could be used in support of conservation.[5]

One of the aims of Qatar National Vision 2030 (QNV) was to acculturate and distribute the weight of tradition and Muslim morality and know-how across various programs that linked modern ideas of natural and cultural sustainability. There had been earlier attempts at establishing a symbiotic support for cultural heritage preservation and natural heritage conservationism in Qatar. While it has been argued that countries of the Gulf region had shown little interest in sustainable development until the mid-1980s, the entanglement of traditional livelihoods, industrialization, and environmentalism was not just a product of strategic development projects.[6] As early as the late 1970s, a United Nations Educational, Scientific, and Cultural Organization (UNESCO) mission to Qatar to provide technical support for the development of the Faculty of Science at the University of Qatar projected a partnership between heritage preservation and nature conservation.[7] UNESCO consultants stressed the significance of including in these initiatives a view from human ecology to retain a knowledge of past customs and skills as they pertain to environmental stewardship, as well as to better engage with the problem of pollution and the danger of too rapid a transition from a nomadic to an urban civilization.[8] Qatar was not a stranger to ecological crises. The first oil workers hired by Shell to set up offshore oil rigs, former pearling divers, were involved in environmental protests in the early 1950s over fears that the company would strip the oyster beds on which their craft had relied.[9] Decades later, during the 1991 Iraqi invasion of Kuwait, environmental warfare resulted in the deliberate pumping of four million barrels of oil into the waters of the Gulf, creating an environmental catastrophe of unprecedented scale.[10]

In some critical ways, the development of a heritage renaissance that aimed to be sustainably connected to local environments ran into the problem of a lack of connection between traditional construction material that is sourced abroad and heritage languages invested in promoting the idea of a uniquely Qatari identity. The Gulf, in general, has very limited amounts of usable construction material that offer the resilience and permanence needed to sustain a traditional heritage fabric over time, so authenticity cannot be aligned with original fabrics. Stone sourced from the coast is too high in salinity to maintain structural integrity over time, and desert sand, while plentiful, cannot be used in concrete aggregate because it is too fine.[11] Construction material for traditional architecture, therefore, was sourced from across the Arabian Gulf and through Indian Ocean trade networks, a practice that was then continued and amplified to broader import networks in the first phase of modernization in Qatar, at a scale that became economically unsustainable. These constraints resulted in the dominant practice of prefabrication and standardization of a modern architecture that could give the perception of being alien to the local environment.[12] Such a lack of association, between the natural and the built visual landscapes of Qatar, reduced among decision-makers the perceived significance of targeting an environmentally situated built heritage.

However, in terms of performed or intangible heritage, the preservation of traditions and the conservation of landscapes were more intimately connected through a dependency on specific traditional activities and their ecosystems: fishing, hunting with Saluki dogs, and falconry required access to viable land and an availability of animal populations.[13] Likewise, those pursuing the traditional practice of establishing winter desert camps, in landscapes that would be dramatically affected by advancing development, were also invested in ensuring environmental stability. In addition, such a connection between culture and nature was maintained at the highest levels of society. Sheikh Saud bin Muhammed al-Thani, whose art collections were a formative part of the establishment of the Museum of Islamic Art, was a well-known naturalist invested in conservationism. In 2014, the *New York Times* reported on how Sheikh Saud had turned the area of Qatar known as al-Wabra into an animal conservation center where he bred endangered wildlife and established an animal hospital and lecturing facilities, and from where he funded conservation programs in other parts of the world.[14] However, despite these legacies, a sustained relationship between Qataris and an interdependent natural and cultural heritage had to be reinvented at a civic level. With QNV engaging stewardship from the perspective of Islam to jump-start and formalize this type of engagement, the Qatari state strategically wedded cultural heritage preservation and environmentalist rhetoric and principles. The resulting initiatives, which ranged from the preservation of mosques to various projects aimed at greening landscapes and buildings, have helped to articulate a vision of heritage preservation grounded in Islamic principles of resource stewardship and sustainability.

Unresolved Regeneration: The Adopting-a-Mosque Campaign

In early 2013, the Department of Architectural Conservation of the Qatar Museums Authority (now Qatar Museums) announced in its *Restoration Newsletter* the launch of a conservation campaign specifically aimed at the preservation of mosques.[15] In collaboration with Awqaf (the Ministry of Endowments and Islamic Affairs) and under the patronage of Sheikha al-Mayassa bint Hamad bin Khalifa al-Thani, this campaign intended to involve Qataris in efforts to preserve their own heritage, and in doing so, to encourage them to repopulate mosques that had fallen out of use. A base map of historical mosques included the name, coordinates, and small thumbnail photograph of each structure. This data was the result of the production of a "Heritage Mosques Map," described in the previous issue of the newsletter by Adel al-Moslamani, head of restoration at Qatar Museums.[16] The map was part of an effort by his office to map key historical resources in Qatar that included the surveying and documentation of "Springs and Wells" and a forthcoming initiative to complete a "Heritage Buildings Map."

Accompanying an image of the map of historical mosques in this announcement, al-Moslamani explained that "we would like to teach, educate Qataris about their Heritage and encourage them help us protect and preserving them [sic]."[17] The emphasis placed on specific goals for this initiative—to *repopulate* mosques and *teach* and *educate* Qataris about their preservation—revealed that priorities in this initiative were twofold. First, this project aimed to coordinate the construction of a recognizable vernacular heritage value through the mobilization of the existing significance of mosques for the daily life and identity of Qataris across the country. Mobilizing the significance of mosques for the growth of stewardship is strategic, as this is an intrinsic value that derives from the continuous practice of Islam in this Muslim-majority country. Second, this effort sought to identify stakeholders that can uphold and validate the preservation of such heritage; that is, a concerned community that supports and sustains preservation initiatives moving forward, which they might come to see as personally rather than symbolically or nationally significant. It was a dangerous proposition— one that revealed the idea that heritage *is* adopted, branded, and bound to specific stakeholders and stewards by the hands of heritage experts. Contrary to a heritage preservation rhetoric imagining a heritage that exists naturally and need only be revealed and cared for through democratic and unobstructed conditions, the Adopting-a-Mosque Campaign used as a point of departure the reality that a majority of the remaining historical mosques across the territory of Qatar were facing rapid obsolescence. As documented officially in the initial survey, and then through my own project of condition assessment a few years later, these mosques showed signs of being largely abandoned, and potentially constituted a historical resource at risk of disappearing in the eyes of preservationists. Encouraging reuse after abandonment might even pose new preservation challenges.

One example of a historical resource of interest to this initiative was the abandoned mosque of Tin Bik in the municipality of al-Daayen (figure 3.1). Rural communities once attached to this and other more remote mosques had relocated to urban centers starting in the second half of the twentieth century, when Qatar ushered in a post-oil era of urbanism marked by increasing migration to the cities and the abandonment of many coastal villages.[18] The inclusion of historical mosques such as this one into the growing catalog of key heritage resources in Qatar suggested that these structures had not been fully forgotten, even if they remained unused. In contrast, the way in which mosques had also been casually but intentionally erased, relocated, and reused throughout periods of redevelopment and modernization across the peninsula put the idea of a "heritage mosque" *stricto sensu* at odds with the growing heritage tradition of Qatar. The heritage value contained within a mosque such as the one at Tin Bik was not necessarily reflected in its derelict minaret, but rather in the survival of its constituent parts: its original wooden doors, beamed ceilings, and even its modernist ceiling fans—as well as its association with coastal subsistence traditions. Significantly, the courtyard of the mosque was covered in *sabban*—very small shell aggregates that were used in traditional courtyard flooring,

FIGURE 3.1.   Mosque in Tin Bik, 2016. Photo by author.

a naturally occurring material sourced from the coast of Qatar. At the time of the surveying, in 2016, *sabban* had already been identified as a protected material by the Ministry of the Environment, which regulated its use to the extent that it could no longer be added to re-create traditional courtyards in new mosque construction. This dictum put modern environmental policies into conflict with cultural preservation approaches striving for authenticity of construction material. In fact, designers for the historical houses of Msheireb Downtown Doha were allowed to source only enough of the material to furnish the courtyard of the Radwani traditional house. However, at Tin Bik, *sabban* poured over from the abandoned courtyard into the gravel streets around it, in apparent careless excess.

Demonstrating the symbolic importance of Muslim places of worship to common conceptualizations of what constitutes heritage value, a former Qatar Museums senior employee observed that "mosques may be the only heritage left in Qatar." He had been involved in early planning efforts to establish heritage trails and public engagement projects for a growing heritage industry in Qatar. He was familiar with the historical mosques because the plan for the heritage trail included a number of old mosques scattered across the Qatari peninsula that had already been mapped and identified. The decay of historical mosques was a known occurrence. In the book *Traditional Architecture in Qatar*, translated by the National Council for Culture, Arts, and Heritage in 2006, Mohammed Jassim al-Kholaifi identified a number of mosques that were already compromised or entirely gone.[19] The book features, for example, photographs of the old mosque in Zubarah, which "no longer exists" and "collapsed and withered away in 1965"; and the mosque and minaret of Abul Gibaib mosque (also Abu al-Gibayeb) "before it was demolished in 1969" or "fell down."[20] In addition, al-Kholaifi mentions the alteration or disappearance of various minarets featured among his photographs: "a minaret of an old none-existent [sic] mosque at Al Khor, that collapsed long ago" and images of minarets "no more existing [sic]" in al-Wakhra (al-Wakrah), al-Asmakh, al-Ariesh (al-'Arish), Doha, and al-Dhakeerah (al-Thakhira).[21] The rate of survival of historical mosques across Qatar was inconsistent. Countless cases, documented in earlier mapping surveys of Qatar, are no longer found. For example, in the relatively well documented World Heritage Site of al-Zubarah, two mosques are captured in aerial photographs taken in the mid-1950s—one of these was famously designed in the domed style of the Qabib mosque in Doha—but they have since fallen into disrepair or been destroyed.

Despite the documented decay of some historical mosques, the list of heritage mosques put together by the Department of Architectural Conservation team of Qatar Museums in 2013 included sixty-six historical mosques mapped across all corners of the Qatari peninsula. They are dated from a generic "19th century" to the year 1965, but most are dated to the 1940s, with a surprising majority dated to the specific year 1940. This distribution reflects the Qatar Museum's assessment of historical mosques aligning with the temporal parameters of Law No. 2 of 1980, which emphasizes pre-1940s urbanism. By that token, any mosque on this list that was built after 1940 was more difficult to explain as an identified heritage resource. The survey, while it included photographic evidence of the condition for each mosque, offered no information on the dates of abandonment, if any. Many of these structures had decayed after abandonment to the point of being almost unrecognizable during my own survey work.

Further alterations or extensive restoration work done since their initial documentation also transformed these structures dramatically, such as the addition of air conditioning units, aesthetic or structural in-filling under arches, or encroachment by other structures. In part, these changes indicated that some mosques had never really fallen out of use after all. At the same time, the launch of the ambitious call for increasing the social significance of mosques as heritage resources was followed by high-profile restoration projects that were projected or completed simultaneously across the country. For example, in the same newsletter announcing the Adopting-a-Mosque Campaign, the Department of Architectural Conservation team provided updates on the ongoing conservation work on the Abu Dholof mosque and the Abdullah Shamsan al-Ruwais mosque rescue projects, the latter a flagship project for the restoration efforts of Qatar Museums.

Qatar Museums reported extensively on the restoration project of al-Ruwais mosque over the years, referred to as the oldest in Qatar. Al-Ruwais is one of the oldest harbor towns on the northernmost coast of the country. The current mosque was built in the 1940s on the ruins of an older mosque thought to date back to the seventeenth century. In the 1970s, after its minaret was hit by lightning, the al-Ruwais mosque was abandoned in favor of newer ones that were equipped with air conditioning and other modern amenities. As a result, the neglected building suffered decay exacerbated by harsh seaside conditions that damaged its foundations. The restoration work on this mosque included strengthening walls (many of which previously had been rebuilt using seashell bricks), removing collapsed sections, monitoring structural cracks and fissures, and adding modern features, such as parking and pedestrian footpaths for visitors. From a preventive conservation standpoint, an analysis of the soil to prevent the negative impact of seawater on the mosque's foundations and walls was reported to be underway. Many of the updates provided on the restoration projects for this and other mosques place a strong emphasis on alignment with international standards—namely, using natural building materials similar to the original ones and using monitoring devices (for cracks and fissures) that were manufactured "locally in accordance with industry accredited international standards under the supervision of Sami Imam and Essam Abbas in a local workshop."[22]

The preservation of mosques in Qatar, in this sense, was not presented simply as a campaign aimed at directing resources toward preserving these specific religious structures. It was also an initiative implicated in constructing a locally grown significance that aims to be at once appealing to universal standards of conservation and to locally grown stewardship and know-how. The development of multiple local industries—the local workshop, supervised by the conservators Imam and Abbas—and, implicitly, the local tourism industry that would follow the rehabilitation of these mosques constitute a case in point. More important, this campaign also responded to a higher calling. The launch of Adopting-a-Mosque called on Muslims to follow guidance from the Holy Qur'an by quoting the following passages: "None should inhabit the mosques of Allah except those who believe in Allah and the last day, establish their prayers and pay the obligatory charity, and fear none except Allah. May these be among the guided ones"; and "Who does greater harm than he who prevents His name to be remembered in the mosques of Allah and strives to destroy them?"[23] These passages highlighted the significance for caring for mosques in a way that make explicit a connection between the goals of preservation and the practices dictated by the Qur'an.

Qatar Museums continued to make progress tackling the preservation of deteriorating mosques across the nation. On 8 December 2016, *The Peninsula* newspaper of Qatar announced the completion of preservation works on two historical mosques: the conservation and restoration of a mosque in Old Salata (a suburb of Doha) and in Fuwairit (a coastal village north of Doha). Ali al-Kubaisi, the chief archaeology officer at Qatar Museums, was quoted in this press release as reinforcing their "commitment to put local communities, young and old, in touch with their past, reminding them of their ancestors' skills, wisdom, and heritage," while the article also praised the work of the Department of Architectural Conservation in maintaining international standards of UNESCO. In addition, the completion of restoration and rehabilitation works at the mosque in al-Ruwais at the end of 2016 marked a significant milestone in the history of preservation efforts in Qatar (figure 3.2).

Unfortunately, despite the considerable preparation that appears to have been put into the launching of this project, the Adopting-a-Mosque Campaign faded unceremoniously. Some informants from within and beyond Qatar Museums explained that the culprit was a lack of institutional and social support for a project that was perceived to overlap with the caretaking responsibilities of the state, and especially of Awqaf. The mosque conservation project folded waqf into a different stewardship regime in ways not dissimilar to how their autonomy was challenged by other political and historical stewardship regimes. For example, under Ottoman rule, and later under new global heritage paradigms, monuments across the Muslim world were caught between preservation systems and standards.[24] The establishment of

Figure 3.2. Al Ruwais Mosque after restoration, 2016. Photo by author.

modern inventories and management strategies in Muslim countries turned waqf buildings into public monuments through other than religious means. This process expressed value in artistic, archaeological, or historical terms without necessarily acknowledging Islam, pre-existing practices and ecosystems of preservation, or its benefactors. Severed in this process were practices for the maintenance of waqf that not only included detailed attention to resource allocation for restoration, maintenance, and repairs, but also, critically important, for means of ensuring the support of local populations.[25] Waqf resources reclassified as heritage under secular management systems and standards were then guided by modern preservation interventions in alignment with various projects of development. Through these changes in guiding principles, space was reorganized and livelihoods were disrupted, resulting in one predominant outcome: "emptying the neighborhoods and buildings of their 'undesirable' occupants."[26] This is not, however, the tension that best describes the status of Qatari waqf resources.

In Qatar, Awqaf reports that 80 percent of Qatari endowments are dedicated to the construction and maintenance of mosques, as well as their preservation; the care of those who work in mosques; and the integration of mosques into the community. This well-rounded approach to stewardship is carried out through sponsorship initiatives to build mosques and their annexes, maintenance plans, educational initiatives that take place within mosques, the sponsorship of libraries in mosques, and the provision of training courses for imams. It may then come as no surprise to imagine that the Adopting-a-Mosque initiative could have been perceived by many as overriding existing legitimate mechanisms to care for these important structures in Qatari society, drawing mosques away from their traditional habitat in Muslim society and thrusting them into a global and extractive discourse of resource-allocation involved in the curatorial mechanisms of modern preservation. It is also true that mosques are perceived to be an indestructible resource that may not need additional protection. During the Traditional Gulf Architecture Week in 2018, Ibrahim Jaidah himself claimed that "nobody would dare to demolish a mosque. . . . That is why they survived."[27] However, the histories of urban development across Qatar would prove him wrong, but this does not preclude mosques from bearing the load of containing heritage value in preservation terms.

The inconsistent rate of survival of mosques in Qatar can also be explained by a documented trajectory of intentional demolition of these structures to make way for new development and adapt to the needs of a growing and modernizing population. It is no surprise, for example, that the Msheireb Downtown Doha project involved the demolition of no fewer than four mosques originally located in the old neighborhood: the Khalifa Mosque, the Abdullah Bin Thani Mosque, the Siran Mosque, and the Imam Hassan Mosque.[28] None of these mosques were preserved; however, their removal was offset by the construction of new, state-of-the-art mosques that mobilize heritage languages and deploy the latest technology in alignment with the goals of sustainable development that informed Msheireb. The urban plan for Msheireb Downtown Doha, in fact, allocated 3,859 square meters to the construction of mosques. This calculation, as well as their location within the project, were not determined by the location of the historical mosques in the old footprint of Old Doha. Instead, the actual location and size of each mosque were negotiated using a triangulation among three metrics: the expert requirements of Awqaf; the urban standards of the Ministry of Municipality and Urban Planning, which oversaw space standards; and the advice contained in the "Mosques" section of the *Metric Handbook of Planning and Design Data*, which determines a standard for the dimensions of a mosque.[29] Msheireb's "Mosque Strategy" eventually located a Friday mosque within each residential zone, calculating a catchment area of 300 radial meters each. After planning, each mosque project was awarded to a different foreign architectural firm through design competitions; and perhaps this might be thought of as the inclusion of a fourth metric—an aesthetic one, guided by a vision of architectural cosmopolitanism that aligns with the brand new architectural language of Msheireb.

Mosque Phase 1A in the Msheireb masterplan was designed by the British firm John McAslan + Partners. The design of this mosque, located in the Heritage Quarter between the Eid prayer ground and the heritage houses, draws on elements from the House of the Prophet in Medina, built in 622 CE, in order to impart "a cultural authenticity."[30] Its design also makes reference to other mosques found in Qatar—al-Yousef Mosque (Old Salata, Doha, 1940), al-Subaiei Mosque (al-Wakrah, 1940), and Abdullah bin Soragah Mosque (al-Rumeila, Doha, 1940)—and includes elements of design commonly found across Qatar such as the ṣaḥn (a courtyard) and liwan (a narrow colonnaded exterior passage). The design language of this mosque combines the dimensions of the prayer rug and the number seven, one of the most significant numbers in Islam.[31] The *Architectural Review* celebrated its "simply composed geometry" and the "keen attention to Islamic geometric principles," which "speaks of an erudite theocentric design and a reverence to regional precedents" (figure 3.3).[32]

Despite a design process primarily outsourced to foreign firms, Msheireb Properties enjoyed guidance from Qataris within the project, and the complicated interplay of expertise and feedback loops among different stakeholders included a place for Awqaf's expertise. To illustrate this, one of the consultants involved in this project explained the process involved in the development of Mosque Phase 1B, designed by another British firm, Allies and Morrison: the firm submitted a design to Msheireb Properties, who sent it to Awqaf for review, who returned comments to Msheireb, who relayed feedback to the designer, and so on. It was in this process that some American- and UK-trained designers whose expertise was commercial offices and luxury residences became attuned to the needs of an Islamic space as best and as fast as they could, but as one of them confessed, in one instance "there was no time to run this change through another cycle of approvals, so someone redrew the minaret in their lunch break." It went under the radar. In another instance, a Mosque Phase 1B meeting between Msheireb Properties and one of its partners in 2013 resulted in a request to revise drawings, specifically, to "add heritage and Islamic elements into the

FIGURE 3.3. Mosque Phase 1A, Msheireb Downtown Doha (right); the National Archives and Bin Jelmood museum (left); Souk Waqif and Fanar Qatar Islamic Cultural Center and mosque (background), 2019. Photo by author.

doors . . . to protect a stronger image of a mosque." The representative for the project liaising with Awqaf was expected to seek approval for decoration details, patterns, and other elements, calling this request for substantial changes at an advanced stage of design "a gut punch." The drawings had already been sent to the construction contractor. The stakes were high for making Mosque Phase 1B thrive in the uncharted territory of a sustainable architectural history in Qatar that was also attentive to the type of stewardship that Awqaf represented. In addition to the responsibility to embody Islamic and traditional elements in a contemporary design and fabric, this mosque was tapped to earn a Leadership in Energy and Environmental Design (LEED) Gold certification in the world's most widely used green building rating system devised by the US Green Building Council in 2009.[33] The project of advancing sustainability as a Muslim cause in the context of specific environmental histories and futures for Qatar was already underway.

Greening Qatar

Resorting to Islam as a way of changing patterns of care and raising a civil society invested in these changes followed a similar pattern as growing a culture of heritage stewardship in Qatar. Environmental and religious literacy were deployed in support of state-sponsored initiatives that invoked Islam as a way to connect with natural resources in the context of national development. Also, as was the case for cultural heritage preservation, this alignment was not laid out based on a conceptual clean slate. The Qatari peninsula was misrepresented in many sources as a barren environment, much as its contemporary cultural landscape had been presumed by heritage experts as barren of heritage. While the neighboring Bahrain has been described as a "legendary oasis," the natural heritage of Qatar had not historically invoked ideas of nature conservatism, greening, or sustainability.[34] An appeal to tradition in support of environmentalism as a moral cause, therefore, required some gymnastics. The former British officer W. G. Palgrave, visiting the area that is today Doha in 1863, described it as "the miserable capital of a miserable province." His harsh description further adds that

> to have an idea of Katar, my readers must figure to themselves miles and miles of low barren hills, bleak and sun-scorched, with hardly a single tree to vary their dry monotonous outline: below these a muddy beach extends for a quarter of a mile seaward in slimy quicksands, bordered by a rim of sludge and seaweed. If we look landwards beyond the hills, we see what by extreme courtesy may be called pasture land, ready downs with twenty pebbles for every blade of grass; and over this melancholy ground scene, but few and far between, little clusters of wretched, most wretched, earth cottages and palm leaf huts, narrow, ugly, and low; these are the villages, or rather the "towns" (for so the inhabitants style them), of Katar.[35]

Soon after this visit, the British diplomat, historian, and colonial administrator J. G. Lorimer described Qatar as an undulating, rocky, and pebbly desert. He added that wells were numerous, the soil poor, and the fields and date groves were almost gone. Such gardens as existed near towns and villages were small and unproductive, while hardly a tree was to be seen anywhere.[36]

The misrepresentation of Qatar as a nation built on an absent ecosystem continued well into the twentieth century and has only been exacerbated by rising industrialization that overpowered the more subdued environmental aesthetic of the desert. In 1945, the Danish anthropologist Klaus Ferdinand described a country in the throes of industrialization as a landscape that was literally on fire, writing that "even the landscape became more and more marked by it. It was not only the new asphalted roads, and the oil-pipelines on the surface; it was also the fantastic inferno-like burning-off of gas at Dukhan and Umm Bab."[37] By the 1970s, Raban noted the effects of this industry and urbanization on the ecosystem, mentioning aerial photos of Qatar pinned to the walls of Qaddumi's office that showed enormous tracts of sand and marsh and a coastal ecosystem that was already in process of being reclaimed.[38] In the same decade, Graham's observations added another dimension of this changing ecosystem, observing that thousands of trees had been planted across Doha and out in the desert, surrounded by sturdy wooden fencing, "evidence of the value of the commodity within."[39] From barren to burning, the nature and significance of the landscape of Qatar were elusive to the untrained observer in search of greening as a visual indicator of a modern nation-state that cares for its natural resources.

These descriptions, together with the particular history of resource extraction attached to the roots of the modern nation-state, lay the groundwork for the idea that to be Qatari is to be unburdened by the current state of the environment. In her ethnographic analysis of Qatar, Anie Montigny brings to the foreground the predominant Qatari view that the petrol and gas resources on which the modern nation was built were bestowed on Qataris by the grace of God, for them to be the principal beneficiaries.[40] Now, confronting an influential modern and global view that associates this resource extraction with unenvironmentalism, Qur'anic verses and the ideals of a return to traditional livelihoods were used to raise awareness of the necessity to prioritize ecological balance in natural heritage preservation.[41] This means that Islam had been mobilized in both discourses—one in support of industrialization and one in support of environmentalism—and now, it was mobilized to negotiate a potential future relationship between these views. Qatar confronted a conundrum in its establishment of a culture of care for natural landscapes and resources that was scientific and morally sound.

The treatment of a Qatari environment as ecologically marginal and in need of improvement authorized a relaxed stewardship by the state.[42] Modernization had yielded rapid changes in urbanization and a high population growth rate that exerted a heavy toll on Qatar's environment, contributing to Qatar reaching the second-largest per-capita ecological footprint in the world.[43] These factors allowed aggressive landscape reconfigurations that accompanied the modernization of Doha, such as the earlier coastal reconfigurations that gave birth to the Corniche and, more recently, the residential mega-project built on reclaimed coastline called The Pearl-Qatar, which generated thirty-two kilometers of new coastline.[44] It was only in 1986 that an Environmental Protection Committee was established in Qatar.[45]

Despite the aggressive liberalization campaigns that Sheikh Hamad spearheaded starting in 1995, environmental protection received little attention from Qatar's leadership until the 2000s. Entering the new millennium, Qatar became invested in disrupting the dichotomous idea that a cultural landscape that was so heavily influenced by the industrialization of the oil era and a culture of conservation of natural and cultural resources were mutually exclusive. In the 2000s, state institutions dedicated to the management of environmental resources were finally established, including legal instruments for the protection of the local and global environment: Environmental Protection Law No. 30 of 2002, an executive by-law (Resolution No. 4 of 2005), and a law on conservation of wildlife and their natural habitats (Law No. 19 of 2004).[46] Efforts toward these reforms were juxtaposed dramatically with the country's continuous high reliance on hydrocarbons, which by 2011 still constituted 90 percent of Qatari exports, and its minimal adaptive capacity in the face of complex climate change factors.[47]

In recognition of the country's deteriorating environmental prospects, QNV sought to include sustainable development as one of its fundamental goals to ensure that the country's prosperity would be preserved and built in a sustainable way starting in 2008.[48] Seeking to shape an environmentally aware population that values the preservation of the ecologies of Qatar and its neighboring states was key, and the concept of natural heritage provided a useful framework through which to enact progress in this regard.[49] The QNV proposed implementing this through administrative and structural changes that included interfacing with the international heritage community.

Recognizing its commitment to environmental protection, in 2008 the Supreme Council for the Environment of Natural Reserves of Qatar submitted a single natural property to the Tentative List of UNESCO as requested by the World Heritage Committee: the site of Khor al-Adaid, a natural reserve also known as the "Inland Sea" located south of Qatar on the border with Saudi Arabia. Other natural landmarks recognized to hold natural heritage value within Qatar included the mangrove forest of al-Thakira Natural Reserve, the Ras Abrouq Nature Reserve (Bir Zekreet), the Umm Tais National Park (established in 2006 during the 15th Asian Games), and the al-Reem Biosphere Preserve, designated in

2007 as one of the thirty-one UNESCO World Network of Biosphere Reserves in the African and Arab States.

Greening also became a key symbolic feature across the built landscapes of Qatar during these transformations. The national Sidra tree (*Ziziphus spinachristi*) was chosen as the logo for the Qatar Foundation, gracing in concrete monumentality the facade of the Qatar National Convention Center in Education City. Acting as a charismatic species[50] that "serve(s) as symbols and rallying points to stimulate conservation awareness and action,"[51] the Sidra tree was chosen to represent a beacon of comfort in the harsh desert environment of the country, allowing life to flourish.[52] At the inauguration ceremony of Education City, in 2003, Sheikha Moza called specific attention to this tree, "with its roots bound in the soil of this world and its branches reaching upwards toward perfection, it is a symbol of solidarity and determination; it reminds us that goals of this world are not incompatible with the goals of the spirit."[53] The worldly goals to which she made reference in this speech included the progressive horizons articulated by the state of Qatar in QNV toward achieving a sustainable future. From participating in the first United Nations (UN) Climate Change Conference of the Parties (COP) for the protection of the environment in Berlin in 1995 to hosting the COP18 conference in Doha in 2012, Qatar had been party to each of the eighteen COP conferences until that time (and continuing now, to twenty-seven and counting).[54]

Explicit reference to greening in the Qatar National Development Strategy 2011–2016 claims that adding a "green dimension to urban planning could strengthen sustainability and make cities more livable."[55] Recommendations in this document included the creation of tree-shaded corridors that are free of car traffic, the incorporation of green spaces in future construction programs, and creating green infrastructure plans. Some of the advantages that were highlighted in these documents in support of greening projects in Qatar were a decrease in noise and air pollution and the protection of animal habitats, such as those of migrating birds. But bidding for the adoption of greening as a sustainable practice regardless of meteorological conditions, soil, topography, geological structure, and petrographic composition was problematic and reinforced the idea that definitions of what constitutes sustainable development in this region can be overly anthropocentric and highly contested.[56]

This paradox was not unique to Qatar. Examining the history of greening in Bahrain, Gareth Doherty explains that "to have and to be green is often presented as a moral imperative, yet the provision of greenery can be morally questionable, especially in arid environments such as Bahrain."[57] Accordingly, the 2012 COP18 in Doha saw the display of greening practices in public urban spaces across the city in the most literal sense: for example, the median on the main road access from West Bay in downtown Doha to the Qatar National Convention Center, where the COP18 was held, was decorated with green Astroturf as a sort of processional road that delegates took from their hotel to the meeting.

Qatar's extreme environmental conditions prevent a greener ecosystem, a fact confirmed by the assessment of the Food and Agricultural Organization of the United Nations, which in 2013 declared Qatar as having zero percent forestry.[58] In 2014, the Ministry of Municipality and Environment (formerly the Ministry of Municipality and Urban Planning) launched an initiative to rehabilitate green areas, combat desertification, and stabilize dunes through the planting of trees and restoration of green areas at Rawdat al-Ghafat, al-Wakrah, and Simaisma. A new National Strategy for Biodiversity was prepared in 2015 to maintain endangered trees and protect them from being overgrazed.[59] Marking trees as a commodity, "heritage trees" became one more building material and heritage artifact in the development of the new city. Across Qatar, rapidly expanding development projects seeking the additional green aesthetics and functions were met with a thin supply of nursery-grown trees, prompting an increase in imports of live trees from the United Arab Emirates and beyond.[60] Mature trees in situ were not always of the desired shape, as described by a designer in Msheireb where greening was carefully curated to reinforce the project's architectural and symbolic languages. Outside Mosque Phase 1A, for example, the grounds are landscaped with plants mentioned in the Qur'an, including pomegranate, olive, and date trees, reflecting a parallel commitment to support preservation and design through religious tradition.

In other areas of redevelopment, the practice of safeguarding mature trees in various demolition projects made trees a part of the archaeological record, marking the boundaries and driveways of former structures— momentarily, that is, before being relocated. Elsewhere in Qatar, the solution to greening was to add more exotic species: Aspire Park proudly featured twenty-three specimens of Argentine floss silk trees (*Ceiba speciosa*), while the al-Hazm designer mall in al-Markhiya, built as a replica of the Galleria Vittorio Emanuele II in Milan, enhanced its authenticity through the addition of mature olive trees (*Olea europaea*).[61] In other areas of the development of Doha, trees were reused and relocated much like historic objects and structures, with many of them repurposed in the landscaping of a new golf course in Education City.

With trees and greenery mobilized as intrinsically valuable and scarce, a productive alliance was forged between heritage preservation projects and practices and greening efforts, staging the ground for raising environmental consciousness and reconfiguring sustainability in authentic, Qatari ways. In 2013, Qatar Museums was not only advertising progress in their restoration projects for the Old Palace, historical mosques, and abandoned villages, but they were also aligning these efforts with the reconstruction of historical and traditional landscapes. These efforts included the rehabilitation of groves of date palm trees (*Phoenix dactylifera*) in the heritage site of Umm Salal Mohammed and in new development projects such as the golf course in Education City. Some conjoining of cultural and natural heritage agendas may have been built on idealism, such as the addition of a courtyard tree to the grounds of the traditional Radwani house against the historical record, which suggests that "the courtyards of Qatari houses were not always enhanced with decorative items. It was said that you were lucky if there was a single tree in your courtyard."[62] Historical archaeologists mapping resources through aerial photographs of old Doha agreed that such a feature would be rare.

The greening strategies that accompanied the heritage renaissance of Qatar were consolidated in a major institution under the Qatar Foundation, tasked with linking biodiversity conservation with cultural heritage viewed through the lens of Islam. In 2007, the Quranic Botanic Garden (QBG) was launched as another center in Education City. It was developed as a joint initiative of the Qatar Foundation and UNESCO with the international and interdisciplinary support and advice of foreign experts and support from Maersk Oil Qatar and Botanic Gardens Conservation International. This project was in line with the vision and mission of the Qatar Foundation to promote the appreciation and preservation of the natural, cultural, and spiritual heritage of Islamic and Arab nations in a global context. The garden in Qatar exhibits about fifty-nine plant species, twenty of which are mentioned in the Qur'an (including al-Zaqqum and al-Daria, both of which are plants that grow in hell), accompanied by the sunna, which gives facts about each plant, the terms associated with it, and how it is cared for and preserved.

The QBG project results from an overarching vision to "provide the people of Qatar and the Gulf Region with a Centre of Excellence for

Research and Education, promoting the conservation of natural and cultural heritage, emphasizing the teachings of the Holy Qur'an and the Hadith . . . and a prime recreational destination."[63] Its educational mission includes the reinforcement of a historical legacy of environmental appreciation in Qatar, driven by oral history accounts and by a spiritual lineage to the heartland of Islamic Arabia through Qur'anic narratives that serve a unified purpose. In line with the ways in which cultural heritage is taught to the citizens and visitors of Qatar, the QBG is involved in a project of acculturation of environmental stewardship that involves highlighting and displaying the significance of specific trees and plants in the Qur'an in order to plant a future environmental consciousness mobilized under Islamic ethics. Through the hadith, the QBG aims to demonstrate that Islam urges people to care for trees and cultivate the land, promoting them as deeds to be rewarded. Overall, the project presents scientific knowledge about the benefits of preserving biodiversity and achieving greater comfort in the harsh climate of Qatar in a way that it is anchored in Allah's instructions for the preservation and stewardship of the environment.

An example of these efforts is the Ghars campaign, unveiled in 2011 by the QBG. Ghars is a name derived from the hadith as narrated by Anas ibn Malik, which says that "there is none amongst the Muslims who plants a tree or sows seeds, and then a bird, or a person or an animal eats from it, but is regarded as a charitable gift for him." At the launch of the campaign, Ghars promised to cultivate 252 trees every year until 2022, with the aim of planting tree number 3,033 by the inauguration of the World Cup in Qatar, in alignment with the United Nations Environmental Programme's Billion Tree Campaign. Reinforcing the connection of this initiative to the teachings of Islam, in 2016 the Ghars campaign reiterated its concern with the preservation of the environment and encouraged all members of society to practice agriculture and tree planting "since Islam urges all of us to do so, as in the Hadith of Prophet Mohammad." Following suit, the Climate Change Department at the Ministry of Municipality and Environment and the Public World Authority, Ashghal, launched their own aligned initiatives under the "Plant a Million Trees" campaigns to fight desertification, enhance biological diversity, improve air quality, and reduce Qatar's carbon footprint by increasing greenery.

In these ways, the project of raising environmental consciousness has been one that connects Qataris to their land as much as it is one that reiterates the significance of Islamic teachings for the environmental well-being of Qatar and the rest of the world. At the plenary lecture for the Second International Forum of the Qur'anic Botanic Garden in 2014, Zaghloul El-Naggar, a faculty member of the World Islamic Sciences and Education University in Jordan, made a compelling case for this integrated view. He argued that a warning about corrupting the environment and advocating for a balanced relationship between humans and their ecosystem had been in the Qur'an for more than fourteen centuries. With all utilitarian concepts proving to have failed in this area, he added, the only way to repair the damage brought about by the advent of industrialization is through an adherence to Islamic environmental ethics that is both faith- and virtue-based.[64] With regional and global interests in mind, the strategic alignment of two institutions, the QBC and the United Nations, was underway along symbiotic cultural and environmental rationales.

Translations

Ghars was not the only campaign that translated global efforts of environmental stewardship into the specific sociocultural context of Qatar. In fact, three kinds of translations were taking place around and through the mobilization of cultural and natural resources in Qatar during this time: a translation of ascendant ideas of global heritage discourse to the specific context of Qatar, a translation of ideas about the natural environment to projects of urban development, and a translation of Qatar's own advances into globally recognized greening technologies and futures that contribute to challenges of desertification and climate change elsewhere. With a focus on the latter, since 2009, another subsidiary of the Qatar Foundation, the Qatar Green Building Council (QGBC), connected Qatar to a global network of other national initiatives under the umbrella of the World Green Building Council. Within Qatar, this nonprofit was established to support Qatar in its journey to advancing a posthydrocarbon knowledge economy. QGBC was instrumental in aligning different sustainability efforts across the developing urban landscape of Qatar, including the implementation of the Global Sustainability Assessment System, a green-building certification system devised by the Gulf Organization for Research and Development that parallels the LEED, Building Research Establishment Environmental Assessment Method (BREEAM)[65] and Estidama[66] assessment and rating systems.[67] Taking Qatarization efforts a step further, in 2022 an organization called Earthna was announced as a different Qatar Foundation subsidiary institution created to act as a center for advocacy for national and global sustainability policy. A much more localized initiative than the QGBC, the name "Earthna" (actually pronounced "irthna," the Arabic for "our legacy") also plays with its meaning in Arablish (Arabic+English) to be read as "our earth."

Throughout its tenure, QGBC had made strides toward leaving a mark on the culture of sustainability in the country and the region. Besides advising development projects across Qatar, they were also part of the team that developed the first Passivhaus in the GCC region, an ultralow-energy villa adapted to a hot climate built in Barwa City, which was well underway by the time of COP18 in Doha and finalized by April 2013. Passivhaus demonstrated the possibilities of a greener livelihood that, unfortunately, very little resembled the spaces, behaviors, and practices of resource utilization of affluent Qatari houses. It foregrounded some climatic adaptations that aligned with cultural practices, such as the preservation of privacy and the use of smaller windowed surfaces and an inner courtyard. However, the Passivhaus concept, developed in Germany in 1990, offered a compact and rationalized living that remained disconnected from the average Qatari lifestyle.

The work of Qatarizing sustainability measures that were, in practical terms, sustainable in Qatar and for Qatari and visitors alike, required more careful compromise than anything this one-off experiment could propose. Other sustainability-oriented initiatives seemed less able to be translated to the specific needs and habits of Qatar; instead, they echoed foreign ideals and values in support of a sustainable living that had been tried and tested elsewhere. For example, the celebration of #WorldBicycleDay, in alignment with the UN declaration of 3 June as International World Bicycle Day, fostered sustainable transportation and promoted healthy habits but paid less attention to the limitations of cultural and environmental constraints in a place like Qatar. Limitations included the difficulty of biking while wearing the long, traditional dress among Qataris of both genders, as well as the unforgiving climatic conditions and a dangerous driving culture of Qatar that is less attuned to sharing streets with cyclists. Other awareness campaigns launched by different state institutions in the spirit of a "green revolution" included a call for moderate consumption that has not traditionally characterized the luxury-oriented lifestyles of affluent Qataris. For example, the electrical company Kahramaa's initiative, Tarsheed, sought public support in their mission to decrease water and electricity consumption by 35 percent and by 20 percent, respectively, as well as to reduce carbon emissions in line with the Conserving Energy and Water Consumption Law No. 26/2008.[68]

What these initiatives were largely missing was a culture of engaging the public in comprehensive dialogue with the government on specific issues that paid attention to processes of acculturation. Relatively low-impact outreach initiatives also suffered from a lack of publicity, so the work of advocacy was left to a small number of concerned nongovernmental organizations (NGOs) involved in raising public awareness about environmental concerns, such as Friends of the Environment, Qatar National History Group, and Qatar Green Centre.[69]

Resorting to the weight of heritage to support and promote cultures of care for natural and cultural resources was prevalent in Qatar but had mixed results. The repurposing of traditional architecture that sought to blend traditional and modern urban development was an effective and sustainable way to disarm a more superficial "green rush" model of change.[70] However, the possibility of finding green and sustainable design and practices rooted in heritage languages and traditional ways often relied on aspirational views and reinvented traditions. At times, for example, claims that traditional cultural forms and architectural practices inherited from the past represented more sustainable futures often reinvented the relationship between the past and the future.[71] The archaeologist Claire Hardy-Gilbert referred to one such discourse as the "wind tower fetish."[72] The *barjeel* (wind tower) is a much-celebrated architectural feature that has been extensively mobilized as an icon of sustainable and traditional architecture. It was the inspiration behind El Kafrawi's design for Qatar University and for the modern 252-meter-tall Kempinski high-rise in Doha, among many other examples.[73] Casual observers of Qatari urbanism interpret the modern prevalence of wind tower–inspired design as a return to tradition.[74] But this Iranian import was not that common a feature on the Arabian side of the Gulf. In the late 1970s, John Moorehead fed into this fetish when he observed that "one last wind-tower survives as a monument to the age before air conditioning," but aerial photography from the 1940s on confirms the rarity of wind towers across the city.[75] The infatuation with the keywords embedded in QNV could, in this way, result in cultural imaginaries that overlooked, and perhaps even flattened, historical records and regional distinctions.

Msheireb Downtown Doha modeled a different and more effective approach to translating sustainability goals into more authentic and locally resonant infrastructures. Self-defined as the world's first sustainable downtown regeneration project, it maintained a convincing claim to promoting authentic livelihoods—aesthetically and spiritually—while featuring the highest concentrations of LEED-certified sustainable buildings. The goal of achieving a 32 percent energy reduction included targeting most buildings in Msheireb to gain LEED Gold or even Platinum certification. The foregrounding of universal standards and goals was mediated by a narrative of origins in support of locality that aligned with Qatarization efforts in two ways. One was the incorporation of existing historic sites in the master plan of the new, modern city, fulfilling the twofold objective of sustainable reuse of structures with a reappraisal of regional materials, as well as the reinforcement of the idea that bygone Muslim society already contained the know-how for passive energy strategies before modernization (including building orientation, urban layouts that encouraged walking, and uses of landscape that supported a local drought-friendly environment). The second appeal to Qatarization was the effective development and use of design languages invoking Qatari urban landscapes and Muslim traditions in finishes, architectural spaces, and urban layout. This reinforced a nod to an Islam-practicing modern society that had not been ravaged by the advent of modernization and could easily assimilate the sophistication of a sustainable city.

Resolving the challenge of creating a traditional yet sustainable future confronted the problem of assimilating two often-opposing perspectives, one oriented to the past and one oriented to the future, in support of behavioral and economic change in the present. Promoting such a multifaceted culture of care for resources required a localizing strategy that could contain Qatari and Muslim identities and remain compatible with the actual natural and built environments in Qatar. Viewed in this way, an emphasis on ecologies as complex systems in which all living things are connected to each other and benefit each another's well-being was as ineffective as an appeal to universal values. Sustaining these transformative projects over time through the cultivation of local stewardship was carried out more effectively through the bonding discourse of Islam, but in other cultural contexts, Islam was used as a divisive force that manifested in obstacles for future cultural development.

CHAPTER 4

The Art of *Mal Lawal*

Creating a Heritage Public That Cares

A thematic tension undergirded the growth
of a civil society that would be concerned with heritage value in Qatar
during the first two decades of the millennium. On the one hand, there
was growing appreciation for Qatari heritage not just as a prescribed
set of symbols inherited from the past, but also as a force linking traditional lifestyles, contemporary productions of authentic art and culture, and future aspirations, especially for sustainable growth. On the
other hand, there was still occasional but outspoken resistance to new
cultural movements that deviated from the strict canon of tradition,
however rooted in or inspired by Qatari heritage they may have been.
The first position was not simply a survival strategy in the face of rampant modernization. Recognizing the continuous production of culture
within the framework of heritage also represented a form of resistance
to the orientalist idea that Middle Eastern cultural riches were exclusively generated in the past, a form of misrepresentation that often went
hand in hand with a distrust of contemporary Muslim societies to protect or steward their own heritage adequately. Negotiations between the
two views for Qatari art and culture were marked by tensions that pitted the past and the present against each other. Moreover, it resulted in
social conflicts that are familiar to the development of heritage cultures
elsewhere, but in Qatar, many of these revolved around a dichotomy

between "us" (Qataris) and "them" (expatriates and migrant workers), thereby posing an existential challenge to efforts to cultivate a broad-based public who cares about, and for, a culture of heritage.

Establishing the contours of what constitutes a legitimate public for the cultural developments of the nation was challenging in the social history of Qatar. The trope of Qataris versus "expats" harks back to the 1950s, when the rudiments of a Qatari identity were forged and encouraged by the ruling family on several fronts. At that time, it was reported that oil strikes that pitted Qatari laborers against Dhofaris (Omanis) and Pakistanis eventually merged into a conflict of Qataris against expats.[1] In this process, merchants weaponized national symbols against foreign contractors and the state created national and commercial laws that defined Qataris and granted them a special status and rights. A further distinction emerged to identify the category of "migrant worker'" as separate from "expatriate," denoting not only different terms of permanence but also class (the distinction between "poor migrant workers" or "low-skilled laborers" and "highly paid professional expatriates," is applicable). By the early 2000s, the distinction between local and foreign was also articulated around a strategy called "Qatarization"; that is, the intentional creation of citizen-workers that can displace the outsourcing of specialized knowledge from primarily Western countries. Qatarization as a government initiative focused on increasing the number of Qatari citizens employed in the public and private sectors to constitute 50 percent of the workforce by 2030. The cultural sector in general, including higher education, constituted an especially significant target of Qatarization. This sector had been predominantly dominated by foreign specialists, known as "expats," occupying and sometimes training the next generation of Qatari experts. In this capacity, they have been described as gatekeepers who translate Qatari culture as passive observants and even benevolent saviors rather than as active participants employing and naturalizing forms of inequality, belonging, and exclusion.[2]

Qatarization was accompanied by official state efforts to articulate a "consolidated civic myth."[3] When Sheikh Khalifa bin Hamad al-Thani came to power in 1972, he expressed his intention to form "an illuminating bridge that links the glorious present with the ancient past."[4] Qatar was lacking the symbolism to go along with this project; hence, his early ruling years were marked by the construction of a symbolic legacy that would clarify and legitimize his claim to rule. Joining the international stage as an independent country gained Qatar status and recognition of its inherited symbols—flags, coins, and anthems. At home, the legacy needed to reconcile past and present in such a way that the modern nation and its historical genealogies and landscapes were integrated into a continuum. Crystal summarizes two challenges in the creation of such a myth: there were not enough Qataris to do it, so inevitably, this required contracting expatriates; and the nation-state myth would have to effectively compete with larger rivals—a Gulfian, a pan-Arab, and a broad Islamic identity. The latter, as Montigny has suggested, "provided the most accessible, evocative, but also flexible and volatile set of symbols."[5] Moreover, a third competing identity was tribalism, which was once repressed as a hindrance to modernization but remained "a crucial element in the Gulf's modernity," acting as "the new aristocratic in the flattening anonymity of twenty-first century transnational movement and cosmopolitanism."[6] A project of normative socialization was henceforth carried out by dedicated institutions charged with guarding history, starting with the newly created Ministry of Information in 1972, the foundation of the National Museum, and ending in nothing less than the Qatar National Vision 2030 (QNV) and all the heritage safeguarding institutions and mechanisms that have already been described in earlier chapters.

Citizen participation in the cultural growth of Qatar along these lines was attempted from the earliest days of the nation. From 1975 on, the governments of the Gulf states sought to compensate for the effects of social change by promoting traditional performances that evoked Bedouin heritage and maritime heritage alike.[7] This effort became particularly visible starting in the 1990s, when traditional performances were encouraged across the Gulf states in support of modern nationalist pride. For example, Montigny also points out that camel breeding and racing were relaunched in the spirit of revaluing Bedouin heritage. Falconry, promoted as another "heritage sport," was not just a way for local communities to maintain self-preservation against foreign forces through traditional performances and practices.[8] It also helped naturalize "a geopolitical order defined by the state system and citizens who 'belong' in some places but not others."[9] What could not be packaged as "tribal modern" for the most conservative segments of society could be neatly put forth in the form of a distilled tradition in such a way that modernity could be allowed to flourish elsewhere. Rather than being driven by nostalgia for pastoral times, the revival of traditional skills had the potential to help younger generations appreciate a time before that which brought progress and technology.[10] In this way, modernization was attenuated through the grand production of festivals celebrating traditional practices that connect urban elites with rural pasts: the revival of festivals of regional and international acclaim and their accompanying cultural institutions, such as al-Gannas, dedicated to promoting traditional Arabic hunting, and their popular Hudud al-Tahaddi challenge, where pure Arabian Saluki (hound) breeds chase a gazelle for over two kilometers.

Similar dynamics played out with more mixed results in arenas such as theater and television. Television and video recordings had "brought alien culture into almost every Qatari home," wrote a British Council observer.[11] Therefore, local producers sought to adapt imported entertainment forms to local tastes and expectations, generating content for Qataris in Qatar. For example, the 1970s saw television shows about traditional Arab medicine as well as folklore, documenting old Qatari stories about fishing, pearling, and nomadic life.[12] Modern theater arrived in Qatar with support from the government, but no formal institutions to advocate for the craft; the most popular play, *Umm el-Zein*, was written in Qatari dialect by a former Shell employee, Abdel Rahman al-Mannai, who then became head of the cultural center.[13] It is remarkable that a theater scene was formed at all. Objections to the setting-up of a theater during the 1960s cited strict Wahabi rules against having women on stage, for example.[14]

In essence, the growth of a civil society that supported the development of arts and culture that are sensitive to the interplay of local and increasingly global legacies needed to support two distinct agendas. One supported the project of growing heritage and tradition as a way to connect the present to the past. The second was the project of adapting to changes brought about by the modern era to connect the present to the future. Public engagement in support of culture would have to be conceptualized in consideration of these rapidly shifting and overlapping conditions. Key in the process of alignment was the generation of a concerned and empowered civil society needed to support the emergence of a culture of heritage preservation in Qatar. The encouragement of various forms of curatorial practices, including the circulation of art, as forms of generating and reinforcing new heritage traditions was a critical staging ground for showcasing these intersections.

Making Heritage Publics for and through Culture

Curating a public concerned with heritage stewardship in Qatar was particularly visible in the mid-2000s, when the latest push for redevelopment had already transformed the central Msheireb district into one of the key faces of the modern city. As redevelopment plans advanced through the nearby al-Asmakh neighborhood, many younger Qataris appeared to rediscover the existence of historical houses that remained encroached in these tightly packed old neighborhoods. The anthropologist Andrew Gardner describes this as the "glow of heritage" that changed perceptions about aging neighborhoods among citizens.[15] The rediscovery, or reappraisal, of these dilapidated structures as historic resources was encouraged through social media and educational programs that served the agenda to promote social attachment to the historical fabric of Qatar. An example of these two mechanisms working in unison, the *Qatar Culture Club*, was active in the curation of cultural debates around the subject of stewardship and globalization from 2011 to 2013.[16] Launched as part of sociology classes at Northwestern University Qatar and Carnegie Mellon University in Qatar, it considered terms like "McDonaldization," "imagined community," and "proletariat" in the context of cultural industries and processes of modernization in Qatar. Another popular blog, *Catnaps*, was a "virtual notebook recommended as an authoritative archive of various aspects of 'old Qatar.'"[17] In this online repository, the British architect, urban designer, planner, and management consultant John Lockerbie maintained an archive of photos and stories of various aspects of Qatari life and development processes. A Qatari designer independently recommended that I join a different living archive, the Facebook group "Doha—The Good Old Days," a private but ever-growing online community primarily composed of expatriates who once lived in Qatar and continued to share archival footage, images, and the occasional anecdote about life in the country in decades past. Crowdsourcing heritage narratives and resources in the new millennium filled the void of archival silences that resulted from a lack of institutional self-reporting and, to some extent, documenting. These public resources reflect the workings of a cosmopolitan community invested in the mechanisms of nostalgia for Qatar.

An accelerated heritage awakening was particularly incited by the presence and advocacy of new graduate programs in museums and archaeology at University College London Qatar (UCL Qatar), which initially became populated by a number of Qatari students sponsored by Qatar Museums. It was in these classrooms and seminar rooms that ideas of rights to access and stewardship of heritage resources in academic debates encouraged student-citizens to reconsider their roles in the new heritage regime. Transporting foreign ideas of stewardship into the particular life-histories of the urban fabric of Qatar was not straightforward. For example, upon learning the identities of the residents who were legitimately occupying the historical houses of the old city—migrant workers from Nepal, Bangladesh, and Pakistan—one Qatari graduate student who had never been to or seen this part of town exclaimed, "But they are destroying *our heritage!*" Such a call to arms, preceded by decades of complete neglect and even ignorance of the historical resources left behind in the center of town, was the kind of energetic stewardship that underpinned contemporary heritage preservation agendas—imagined by many as possible to execute only by "insider" Qatari citizens.

As has been discussed for other cities of the Gulf, an entire generation of Qataris had been asked, twice, to acquiesce to a future-oriented narrative of progress in support of two opposite orientations. The first time, Qataris were asked to detach from the urban fabric of Qatar to make way for processes of urban destruction and redevelopment that they were experiencing through the project of modernization.[18] This was a time when the Museum of Modern Development, across the square from the Emiri Palace, boasted of the vast oil revenues and how they were being spent.[19] The second time, more recently, the future-oriented nation-building narrative based on articulating a shared civic heritage had to find ways to successfully reconcile Qataris with their traditional urban fabric, despite much of it already having been replaced in the process of modernization. To make things more complicated, there were instances in which what remained, as was the case in al-Asmakh, had been cared for by migrant workers for decades. In a less orthodox practice of "preservation," these noncitizen tenants had maintained historical houses that functioned as homes and shelters rather than being relics of the past. The coup de grâce was the fact that the migrant workers legitimately living in the historical houses in the old neighborhood were the same type of migrant workers (construction workers) who had been trained in authentic crafts and techniques needed to reconstruct authentic heritage fabrics across Qatar. Through habitation, skills, and formal and casual practices of care, the residents of al-Asmakh acted and performed in practical terms as a sort of steward for a neighborhood that had been largely ignored by the majority of the Qatari public for decades. However, noncitizens who acted on necessity and survival rather than loyalty to perform Qatari identity politics were not recognized in official discourse. Even more, as my former student's comment suggests, their presence could be considered detrimental to the well-being of heritage assemblages.

The shift in state-sponsored attitudes toward the historic urban fabric presented a fresh opportunity to acculturate Qataris and non-Qataris alike into its culture of heritage preservation—if it could successfully smooth over contradictions raised by these efforts, especially insider-outsider tensions. In particular, the demolition of the central neighborhoods of Msheireb, al-Asmakh, and al-Najada provided opportunities for crafting a specific heritage public in Qatar that was responsive to the type of preservation that Qatari institutions were conducting. Around these sites, the Qatar Foundation and Qatar Museums launched a series of public and professional engagement initiatives that aimed to bring together a broader public invested in heritage preservation and simultaneously placed visible projects such as Msheireb as places of transnational cultural collaboration and exchange.[20] For example, Msheireb Properties launched in 2009 the Echo Memory Project (*Sadaa Thakerat al-Makan*), headquartered in the Msheireb Arts Center (MAC) in the abandoned old Girls' School, al-Wassad, of al-Asmakh. Here, the artist and curator Ben Barbour oversaw rooms full of *ashya* (things); that is, the old remnants of what had been the Msheireb neighborhood before demolition. This assemblage was the result of a systematic collection, documentation, and safeguarding of what they called "found objects" of the former version of the Msheireb neighborhood up until its redevelopment. In these rooms, the human and architectural past of Qatar was reduced to piles of ceiling fans, neon lights, and commercial signage of every shape and color. It offered a visual archive of a modern turn in Qatar that adapted traditional architectural spaces to the needs of a fast-growing cosmopolitan society defined by technological advancement.

An estimated 3,000 to 4,000 objects were gathered as part of this project, many of which were displayed and stored at MAC while others remained in an oversized storage facility in Industrial City, an unglamorous urban grid dominated by auto body shops, wholesale stores, and small industrial facilities that were a far cry from the manicured production of a new Doha. In fact, Industrial City caters specifically to the social lives of low-income migrant workers.[21] In this offsite storage space, there was an unlikely heritage collection-in-waiting of a different order of magnitude from the collections at MAC: wooden and metal doors, light fixtures, concrete and metal sections of *mashrabiya*, decorative fences, shop signage, but also bundles of danshal wood beams, bits of masonry, columns, entire arches and walls, old television units, mannequins, and other items. Here, the eclectic collection of what once

FIGURE 4.1.   Heritage in storage, Industrial City, 2011. Objects and architectural features collected and stored prior to the demolition of the Mshreireb neighborhood in central Doha. Photo by author.

constituted the urban fabric of Msheireb was waiting to be reassembled along a new cultural narrative. Some of these fragments of Old Doha were carefully supported and wrapped in plastic film, while others were piled by type following no obvious chronological or stratigraphic order: wood with wood, doors with doors, shop fittings with shop fittings, and so on (figure 4.1). Were it not for the Arabic script on many of these objects whose existence mark the turn to modernity, they could have come from practically anywhere else in the world: Jakarta, Buenos Aires, a Muslim-majority urban center, or elsewhere. The remnants of a generic modernity that defined entire decades of life in Doha marked the end of traditional time but also proposed the 1950s onward as a time when domestic and commercial livelihoods could, in theory, exist independent of Islam, even endangering the more religious cadences of life of a Muslim city.

One of the organizers of this curatorial effort, Tim Makower, stressed the collaborative nature of this initiative as resulting from a strong link between London and Doha in the fields of art and culture, while also referring to this output as "remaining uniquely Qatari in its identity."[22] Makower was the architect leading the task of defining and establishing the architectural language guidelines for the Msheireb project. He was also the expert behind efforts to connect the heritage assets of Old Doha with a long tradition of UK expertise in matters of cultural development. For example, a design charette followed the documentation efforts of Old Doha with the aim of examining ways to raise awareness among government agencies and the public and offer a model that could turn lessons of Doha's past into an environmentally and socially sustainable vernacular for the future.[23] These initiatives were backed by the British Council and Qatar Museums and supported by Msheireb Properties and the Royal Institute of British Architects, which ran an open competition for small and newly established UK-based architectural practices to partner with Qatari practitioners for a weeklong project in Doha.[24]

Making art out of displacement in Msheireb was more geared toward a loose interpretation of what it meant to salvage a "memory of place" through the documentation of objects from a lost era rather than an investment in recognizing publics and deploying public engagement strategies for Qatar.[25] In fact, it could be argued that the primary benefactor of Echo Memory was a team of artists from the Prince's Drawing School in London who worked with students from Qatar University over a period of six days in the fall of 2010 to record this neighborhood at a moment of significant change. Only four drawings in the publication were made by members of Qatar University. However, the goal to generate more engaged heritage publics through the arts spawned myriad other projects with similar methods around sites that were relatively orphaned in terms of stewardship. A different initiative at Msheireb, called a "Drawathon," was organized by Qatar-based artists on 9 November 2013 and exhibited at the Student Center Art Gallery of Hamad Bin Khalifa University in Education City. The Drawathon was an initiative brought to Qatar with roots elsewhere—namely, the Big Draw's annual monthlong series of events promoting drawing and visual literacy in the United Kingdom. Importing foreign ideas of community arts programming in Doha's emergent cultural landscape was another side of the same coin that brought global arts agendas to Qatar. The influence of the United Kingdom over the cultural development in Qatar remained consistent with the British Council's earliest intentions and interventions in the 1970s.

Initiatives more attentive to local publics, professional collaborations, and training programs such as the Mapping Old Doha project, run by UCL Qatar and Qatar Museums, focused on mapping architectural heritage resources across al-Asmakh and al-Najada. It was during one of the field components of this initiative, in 2014, that a firsthand experience with the realities of displacement and demolition in al-Asmakh resulted in a sort of "open house" to collect grievances and experiences from migrant residents of the neighborhood at the MAC. The event was organized by a team of faculty members and students from University College London (UCL) and the arts team of Msheireb Properties and involved opening MAC to offer tea, biscuits, and conversation. One of the rationales behind this event was the understanding that this segment of the public, constituting noncitizen migrant workers, was discouraged from playing an active role in the heritage-making plans for Qatar. In contrast, local Qatari publics were directly targeted through the platform of official archaeological and heritage sites. For example, in anticipation of al-Zubarah's likely addition to the World Heritage List, Qatar Museums Authority and the University of Copenhagen launched an outreach program at the al-Zubarah archaeological site to build relationships with Qatari people, especially school-aged children and those living closer to the site.[26] In Education City, institutions observed the principles for engaging with the public as dictated by their own main campuses. It was, after all, a large part of their brand. In this way, UCL Qatar, a satellite campus of UCL in the United Kingdom, deployed engagement strategies "focused on UCL's ethos of inclusivity by reaching out to those in society who are often sidelined."[27] From children's storybooks to graduate training programs, the educational ideology of UCL Qatar built heritage literacy into Qatar but maintained the primary remit, as part of the Qatar Foundation, to bring about a heritage awakening among Qataris.

However, the modern educational ethos of a UK-based institution like UCL Qatar promoted a broader engagement with heritage value and the arts in general than the specific context of Qatar could, or would, accommodate. The view from the United Kingdom was guided by concerns about inclusivity, diversity, and equity, a mismatch with Qatar's societal norms and system of government, where the state was the primary architect of preservation, censorship of countervailing visions was feared, and access to the most basic public spaces was heavily policed—to reiterate, bachelors (another term for migrant workers) were excluded from many shopping centers on family days. The tensions between, on the one hand, the academic imperative to engage *all* publics in line with modern heritage preservation ethics and, on the other hand, the institutional mission in the Qatar Foundation to educate *some* publics was palpable.

Crowdsourcing Heritage Significance

The public as imagined by Qatari institutions was simultaneously served academic, state-driven, and popular heritage narratives. For example, at the same time as the Museum of Islamic Art hosted the niche academic conference and training workshop "The Illuminated Word, Historic Qur'ans: Codicology and Conservation" (April 2014), Qatar Museums launched the first of three exhibitions that highlighted the more personal and popular dimensions of collecting and accruing heritage value. The exhibition "Mal Lawal"—meaning "from the old days," in Qatari dialect—showcased objects owned by individuals and families who were approached for this initiative in their capacity as "private collectors" in Qatar. A promotional video for the first Mal Lawal exhibit invited viewers to a cultural project of showcasing various collections from the people of Qatar accompanied by an exhibition of contemporary Qatari artists. The curatorial effort to blend the materiality and narratives of heritage with the innovation and expressions of artistic creation as part of one continuum unfolded over three events during the second decade of the new millennium. Mal Lawal 1 (Al Riwaq exhibition space, 12 September–11 October 2012) was such a success that it was followed by two more installments, each one held in bigger and more important venues: Mal Lawal 2 (Doha Exhibition Center in Dafna/West Bay, 28 February 2015), and Mal Lawal 3 (National Museum of Qatar, 18 June–15 September 2021).[28]

Crowdsourcing heritage value in this way was not an entirely new approach to raising public engagement in Qatar. Back in 1975, the preparatory work for the opening of the National Museum included the formation of a committee of distinguished Qataris, established by Sheikh Khalifa, to advise on the collections of the museum and the curation of traditional and ethnological materials. Michael Rice described how, through the Ministry of Information, a call was put out to the public to bring any materials that they thought likely to be of possible interest to the museum to a collecting center in Doha.[29] This call for contributions complemented other curatorial strategies, such as conducting interviews with older members of the al-Thani family and collecting and examining old photographs from a variety of archives. As was the case with the Mal Lawal initiative, collection-making strategies for the original National Museum prepared to outfit a historical period of Qatar that was thin on historical resources—namely, the transition between nomadic and settled life in the Arabian Gulf littoral. Even in 1975, crowdsourcing was the pathway to resist a chronological alienation imposed by other official and art historical heritage constructs and collections such as the ones later held at the Museum of Islamic Art, where it has been argued that Qatar's history is not represented in the permanent collection.[30]

Collection completeness was only one of the motivations for crowd-sourcing heritage objects and accompanying narratives. Another key rationale was the need to raise a heritage public attuned to the significance of stewardship. As Sheikha al-Mayassa bint Hamad bin Khalifa al-Thani, chairperson for Qatar Museums, explained, significant collections begin with a personal obsession or a motivation to preserve and archive history through objects, a conscious decision to collect and preserve, which raises a common trope in museum studies that claims that the imperative to preserve is a natural human, and therefore also Qatari, inclination.[31] Mal Lawal was, then, aimed at instilling a love of preserving heritage objects.[32] Growing a community of collectors under the umbrella of Qatar Museums made the private accessible to the public without being driven by the commercial market in an initiative that "reminds us that cultural growth is a joint effort between the government and its people."[33] The Mal Lawal platform could also expertly navigate the politics of tribal representation through curatorial negotiations, maintaining a balance between family or tribal units in this visible and status-granting platform. These efforts resulted in eclectic collections: the first Mal Lawal included weapons, coffeepots, a ceramic vessel with Arabic calligraphy from around the twelfth century, wooden chests, a giant clam, fossils, Sumerian carvings, a mid-twentieth-century radio, cameras, pocket watches, Qur'anic scrolls, an astrolabe, furniture, coins, maps, jewelry, and, of course, pearl items. Many, but not all, of these objects featured Islamic patterns and Arabic writing.

The organizers for this initiative, as well as the observers and commentators, considered the Mal Lawal events to be a huge success.[34] From a promotional video that invited contributors to participate because "your collections represent you, and you represent Qatar," to the lectures, workshops, and outreach and education programs that were launched to encourage audiences to connect with the content being displayed, the importance of collecting as a mechanism for shaping the past, present, and future of the nation was imparted to collectors and amateur enthusiasts alike. It articulated, in a sense, a collective form of collecting. Exhibiting the privacy and complexity of Qatari home life on a public platform challenged the outsider reporter Helga Graham's observations in the 1970s that Qataris do not like old, nor "eastern" things.[35] But this opening of private life to public consumption and scrutiny came at a cost. According to Qatari informants, Mal Lawal was a dangerous territory that made evident that culture in Qatar was grown and performed in "secular spaces" that circulated "secular objects" of modernity. In a Wahabi-oriented household through the 1950s to the 1980s, they claimed that one would not own, or admit to owning, a record player or a television set. Over the past fifty years, the religious and cultural stigma associated with music performance resulted in a mixed attitude toward this practice. Islamic apprehensions concerning music are well known throughout the Middle East[36]—so much so that Harry St. John Philby, the British explorer and historian, once described Arabia as a "musicless land."[37] Salafi puritanism and negative associations with singing as an unsuitable profession for a free-born Arab have given way now to a passion for music and tradition in modern celebrations of Qatari song, such as the Qatari Song Night Festival.[38]

The question of whether a new or traditional activity was aligned with being Muslim became a central tension in the arts and culture scene of Qatar, which pitted authentic archival and oral sources against contemporary cultural politics. The UCL Qatar–based research project "Origins of Doha and Qatar" (ODQ) also invited the public to participate in their research initiative by contributing primary and personal items—family photos, videos of Doha, and others. Within this initiative, Tammi Moe and Fahad al-Obaidly aimed to capture the experience of the development of the town and its transition from a traditional settlement to a modern city. The ODQ project reviewed data from earlier efforts by the Gulf Folklore Centre, the National Museum of Qatar, and the National Archives, complementing the palimpsest of data produced by archaeological excavations, archival and oral histories, and ethnographic interviews.

During this phase of the ODQ project, the team encountered different forms of resistance to the display of faith-specific religious objects, historical photographs, and sensitive oral histories.[39] Their experience suggested that display of potentially *makruh* (discouraged) or possibly *haram* (forbidden) activities as constituent parts of the recent historical periods of Qatar was a disturbance of the careful dissonance that the younger generation perceived as sustaining the heritage renaissance of Qatar or, as one of these young Qatari informants called it, "a living image of state schizophrenia."

The prolific use of participatory collecting and oral history projects to construct knowledge and provide a causeway to incentivize public engagement in the growth of heritage industries had its downsides when it was not properly incorporated into a research project such as ODQ. The mobilization of oral history as *artifacts*—objects of cultural or historical interest made by a human being and extracted through investigative procedures—was sometimes weakly contextualized. For example, the ease with which oral history projects were deployed by various educational institutions often failed to consider a critical problem with this mode of engagement: the conditions under which the data was obtained, curated, and later put to work, transgressing the boundaries of private and public life that are particularly significant in Qatari culture. Undergraduate students thrust into oral history projects as part of their coursework across US campuses of Education City explained later that they were not instructed on their right to refuse to participate in these initiatives, nor were they told about the treatment of the resulting data that later became public through publication initiatives.[40] In addition to problematically erasing "the text-producing activities of the interviewer," the popularization of such an extractive methodology by powerful institutional knowledge-brokers raised ethical concerns as certain cultural norms were forced to shift in the name of heritage-making.[41]

Addressing Broken Engagements

The project of engaging and educating a public in Qatar demonstrates the ways in which the observance of cultural norms aligning with Islam could be a moderate disruptor of the development of a new vernacular. Islam has, in many ways, been mobilized as a strong divisive force in cultural developments in general. Sheikha al-Mayassa explicitly referred to this when describing the aims of the Museum of Islamic Art, which she envisioned as a place of resistance against predominantly negative views of Islam as a violent religion. Instead, she expressed, the nascent institution seeks "to showcase, with evidence, that Islam is a peaceful religion at the heart of the most intellectually and culturally sophisticated societies throughout history."[42] At the same time, however, this museum seemed to downplay the notion that its collections are predominantly religious. For example, the British Museum's 2012 traveling exhibition "Hajj: Journey to the Heart of Islam" changed its title to "Hajj: Journey through Art" at the Museum of Islamic Art in 2014.[43] Such a shift hints at an antimodernist view that excludes and minimizes the significance of a social context for a lived Islam.[44] The museum consultant Karen Exell observed that the Museum of Islamic Art aligned more with "a disciplinary, Western imagining of an Islamic world unrelated to the contemporary Islamic culture of Qatar," in such a way that its exhibits could not communicate the placatory message about Islam that al-Mayassa anticipated.[45]

Exell concluded in her work that intentional secularization in the museum's collecting and exhibiting practices was a necessary attempt to project cultural fluency in the international language of taste. And yet, scandal over the "showing of exhibition of artworks believed to violate Islamic principles" surfaced with some frequency within and beyond the space of the museum.[46] To accompany this potential confrontation, efforts to acculturate the public to new forms of expression included initiatives such as Fannek, a monthlong public art initiative that provided a gateway to explore Qatar's public art scene through tours, talks, and workshops; and Menthaar, another outreach program that explored, through a series of tours and webinars, Qatar's heritage, culture, environment, and vision for the future. Despite these, tensions over what kinds of art were appropriate to show in a predominantly Muslim society manifested in the public sphere with the incendiary force that only social media can generate.

Exell curates some of the scandals that marked specific exhibitions and institutional initiatives throughout an eventful 2013. In August, an article outing the misuse of funds and uneven treatment of Qatari and Western expertise at Qatar Museums was published in the Qatari newspaper *Al Arab*, provoking a storm in social media. Among the grievances expressed through this medium was the prioritizing of Western art and artists and the exhibiting of artwork believed to violate Islamic principles and local codes of conduct. She further recounts how, in this same year, protests erupted on social and traditional media following the installation on the Corniche of the Algerian artist Adel Abdessemed's *Coup de Tête* statue, depicting the disgraceful moment in sports history when the French footballer Zinedine Zidane head-butted the Italian player Marco Materazzi at the World Cup in 2006. Perhaps the most recognizable expression of this tension took place the same year following the unveiling of Damien Hirst's sculptural piece outside Sidra Hospital, which specializes in children and women's health. Titled *The Miraculous Journey*, this installation features fourteen giant bronze sculptures depicting stages of fetal development from conception to birth. After being unveiled briefly in 2013, they were covered almost immediately to (allegedly) protect them from ongoing building work at the hospital.

The outcry on social media was instantaneous at the first unveiling. Led by an older generation, callers flooded the radio show *Good Morning*

Qatar to express outrage about the Sidra babies. The representation of the human form in art pieces such as this one was justified on scientific and educational grounds—a medical alibi that allows contemporary art to subtly liberalize Qatar's local culture, provoking debates about public representation of the body and freedom of expression.[47] *The Miraculous Journey* was finally uncovered again, much later, in November 2018. One of the ways in which officials acculturated this project, the first naked sculpture in the Middle East, was by arranging for a boy to recite a passage from the Qur'an about the formation of life.

Hirst's sculpture was one of a series of modern art installations commissioned by Qatar Museums that provoked a negative reaction among Qatari audiences. Many of these provocative artworks featured nudes and the word "God" in the title—which was not translated into Arabic. Notably, in 2013, the government of Greece was forced to recall two nude statues that were part of the exhibition *Olympics—Past and Present* at the 3-2-1 Qatar Olympic and Sports Museum.[48] In April 2021, a replica of the Charioteer of Delphi, a gift from Greece to Qatar, was unveiled at Doha's Hamad International Airport metro station. Immediately the religious conservatives in Qatar asked for the removal of this human figure as an expression of *shirk* (idolatry), asking how Qatar Museums could put up a Greek, Western deity on Qatari grounds. Surprising many observers even within the organization, Qatar Museums did not engage with this conflict on social media channels. Elsewhere—everywhere—in the country, a surge in nationalist sentiment during and following the years of the blockade that isolated Qatar from its neighbors between 2017 and 2021 had manifested in the prolific dissemination of a different representation of the human figure: a stencil of the ruler's profile, Emir Tamim bin Hamad al-Thani, created by the Qatari artist Ahmed bin Majed Al-Maadheed. This image went viral on social media and on the fabric of the city itself. Accompanied by the inscription "Tamim al-Majd" (Tamim is Glory), this figurative depiction of the ruler can still be appreciated in diverse formats, from small decals decorating cars to enormous banners gracing the facades of buildings (figure 4.2). Its prolific use suggests that the visual culture of the Qatari modern project negotiates an iconism and a figurative art at will in support of reinforcing nationalist ideals, even if they are less attentive to conservative Muslim sensibilities.[49]

When alignment with Islam was not the primary vehicle for a backlash against forms of representation, attacks against new cultural expressions revolved around the lack of indigeneity and locality in design and authorship. Questions about the commissioning of artwork to foreign artists instead of local Qatari artists were prevalent and met with

FIGURE 4.2.   Tamim al-Majd banners hanging on buildings in al-Sadd, Doha, 2019. Photo by author.

suitable justifications that localized the intentions of the artist. For example, the installation of a giant *Untitled Lamp Bear* by the Swiss artist Urs Fischer at the center of the departures hall of Hamad International Airport terminal in 2016 was described in the précis accompanying the artwork as a sculpture "celebrating the idea of travel."[50] Meanwhile, a nearly identical sculpture installed at Brown University (2016–2020) was celebrated for referencing the institution's mascot, the Kodiak bear. In 2021, *Falcon* by Tom Claassen was installed outside the departures hall of the same airport. Depicting Qatar's national bird, it features lines that represent "the aviation routes from Qatar to the rest of the world," consolidating its purpose and location.[51] Adding to this justification, Claassen explained that *Falcon* takes its inspiration from and speaks to Qatar in "the curves that can be found in Arabic calligraphy and the folds in the fabric of traditional attire" (figure 4.3).[52] These more abstract attempts at conversing with the visual culture represent-ing national identity were likely lost to much of Qatar's audiences. Still, on social media, public discontent was vocal, with some critics asking if the costs of commissioning and installing the giant golden bird of prey instead be put toward charity or the building of mosques. In this example, efforts to localize can be ultimately condemned by local voices as a failure to align with a suitable Muslim stewardship of the arts.

FIGURE 4.3.   *Falcon* by Tom Claassen, Doha International Airport, 2021. Photo by author.

Backlash surrounding public sculptural art through the 2010s and into the 2020s conformed a visible platform for venting public grievances about cultural developments and cosmopolitan art initiatives of Qatar Museums that fell out of line with the expected national and cultural identity of the nation. Islam, and being Muslim, were often at the center of these encounters. It was therefore no surprise to note the frequency with which foreign artists and creators appealed to the semiotics of Islam in their artwork. The use of Arabic script as a form of Arabizing (and sometimes Islamicizing) art was ubiquitous. In 2013, the French-Tunisian graffitist eL Seed, not a native Arabic speaker, was commissioned to give the four underground tunnels of Salwa Road an urban facelift with his iconic "calligrafitti," inspired by Qatari poems.[53]

On the grounds of the National Museum of Qatar, the French artist Jean-Michel Othoniel designed an ensemble of 114 fountains titled *Alfa*, whose designs were inspired by reeds in the desert used to weave baskets in an unspecified area of what he called the "Golphe Persique." At the Public Art and Heritage panel aligning with the opening week of the National Museum, he invoked the abstract beauty of Arabic calligraphy, a script and language that he admitted he could not read or understand, as a source of inspiration for crafting the functional but linguistically incoherent fountains. Moderating for this panel, Tom Eccles, the Public Art adviser to Qatar Museums, joked that the source of inspiration from Qatari culture in artists' work was "Qatar Airways."[54] Perhaps the truth was not far from this for many of these foreign artists. Observing the new lighting towers that line the road to Hamad International Airport, which are decorated with an Arabic-looking pattern, a young Qatari informant critiqued the use of Arabic lettering as nonsensical pattern calling it "a sad theme of lingering imperialism."

What these forced encounters generated, between foreign visions and heritage traditions, was a sense of inadequacy of the role of Qatar Museums as a steward of Qatari identity. In this sense, the cultural institution was put in the difficult position of negotiating multiple geographical and temporal orientations that coexist under the rubric of "tradition" in Qatar. This role required both supporting and decultivating a Wahhabi narrative of state in its handling of old and new visual heritage, particularly with relation to the circulation of images. In addition, the opening of each new thematic museum across Qatar often required paying homage to an idealized original Qatar National Museum, believed locally to have represented Qatari heritage and culture more authentically through its exhibitions and collections. Thus, the new National Museum was wrapped up in a rumble of controversy as soon as it opened: some informed observers noted that the adaptation of traditional clothing for the immersive 2019 film on pearl diving, *Nafas*, directed by Mira Nair, was made to align with modern ideas of modesty rather than the practical and historically accurate dress length of a seafaring community. Historical accuracy, conveyed through photographic and film archives such as the archival artifacts generated by the Danish anthropological documentation of Qatar in 1959, could become inconvenient when they failed to fit into new civic myths.[55]

Throughout these challenging attempts at successfully engaging a public in Qatar, Islam was often summoned as an arbiter of public engagement. At the heart of these tensions, there was often an unspoken, driving question: How much do Qatari art and culture observe the concerns of an Islam-practicing society? This tension manifested in diverse and bewildering situations where institutional agendas responding to aspects of QNV clashed with what some informants in the arts sector called religious hardliners. The frequency and thematic consistency of this pushback suggested that public engagement with and support of the modern production of culture and art as a legitimate extension of traditional aesthetics would never be successful. *Shirk* could manifest in every corner. It did not help the project of reconciliation of different value systems that, until this time, prolific literature on museums across the Gulf paid little to no attention to the specificities of Muslim contexts and voices in their analysis and dissemination of the work of local museums and exhibitions. Limited trajectories in Qatar on the training of localized heritage expertise, resources, and preservation contributed to this detachment.

UCL Qatar was charged with such an educational project, supporting an institutional and disciplinary growth of ideas of heritage stewardship. Like other satellite campuses in Education City, this institution was run by a community of academics that was primarily foreign, European, and non-Muslim. The first UK-based team that inaugurated the UCL Qatar campus was comprised of scholars of European nationality and training, of which only one was a known specialist in the archaeology and heritage of the Gulf and Qatar. The rest generally lacked the regional experience that could have led them to seize the opportunity to create a curriculum that was attentive to Muslim voices of authority. The lack of published academic debates and experiential knowledge of regional contexts—culture and religion included—inevitably resulted in the establishment of curricula for training in heritage and museums that could have been crafted and taught in practically any other part of the world. The emphasis of these educational opportunities remained instead on an approach informed by global and scientific standards of practice that were characteristic of a Eurocentric intellectual tradition. In this way, the educational portal of Qatar aligned effectively with what Denis Byrne has called a process of ideology transfer in heritage management across the non-Western world.[56] In this global model, the nuances of public engagement for Qatar were lost to universal standards and utopian aspirations. A Muslim-friendly culture of heritage needed to be cultivated instead through new standards recognizing that the rigidity of heritage discourse means that being "traditional" in Qatar may imply choosing between observing the cult of heritage or that of religious traditions. Creating opportunities for hybridity between these two ontologies, therefore, has been central to the modern project of heritage-making.

Cultivating (Invented) Traditions

Heritage industries in Qatar have come a long way since Montigny observed the marginal space intentionally given to Islam in the heritage imagination of the young nation. Islam has been increasingly mobilized in the messaging and public response to a highly orchestrated industry that often includes traditional heritage and artistic developments in one continuum. Yet exactly how invested the state has been in cultivating a heritage stewardship tradition that foregrounds Islam remains obscured by how much of the heritage landscape survives in different states of waiting to be reassembled and acculturated into a single heritage tradition. In large part, this is due to the complexities of heritage stewardship. For example, in the project of restoring and maintaining the most representative of Muslim historical spaces, the mosque, becoming official heritage often involves a certain isolation of a place from its actual and potential publics and uses.[57] While the mosque of Tin Bik (discussed in chapter 3) continued its journey of slow ruination, the restoration of a nearby historic mosque at Umm al-Suwaijah was completed (figure 4.4). Currently, this site remains inaccessible to the public, visibly ready for visitation but surrounded by tall fencing around the entire settlement. Its physical alienation from visitors hinders the role and performance of the site as a stage for making heritage publics. In this way, the absence of a public, a user, an invested stakeholder, or a steward is a condition that simultaneously leads to and is produced by a site's physical or discursive stagnation or erasure. Other, possibly more architecturally iconic, mosques were denied the opportunity to be part of such a heritage ecosystem. The al-Hilal Mosque in Doha, an impressive piece of International Islamic Architecture style built in 1983, was demolished by 2020 despite being a strong candidate for preservation as postindependence and modernist heritage alongside the Sheraton Hotel.[58] Its distinctive minaret, however, was salvaged by the Qatar Museums Public Art Department, with support from Ashghal, for the purpose of being exhibited at al-Bidda park along the Corniche in the form of sculptural art, inviting an entirely different kind of stewardship.[59] The entanglement of heritage and public art is thus reinforced in innovative and invented traditions in Qatar—a project of heritage

FIGURE 4.4. Umm al Suwaijah, al-Khor, 2016. Photo by author.

reprogramming that also intended to curate roundabout art such as the Clock Tower, the Tea Pot, and the famed Oryx Roundabout.

Invented heritage preservation traditions require invented heritage publics. In Qatar, as in many other places, this coordinated effort is based on strategic and controlled calls for participation in heritage use and management that simultaneously limit public access and an ability to partake in heritage practices and decisions. The separation of expert and public views and responsibilities is a structure inherent to the channels of authority and knowledge production in heritage preservation frameworks. In a Qatari context, the mythologized local voice, on which heritage preservation models relies, is further obscured by the inability of heritage narratives to circulate along deliberative democratic channels, obstructed by the known fear of opposition. It is because of this underlying condition that earlier versions of public art in Doha, and across the Arabian Gulf, manifested in monumental coffeepots and pearl shells, innocuous representations that could navigate modernization and censorship.[60] As acknowledged by Jean-Paul Engelen, former director of public art programs for Qatar Museums, public education has become "as much a part of the program's mission as is the installation of the artworks themselves."[61] Qatar in the twenty-first century presents a compelling example of the ways in which practices of care beget the naturalization of heritage and its preservation, and vice versa.

The work of creating subjects who care for resources is as important as identifying, creating, and institutionalizing those resources. In other words, the subjects of heritage—and how they come into being in the first place—are as important to understand as the objects that a culture of heritage preservation seeks to safeguard and manage or the approaches and ideologies through which it proposes to accomplish its goals. Heritage preservation strategies are, therefore, a quintessential arm of the cultural branding efforts of Qatar. In curating stewardship roles and channels that align with these efforts, the inclusion of Muslim-associated concerns and voices of authority are carefully guarded as potential sources of dissonance. The establishment of heritage stewardship as a civic aspiration is caught between the rise of international heritage stewardship and its governing structures, a landscape of expertise still marked by the transition from protectorate to sovereign nation, and a regional tradition of heritage preservation that has centered on conflict. How stewardship is made to navigate these tensions reveals a marginalization of Islam as the rationale for curatorial projects not so much through exclusion, but through segregation, operating only within the confines of specific topics and initiatives.

In this strategy, Qatari leadership appears to mix symbolic elements of the old social discourse, at times retaining "only the rubble" of traditional religious discourse, enough to seduce, mobilize the social imagination, and attract the public to an "ideological palace."[62] Yet integrating Islam and its moral values, as the foundation of cultural development, into new professional codes of ethics has also served the government to mobilize Qataris more strongly as a cultural labor force. The cultivation of citizens in the future orientations of Qatar has ushered in new state-society relations "via the two-fold Qatari cultural identity anchored in both futurism and heritage" as a reliable source of future state survival.[63] Disrupting the dichotomous identification of tribal versus modern, or local versus foreign, heritage as a powerful apparatus for cultural production reinforces "new loyalties to the abstract notion of the Qatari state beyond the smaller circles of belonging, namely the individual, the community, the family or the tribe."[64] In these ways, the emergence of a culture of heritage preservation in Qatar reveals the operating mechanisms of any other invented tradition of preservation.

Conclusion

Heritage Observed

On 5 January 2021, the emir of Qatar, Sheikh Tamim Bin Hamad al-Thani, descended the steps from his private airplane to the tarmac of the airport in al-Ula, Saudi Arabia. There, he was embraced by the crown prince of the kingdom of Saudi Arabia, Mohammed bin Salman. This greeting marked a historic moment in the forty-first summit of the Gulf Cooperation Council (GCC): the end of the forty-three-month blockade of Qatar by Saudi Arabia, the United Arab Emirates, Bahrain, and Egypt. From 5 June 2017, until that moment, a diplomatic crisis had redefined relationships between Qatar and its neighboring nations and their allies, who accused the state of supporting Islamist groups such as the Muslim Brotherhood, al-Qaeda, and the Islamic State of Iraq and the Levant (ISIL). Qatar, instead, claimed allegiance to the war on terrorism through its close relationship with the United States, while remaining, invariably, a profoundly Muslim nation whose official state religion is Sunni Islam and has been known to offer refuge to Wahhabi preachers.

The historic reconciliation of GCC leaders was choreographed in the breathtaking archaeological and natural features of al-Hijr (also known as the Madâin Sâlih and Hegra Archaeological Site), the first site in Saudi Arabia to be successfully nominated to the World Heritage List of the United Nations Educational, Scientific, and Cultural Organization (UNESCO).

Al-Hijr is the largest-known conserved Nabatean site, boasting 111 monumental tombs and extensive hydraulic systems belonging to a pre-Islamic culture that has been more widely popularized in the World Heritage Site of Petra, in Jordan.[1] Like other World Heritage Sites, al-Hijr satisfies a trilogy of roles: a contributor to national identity, a site representing an ancient, pre-Islamic religious system, and a modern tourist destination in the fast-growing Muslim and cosmopolitan Saudi Arabia. Its ability to reconcile these orientations and its role as a platform for peace building is precisely what the World Heritage List strove to provide since its inception.[2] Therefore, in 2021, al-Hijr provided for this moment a certain symbolic neutrality as ancient Arabian heritage that stands in allegiance to global and universal values. That leaders of Muslim-majority nations resorted to a pre-Islamic site to stage a highly mediatized diplomatic milestone fell in line with a prominent theme for the region that intensified throughout the twentieth and twenty-first centuries. As convincingly demonstrated by Qatar, the Muslim world overall had been gaining positive visibility and authority in questions of global, regional and local heritage conservation over the decades leading up to this juncture. This included, as I have argued throughout this book, stewardship of historical resources that are both considered to be Muslim and non-Muslim legacies. The staging of a successful diplomatic rapprochement between Qatar and their neighbors at a World Heritage Site symbolized the successful Muslim stewardship of all cultural heritage. It was a moment weighty with symbolism.

Far from the utopian ideology of UNESCO, which anticipated a heritage regime without stated politics or ulterior motives, nations like Saudi Arabia and Qatar know well that heritage is made to be seen and exhibited, to act as a platform for the concerns and negotiations of the nation-state, and to be mobilized in diplomatic exchanges and tugs-of-war such as the recent diplomatic crisis. The mastering of heritage in these ways requires making some concessions in the project of aligning local and global agendas such that heritage languages remain translatable across both spheres. Therefore, this book has centered on finding, not defining, the elusive subject of religion in the establishment and circulation of heritage preservation cultures that serve multiple roles within and beyond the nation-state.[3] Finding Islam in the culture of heritage preservation entails observing the circulation of heritage value at the surface and the underground, recognizing that heritage value resides in the visible and the invisible and in formal and informal venues, and is expressed in blunt and unspoken ways. The plasticity of heritage value, then, transcends the rigidity of the study of heritage-making and preservation practice as discoverable and translatable objects and languages. Throughout the chapters of this book, I have argued that the perspectives contributed by religious traditions in the world of heritage culture-making in Qatar has been hard to isolate in a purified form. In part, this is because, as Geertz argues in *Islam Observed*, "the religious perspective, like the scientific, the aesthetic, the historical . . . is after all adopted by men only sporadically, intermittently."[4] I argue throughout this book that it matters who the "men" are in various discussions of the significance and roles for different experts and expert forms of knowledge.

Through these brokers, official and non-official dialogues surrounding heritage projects across Qatar put emphasis on the project of *rediscovering* local heritage and culture, as if cultural development until then had all but disappeared. A senior researcher from a foreign university involved in the preparatory work toward the new legal instrument in support of heritage safeguarding explained in private that "Qataris do not know what they want," a tired trope that has revived the specter of colonialism to enable foreign access to local cultural resources. What Qatar should preserve, they explained, is the city skyline of Doha, with its iconic towers. This voice is overlayed on the assessments of prior foreign experts who argued, for example, that "the only genuine Qatari elements were the architectural fragments, which reflected an earlier Qatari architectural aesthetic dating to the period when more affluent settled lifestyles were possible following the discovery of oil in 1939."[5] Expert-led discourses, which become authoritative archives of contemporary Qatar in the relative absence of locally grown expertise, thus ridiculed the nation for the quality of its resources from the past, as well as its efforts to maintain a contemporary sense of place. The notion that existing cultural institutions could not teach themselves how to chart a coherent future loyal to their own cultural norms has been the most evident sign of a rampant Orientalist and colonial trajectory in heritage discourse.

It also matters that this project of construction of heritage languages and standards is circumscribed by the strict empiricism that underpins a global and influential culture of heritage preservation—one that is always driven by international agendas and the choreographies of cultural diplomacy that, historically and politically, tend toward dismissing Islam as a legitimate context for the examination of agency. Over the last five decades, the heritage industry in Qatar has grown and thrived under four different rulers and in accordance with shifting organizational and state agendas that were nonetheless united by a common denominator: the mobilization of largely Western forms of expertise and knowledge. Through the work of knowledge brokers who were primarily not Qatari, nor Arab, nor Muslim, and a disciplinary lens designed to bypass religious orientations, the mobilization of Muslim voices, forms of authority, and institutions was expected to be sidelined in the process. It is not surprising, therefore, to observe that the majority of commentators and advocates for a Qatari heritage industry undermine the predominantly Muslim context in which heritage is created and performed. Searching for "Islam" as a keyword in this growing corpus of literature continues to yield little else than the name of the Museum of Islamic Art. The keyword "Muslim" has been practically nonexistent in much of the gray literature that I have examined throughout the periods that this book concerns itself with. Rather than explicitly excluding a lived Islam from the growing history of heritage principles and approaches that result from these observers and practitioners, this overwhelming exclusion is performed by omission in the articulation of heritage assemblages, priorities, approaches, and legal frameworks.

As a compelling example of this omission, in October 2018, the *Gulf Times* announced the intention of Qatar Museums and University College London Qatar (UCL Qatar) to develop a new cultural heritage law by October 2020, in alignment with the Qatar National Vision 2030 (QNV).[6] Experts from both institutions sought to capitalize on their experience and familiarity with global frameworks for cultural development, such as UNESCO, to modernize and update Law No. 2 of 1980 on antiquities in alignment with internationally recognized standards. This project was officially launched at a two-day workshop that included government agencies and international experts from the University of Siena and the University of Geneva. Awqaf, one participant reported, was not among the agencies invited to contribute to these discussions, despite clarifying that compliance with sharia law was expected. According to one of the project leads, the new legal framework aimed to allocate responsibilities to the public sector, private entities (industry and individuals), and the general public. But it was clear through the material circulated in various press releases that this initiative was primarily intended to target Qatar's compliance with the standards of international and global heritage institutions rather than to support a local and locally relevant consumption and use of heritage resources. This is particularly revealed in the main foci for the preparatory work toward the drafting of this law: update the definition of heritage typologies and reinforce the role of Qatar in the illicit trafficking of cultural property and the protection of heritage during armed conflict. To drive these points home, throughout 2021 Qatar was invited to join UNESCO's twelve-member Committee for Protection of Cultural Property in the Event of Armed Conflict, established by the 1999 Second Protocol to the Hague Convention. In the same year, Qatar brokered a ceasefire between Israel and Hamas and, later, facilitated talks with the interim Afghan government during the Taliban takeover of Afghanistan. While supporting a universal aspiration for a "heritage for peace" through cultural diplomacy, the project of legislative modernization was still expected to maximize "the social and social-economic benefits of arts and culture," as explained by Qatar Museum's acting chief executive officer at the time, Ahmad al-Namla.[7] The culture of heritage preservation in Qatar was, once again, thrust into the secularizing order of global heritage that it simultaneously works to support and reconfigure.

The idea of examining a modern Islamic heritage practice as the linchpin in this reconfiguration has been an ontological and epistemological challenge outside the confines of a strict study of Qur'anic exegesis. As an analytical lens, artificially isolating "the Islamic" in the world of heritage preservation fails to explain the cultural gymnastics involved in branding a modern Qatar through its heritage. Qatar is not exceptional in this. The same applies to any modern nation-state whose heritage and tourism industry are so deeply entangled with the needs of cultural diplomacy, cultural exchange programs, and bilateral international collaborations, as well as the production of an elite-driven national identity narrative for domestic consumption.[8] Such an internationalization of Qatari heritage—in the sense of traditions and legacies—was exponential and multifaceted during the period of research covered in this book, suggesting other productive avenues for inquiry. During this time, the Qatar Foundation's commitment to forging cultural products attentive to national identity with a nod to Islam was matched by its commitment to secular internationalism. A subsidiary organization based in the United States, Qatar Foundation International, promoted Arabic-language programming in the United States, Canada, Great Britain, and Brazil since 2009.[9] Their other major international program was the establishment of the World Innovation Summit for Education, an international platform that supports new collaborative approaches to education.

Bilateral cultural cooperation has had a strong presence in Qatar. In 2012, Qatar Museum's office of strategic cultural relations inaugurated a multicultural initiative called "Years of Culture—Building Bridges between Nations," resulting in mutual exchanges of art, culture, heritage, and sports. Strategically, each Year of Culture (Japan 2012, United Kingdom 2013, Brazil 2014, Turkey 2015, China 2016, Germany 2017, Russia, 2018, India 2019, France 2020, and United States 2021) was aligned with related economic and political interests under tightly curated representations of internationalism—a seed project to represent Eid celebrations in Brazil for 2014 was promptly shut down by Qatar Museums. Russia 2018 coincided with Russia's hosting of the FIFA World Cup in anticipation of Qatar's hosting of the event three years later, while Japan 2012 was also the year that Qatar announced the establishment of a $100 million Qatar Friendship Fund to support Japan after it was hit by a devastating earthquake in 2011.[10] This platform disseminates a privileged narrative of Qatar as a cultural hub that is ambitious, innovative, cooperative, and significant.[11] For the ten-year anniversary of this initiative, and aligning with Qatar FIFA 2022, the Year of Culture 2022 celebrated internationalism at a different scale: MENASA, the variety of cultures from across the Middle East, North Africa, and South Asia. As a theme, it was chosen to contest international critiques of Qatar as an oppressive regime toward migrant communities from these regions whose labor helped build the infrastructure for international events such as the World Cup.

Meanwhile, in Qatar, a growing tourism industry promoting a heritage tradition attentive to its Muslim context sometimes showed a glimpse of itself during the second decade of the millennium. The Qatar-based company Regency Holidays promoted "101 Things to Do in Qatar," an eclectic list that included mall tours, visits to seemingly ordinary places such as the Qatar Bowling Centre, the touring of historic and archaeological sites such as al-Koot fort and Jassassiyeh rock carvings, and traditional experiences such as overnight camping at the Sealine area, south of Qatar. These heritage tours also curated different aspects of Muslim life, such as the exploration of al-Khor mosques, north of Doha, and visits to Fanar Cultural Center, "where cultural and religious traditions are enacted in more depth."[12] Such a tourism experience was not projected for local consumption. Economic investments by Qatar Holding LLC (part of the Qatar Investment Authority) better reflect cultural consumption by many elite Qataris: this portfolio included Harrods luxury department store, real estate in London's Olympic Park, high-end luxury boutique hotels in Switzerland, ownership of the Paris Saint-Germain football team in France, and sponsorship of F. C. Barcelona in Spain, not to mention global luxury brands such as Valentino, Louis Vuitton, and Porsche.

Reassembling, Waiting

With these and more developments unfolding beyond the scope of this book, the question of how Qatar mobilizes their hard-earned leadership role and orients their unique heritage preservation strategy into the future splits into multiple avenues that transcend the chronological frontiers of this research project and the methodological scope of a heritage ethnography. As is true with any given point in time during the period that this book is concerned with, Qatar could appear to align its cultural development with cosmopolitan or insular tendencies in nonlinear ways. These seamless transitions were well developed in the day-to-day life of Qatar. The radio programming playing profanity-laced hip hop in English could be easily interrupted for the *adhan*, the call for prayer, while the Qatar Philharmonic Orchestra at the Museum of Islamic Art performed an incredible rendition of the American heavy metal band Metallica's greatest hits during one well-attended public program in May 2018. The oryx statues that had disappeared from public view for years, supported by an "anti-Islamic" alibi in 2013, reappeared unceremoniously on the ground, decorating the parking lot of Darb al-Saai, the fairgrounds located in the relatively central neighborhood of al-Saad, built to celebrate traditional events such as National Day.

In other spheres, the orientation of a Qatari heritage brand that aligned itself more intentionally with a Muslim culture became more intelligible by the end of this project. The reopening of the Museum of Islamic Art in late 2022 featured a reimagined curatorial representation of Islam in their galleries that focuses on the life histories and uses of objects rather than the objects themselves. In particular, the centrally located gallery called "Religious Life in the Islamic World" foregrounds a diverse *umma* and the practices of a lived Islam through the representation of the five *arkan al-Islam* (pillars). The central view of this gallery features an impressive *sitara* (door textile) of the Ka'ba from the late Ottoman period to celebrate the Hajj, and the main entryway is flanked by the two keys of the Ka'ba in the museum's collection, which previously had been buried in display cabinets of other galleries.

More recently, the temporary exhibit "Mosques in Qatar: Then and Now" (22 June–12 August 2023) showcases traditional mosques across the Qatari peninsula, from archaeological (the Murwab Mosque) to modern (the Education City Mosque), highlighting the social and religious landscape that supports these special places and the investment of

Qatar Museums in the restoration and recognition of heritage mosques. The collection of photographs and architectural models exhibited at this point in time also makes evident the budding relationship between Awqaf and Qatar Museums: labels include the "Waqf name" of the mosque and the "date of receiving." In fact, the exhibition was possible thanks to a collaboration between the Ministry of Endowments and Islamic Affairs (Awqaf) and the sponsorship of the Seashore Group, a multifaceted business organization.

Beyond cultural institutions and analogous with a local tourism industry, the new millennium saw the burgeoning of "Islam as heritage" within Qatar in other ways. In March 2022, the Zulal Wellness Resort by Chiva-Som opened in Khasooma, a private coastal location in the north of Qatar. It lauded itself as a pioneering destination in the Middle East that blends traditional Arabic and Islamic medicine with a holistic health and well-being philosophy popularized by Chiva-Som's internationally acclaimed wellness resort in Hua Hin, Thailand. This enterprise was also localized through toponymy—"Zulal" means "pure natural water" in Arabic, a term used to reflect the rejuvenating properties of the natural water found in the desert—and through the language of heritage. The resort was designed by Msheireb Properties soon after completing Msheireb Downtown Doha, with "deep respect for Qatari culture and customs," as described in their promotional material. In line with the discourses that have defined the rise of a culture of heritage preservation in Qatar for the last three decades, the Zulal spa referred to itself as a place where past tradition meets future health, bringing ancient philosophy into a contemporary context. Heritage culture in Qatar had thus gained undisputed authority to market practically anything as authentically Qatari, and making aspects of Islam more visible was effectively a key part of this branding strategy.

In the aftermath of hosting FIFA's 2022 World Cup, the journey of branding heritage in Qatar remains a powerful lesson in how important and fruitful it is to pay attention to the interplay between heritage and religious traditions in a framework that is much larger and more impactful than simply taking an interest in a prescribed religious heritage. This case study suggests that attention to Islam in the workings of heritage in Qatar constitutes a specific "heritage gaze"; that is, a way of seeing that not only makes visible the role of Islam in the culture of heritage in Qatar, but also remains attuned to the ways in which religious beliefs and practices can and should alter the trajectories of heritage cultures and traditions of care in a variety of ways.[13] Sometimes a religious context and its practitioners have significant agency in giving shape to this process, supporting the delimitation of what constitutes, in this case, constructing and caring for a "Muslim" heritage. Other times, religious traditions are encoded into different heritage histories and functions in subtler ways that navigate the overarching secular forces of global heritage preservation traditions.

In the worst but most well documented of cases known in global heritage history, religious traditions are simply eliminated from exerting any influence on heritage and its care. Each chapter in this book, therefore, explored a specific locale where secularism and religion were negotiated, demonstrating how heritage traditions and their accompanying debates and forms of expertise traverse, and sometimes avoid, disciplinarily defined "Muslim" spaces and practices. Beyond calls for "revivalism" or "modern traditionalism" in Qatar, to foreground a cultural heritage preservation tradition that remains connected to religious traditions is to speak of a form of caring that connects the past with the future, and also connects Qataris to each other and to the rest of the world.

NOTES

Introduction

1. UNESCO, *Proceedings of the Doha Conference of 'Ulama on Islam and Cultural Heritage. Doha, Qatar. December 30–31, 2001* (New York: UNESCO, 2005). In the Doha Statement itself (included in this publication), the event is referred to as the "International Symposium of *'Ulamâ* on Islam and Cultural Heritage."

2. UNESCO, *Proceedings of the Doha Conference of 'Ulama on Islam and Cultural Heritage*, 30, referring to the Pan-Arab newspaper *Asharq al-Awsat*, 13 March 2001.

3. UNESCO, *Proceedings of the Doha Conference of 'Ulama on Islam and Cultural Heritage*, 6.

4. Trinidad Rico, *Global Heritage, Religion, and Secularism* (Cambridge: Cambridge University Press, 2021); Trinidad Rico, "Muslim Heritage Preservation Stewardship under UNESCO," Special Issue, "UNESCO World Heritage at 50: What Future for the Past?," *Change over Time* 11, no. 2 (2022): 182–199; Trinidad Rico, "Heritage Preservation in Religious Landscapes: Disciplinary Challenges for the Middle East and North Africa," *Archaeological Dialogues* 28, no. 2 (2021): 111–120.

5. Mounir Bouchenaki, "Safeguarding the Buddha Statues in Bamiyan and the Sustainable Protection of Afghan Cultural Heritage," in *The Future of the Bamiyan Buddha Statues: Heritage Reconstruction in Theory and Practice*, ed. Masanori Nagaoka (Paris and Kabul, Afghanistan: UNESCO; Cham, Switzerland: Springer, 2020), 19–30.

6. Transliterated as "Youssef Kardaoui" (in the French tradition), in Bouchenaki, "Safeguarding the Buddha Statues in Bamiyan."

7. Peter Morey and Amina Yaqin, *Framing Muslims: Stereotyping and Representation after 9/11* (Cambridge, MA: Harvard University Press, 2011), 2.

8. Denis Byrne, *Counterheritage: Critical Perspectives on Heritage Conservation in Asia* (London: Routledge, 2014); Denis Byrne, "Prospects for a Postsecular Heritage Practice: Convergences between Posthumanism and Popular Religious Practice in Asia," *Religions* 10, no. 7 (2019): 436.

9. Cf. Homi K. Bhabha, *The Location of Culture* (London: Routledge, 1994).

10. Jürgen Habermas, "Notes on Post-Secular Society," *New Perspectives Quarterly* 25, no. 4 (Fall 2008): 17–29.

11. Lynn Meskell, *A Future in Ruins: UNESCO, World Heritage, and the Dream of Peace* (Oxford: Oxford University Press, 2018).

12. Rico, *Global Heritage, Religion, and Secularism*.

13. UNESCO/Prep.Com./51, 3 July 1946. Progress Report on the Programme of the United Nations Educational, Scientific and Cultural Organisation (Annex III-G.1.) II. Sub-section on Philosophy.

14. UNESCO/Prep.Com./51 (Rev 1) Chapter I, 16 August 1946. Revised Progress Report on the Programme of the United Nations Educational, Scientific and Cultural Organisation. Chapter I. 2: The Philosophy for UNESCO.

15. Letter from Naji al-Asil, Head of the Iraq Delegation, to President of the Preparatory Commission, 19 November 1945. UNESCO Archives, file reference UNESCO/Prep.Com./6. For a repeat performance a few decades later, see the description of the pioneers involved in the drafting and implementation of the 1972 World Heritage Convention in Christina Cameron and Mechtild Rössler, *Many Voices, One Vision: The Early Years of the World Heritage Convention* (London: Routledge, 2013). Al-Asil was also director-general of the Iraq Antiquities Department from 1944 to 1958.

16. Aike P. Rots, "World Heritage, Secularisation, and the New 'Public Sacred' in East Asia," *Journal of Religion in Japan* 8, no. 1/3 (2019): 151–178; Byrne, *Counterheritage*.

17. Charlotte Joy, *The Politics of Heritage Management in Mali: From UNESCO to Djenné* (London: Routledge, 2013), 22.

18. Charlotte Joy, "UNESCO Is What? World Heritage, Militant Islam and the Search for a Common Humanity in Mali," in *World Heritage on the Ground: Ethnographic Perspectives*, ed. Christoph Brumann and David Berliner (London: Berghahn, 2016), 60–77.

19. Rico, *Global Heritage, Religion, and Secularism*.

20. Theodosios Tsivolas, "The Legal Foundations of Religious Cultural Heritage Protection," *Religions* 10, no. 283 (2019), https://doi.org/10.3390/rel10040283; Tuğba Tanyieri-Erdemir, "Historical Trajectories, Institutional Particularities: The Funding Regime for Religious Heritage in Turkey," in *Funding Religious Heritage*, ed. Anne Fornerod (Farnham, UK: Ashgate, 2015), 213–226. Belief systems and "spirits and feelings" were articulated as legitimate forms of knowing in doctrinal documents such as the Nara Document on Authenticity of 1994.

21. Lynn Meskell, "Negative Heritage and Past Mastering in Archaeology," *Anthropological Quarterly* 75, no. 3 (2002): 557–574; Deborah Stein, *The Hegemony of Heritage: Ritual and the Record in Stone* (Berkeley: University of California Press, 2018); Finbarr Barry Flood, "Between Cult and Culture: Bamiyan, Islamic Iconoclasm, and the Museum," *Art Bulletin* 84, no. 4 (2002): 641–659; Jamal Elias, "(Un)making Idolatry: From Mecca to Bamiyan," *Future Anterior: Journal of Historic Preservation, History, Theory and Criticism* 4, no. 2 (2007): 13–29.

22. Rots, "World Heritage, Secularisation, and the New 'Public Sacred,'" 155–156.

23. Byrne, *Counterheritage*, 1.

24. Rots, "World Heritage, Secularisation, and the New 'Public Sacred,'" 160–161.

25. Brenda D. Schildgen, *Heritage or Heresy: Preservation and Destruction of Religious Art and Architecture in Europe* (New York: Palgrave, 2008), 14–15; cf. Trinidad Rico, *Constructing Destruction: Heritage Narratives in the Tsunami City* (London: Routledge, 2016); Glenn Bowman, "Introduction: Sharing the Sacra," in *Sharing*

the Sacra: The Politics and Pragmatics of Inter-communal Relations around Holy Places, ed. Glenn Bowman (New York: Berghahn, 2012), 5.

26. Ömür Harmanşah, "ISIS, Heritage, and the Spectacles of Destruction in the Global Media," *Near Eastern Archaeology* 78, no. 3 (2015): 170–177.

27. Anna Karlström, "Spirits and the Ever-Changing Heritage," *Material Religion: The Journal of Objects, Art and Belief* 9, no. 3 (2013): 396.

28. Byrne, *Counterheritage*, 19.

29. Lawrence Rosen, "Proceeding of the Doha Conference of 'Ulama on Islam and Cultural Heritage. Doha, Qatar. December 30–31, 2001. Pp. 73 in English and Arabic each. New York: UNESCO, 2005," *International Journal of Cultural Property* 15 (2008): 101–103.

30. Mirjam Brusius and Trinidad Rico, "Counter-archives as Heritage Justice: Photography, Invisible Labor and Peopled Ruins," *Journal of Visual Culture* 21, no. 3 (2023): 64–92.

31. Karen Exell and Trinidad Rico, "Introduction: (De)constructing Arabian Heritage Debates," in *Cultural Heritage in the Arabian Peninsula: Debates, Discourses and Practices*, ed. Karen Exell and Trinidad Rico (Surrey, UK: Ashgate, 2014), 1–15.

32. Susan Pollock and Reinhard Bernbeck, "Introduction," in *Archaeologies of the Middle East: Critical Perspectives*, ed. Susan Pollock and Reinhard Bernbeck (Malden, MA: Blackwell, 2005), 2.

33. Trinidad Rico and Kim Lababidi, "Extremism in Contemporary Heritage Debates about Islam," *Future Anterior: Journal of Historic Preservation History, Theory, and Criticism* 14, no. 1 (Summer 2017): 95–105; Kishwar Rizvi, "It's Harder Than Ever to Teach Islamic Art—But Never More Important," *Washington Post*, 6 January 2017, https://www.washingtonpost.com/posteverything/wp/2017/01/06/its -harder-than-ever-to-teach-islamic-art-but-never-more-important/.

34. Mirjam Shatanawy, "Curating against Dissent: Museums and the Public Debate on Islam," in *Political and Cultural Representations of Muslims: Islam in the Plural*, ed. Christopher Flood, Stephen Hutchings, Galina Miazhevich, and Henri Nickels (Leiden, Netherlands: Brill, 2012), 177–192.

35. ATHAR Regional Conservation Centre (Architectural-Archaeological Tangible Heritage in the Arab Region), Sharjah, United Arab Emirates.

36. John Irish, "UNESCO Chief Says U.S. Funding Cuts 'Crippling' Organization," *Reuters Science News*, 11 October 2012, https://www.reuters.com /article/us-unesco-funding/unesco-chief-says-u-s-funding-cuts-crippling -organization-idUSBRE89A0Q620121011.

37. Lynn Meskell, "UNESCO's World Heritage Convention at 40: Challenging the Economic and Political Order of International Heritage Conservation," *Current Anthropology* 54, no. 4 (2013): 483–494.

38. UNESCO, "Decisions Adopted by the World Heritage Committee at Its 37th Session (Phnom Penh, 2013)," World Heritage Committee Thirty-Seventh Session, Phnom Penh, Cambodia, 16–27 June 2013. WHC-13/37.COM/20.

39. UNESCO, "Statement from the Chairperson of the World Heritage Committee," *UNESCO News*, 31 March 2011, https://whc.unesco.org/en/news/735.

40. UNESCO, "Draft Decision: 36 COM 8B.19," Item 8 of the Provisional Agenda: Establishment of the World Heritage List and of the List of World

Heritage in Danger, 8B. Nominations to the World Heritage List, Convention Concerning the Protection of the World Cultural and Natural Heritage, World Heritage Committee, Thirty-Sixth Session, Saint Petersburg, Russian Federation 24 June–6 July 2012 WHC-12/36.COM/8B, Paris, 11 May 2012.

41. Meskell, *A Future in Ruins*, 196.

42. UNESCO, "UNESCO Director-General Condemns Destruction to the Museum of Islamic Art in Cairo, Egypt," *UNESCO News*, 24 January 2014, https://whc.unesco.org/en/news/1081; UNESCO, "Reconstruction of World Heritage Mausoleums Starts in Timbuktu (Mali)," *UNESCO News*, 14 March 2014, https://whc.unesco.org/en/news/1112; "Final Report and Action Plan for the Rehabilitation of Cultural Heritage and the Safeguarding of Ancient Manuscripts in Mali," International Experts Meeting for the Safeguarding of Mali's Cultural Heritage, Paris, 2013 [1] 2013. Monday, 18 February 2013, UNESCO Headquarters (Paris), p. 6. Item 13; UNESCO, "UNESCO Announces the Bamiyan Cultural Centre Design Competition," *UNESCO News*, 16 November 2014, https://whc.unesco.org/en/news/1198.

43. UNESCO, "World Heritage Committee Meeting Opens in Doha," *UNESCO News*, 15 June 2014, https://whc.unesco.org/en/news/1143.

44. UNESCO, "World Heritage Committee Meeting Opens in Doha."

45. UNESCO, "Qatar Development Fund Boosts UNESCO Heritage Emergency Fund," *UNESCO News*, 8 December 2015, http://whc.unesco.org/en/news/1403.

46. UNESCO, "Conservation Completed on Lion of Al-lāt Statue from Ancient City of Palmyra, Damaged by ISIL," *UNESCO News*, 5 October 2017, https://whc.unesco.org/en/news/1727.

47. UNESCO, "UNESCO Hosts First International Coordination Meeting for the Recovery of Aleppo's Heritage," *UNESCO News*, 9 March 2017, https://whc.unesco.org/en/news/1639.

48. "Foreword," *Heritage Emergency Fund: Annual Progress Report*, 2018. 2019, p. 7. CLT/HEF/Annual Report 2018.

49. Associated Press, "France's Audrey Azoulay Wins Vote to Be Next UNESCO Chief," 13 October 2017, https://apnews.com/article/2fa44c4781524a48a7fb62 22bd375ab2.

50. UNESCO, "Interview with H. E. Sheikha Al Mayassa Bint Hamad Bin Khalifa Al Thani," *World Heritage* 72 (June 2014): 6–7.

51. Herb Stovel, "Conserving the Sacred: Special Challenges for World Heritage Sites," *World Heritage Review* 51 (2008): 26–33.

52. Robert Wild, Christopher McLeod, and Peter Valentine, *Sacred Natural Sites: Guidelines for Protected Area Managers* (Gland, Switzerland: IUCN, 2008).

53. ICOMOS, *17th General Assembly of ICOMOS, Paris, France, 27 November to 2 December 2011*, 2011, 20, https://whc.unesco.org/uploads/activities/documents /activity-646-1.pdf.

54. "Convention Concerning the Protection of the World Cultural and Natural Heritage, World Heritage Committee, Thirty-Seventh Session, Phnom Penh, Cambodia, 16–27 June 2013," Decisions Adopted by the World Heritage Committee at Its 37th Session (Phnom Penh, 2013). WHC-13/37.Com/20.

55. "In Support of the Future of the Past: The Qatar-Sudan Archaeological Project," *World Heritage* 89 (October 2018): 26–27.

56. The full name of the school is SMKN 1 ROTA Bayat School, Java, Indonesia.

57. Daniel Eddisford and Robert Carter, "The Vernacular Architecture of Doha, Qatar," *Post-Medieval Archaeology* 51, no. 1 (2017): 107–181.

58. Lara Deep and Jessica Winegar, *Disciplining the Middle East* (Stanford, CA: Stanford University Press, 2015).

1. Institutions and Expertise

1. Report about the creation of a center for cultural cooperation in the Near and Middle East, 14 September 1948, UNESCO Archives, file reference 008 (5-011) A 31.

2. Report of 5 years spent in Doha from British Embassy in Doha, 25 September 1974, UK National Archives, file reference p. 3.

3. This rhetoric was echoed and reinforced in academic channels; for example, Rupert Hay, "The Impact of the Oil Industry on the Persian Gulf Shaykhdoms," *Middle East Journal* 9, no. 4 (Autumn 1955): 361–372.

4. Progress Report on the Programme of the United Nations Educational, Scientific and Cultural Organisation, 3 July 1946, UNESCO Archives, file reference UNESCO/Prep.Com./51. Annex III-G.1.

5. Revised Progress Report on the Programme of the United Nations Educational, Scientific and Cultural Organization, 16 August 1946, UNESCO Archives, file reference UNESCO/Prep.Com./51 (Rev 1).

6. Near and Middle East Cultural Centre, UNESCO Archives, file reference 008 (5-011) A 31.

7. Letter to Dr. Raadi from J. J. Mayoux, Directeur de l'Enquête sur la Philosophie et les Humanités, 1 September 1947, UNESCO Archives, file reference 008 (5-011) A 31.

8. Letter to Dr. Mohamed Awad (Egypt), 20 January 1948, UNESCO Archives, file reference 008 (5-011) A 31.

9. Correspondence with Dr. Maulana Abul Kalam Azad and J. J. Mayoux, 17 February 1948, UNESCO Archives, file reference 008 (5-011) A 31.

10. Letter from P. Bosch-Gimpera to M. Joan Thomas, 23 April 1948, UNESCO Archives, file reference 008 (5-011) A 31.

11. Letter from Dr. Raadi to the Director-General, Constatations de fait et suggestions de principe concernant la création d'un organe de liaison culturelle dans le Proche et le Moyen Orient, 28 June 1948, UNESCO Archives, file reference 008 (5-011) A 31.

12. Representation of UNESCO in the Main Cultural Areas of the World. Report of the 8th Session of the Executive Board, 6 July 1948, UNESCO Archives, file reference 8/EX/ 19.

13. Letter from Acting Head, Bureau of Administrative Management and Budget, to Assistant Director-General for Cultural Activities, Division of Philosophy and Humanistic Studies, 6 August 1948, UNESCO Archives, file reference 008 (5-011) A 31.

14. Laura E. Wong, "Relocating East and West: UNESCO's Major Project on the Mutual Appreciation of Eastern and Western Cultural Values," *Journal of World History* 19, no. 3 (2008): 349.

15. Statutes of the Advisory Committee on Mutual Appreciation and Eastern and Western Cultural Values, 7 January 1957, UNESCO Archives, file reference 46 EX/Decisions Annex.

16. Wong, "Relocating East and West."

17. Conference on Archaeology and Cultural Heritage in the Arab World (translated from Arabic). Retrieved 14 September 2022. http://culture.alecso .org/heritagecongress/.

18. Conclusion d'un arrangement avec l'organisation arabe pour l'éducation, la culture et la science (ALECSO) en vue de l'application de l'accord passé entre l'UNESCO et la Ligue des États Arabes, 10 Octobre 1972. UNESCO Archives, file reference 90 EX/33.

19. Resolutions and Decisions approved by the Executive Committee in its 99th Meeting, Paris, 26 April to 26 May 1976. UNESCO Archives, file reference 99 EX/Decisions 5.4.5.

20. Creación del comité consultivo de la cultural árabe, 26 Abril 1976. UNESCO Archives, file reference 99 EX/15; 99 EX/62.5.4.5.

21. Agnès Borde Meyer, "Safeguarding Iran and Afghanistan: On UNESCO's Efforts in the Field of Archaeology," in *A History of UNESCO: Global Actions and Impacts*, ed. Poul Duedahl (New York: Palgrave Macmillan, 2016), 300–312.

22. UNESCO, International Symposium on Conservation and Restoration of Islamic Architectural Heritage, 7th to 13th April 1980, UNESCO Archives, file reference CTL-83/WS/41, 23.

23. UNESCO, International Symposium, 21.

24. René Maheu, Rapport du Directeur général sur l'activité de l'Organisation en 1962, présenté aux États membres et au conseil exécutif conformément à l'article VI.3.b de l'Acte constitutif. UNESCO. General Conference, 13th, Paris, 1964. UNESCO Archives, file reference CPG.63/I.17.

25. This was a contribution amounting to $55,000 paid by December 1964. UNESCO, "Extra Time to Save Abu Simbel," *The UNESCO Courier* 15, no. 2 (February 1962): 34. René Maheu, Informe del Director General sobre las actividades de la Organizacion en 1964, presentado a los Estados Miembros y al Consejo Ejecutivo en cumplimiento del articulo VI.3.b de la Constitucion. UNESCO. General Conference, 14th, 1966, p. 80. UNESCO Archives, file reference CPG.65/I.19.

26. Ghosh was the UNESCO consultant for Qatar (1968), Bahrain (1968), Saudi Arabia (1968–1969), and Yemen (1970). Amalanda K. Ghosh, "Qatar—Report on the Protection of Cultural Heritage and Development of a Museum: Qatar—(Mission), February-March 1968." UNESCO Archives, file reference 788/BMS.RD/CLT.1968.

27. Ghosh, "Qatar—Report," 7.

28. Arab Gulf States Folklore Centre, Establishment of an Information Centre. Restricted Qatar Technical Report. UNESCO Archives, file reference FMR. PGI.OPS.84/201.

29. UNESCO Fellowship Study Program, UNESCO Archives, file reference 069: 72 (536) [AMS SITES AND MONUMENTS QATAR. Code: 151.9479.QAT.81].

30. UNESCO Archives, file reference 5C/ECO/5865/8.51(309), REF 3/1D /89/022 8 February 1989; DG/2.6/5864/309, 18 April 1989.

31. "UNESCO Chief Lauds Qatar's Role," *Gulf Times*, 21 February 1985, 5.

32. Address by Federico Mayor, director-general of UNESCO, at the ceremonial session to mark the tenth anniversary of the International Campaign for the Safeguarding of the Cultural Triangle of Sri Lanka; Colombo, 11 December 1990. UNESCO Archives, file reference DG/90/49. Lynn Meskell, *A Future in Ruins: UNESCO, World Heritage, and the Dream of Peace* (Oxford: Oxford University Press, 2018), 102, 105-106, 165.

33. Report on the Evaluation of UNESCO Field Offices in the Arab States Region, One Hundred and Fifty-Second Session, Paris, 10 September 1997, Item 6.2 of the provisional agenda. UNESCO Archives, file reference 152 EX/24.

34. Final Report of the Tenth Session of the Executive Council of the Islamic Educational, Scientific and Cultural Organization—ISESCO—Rabat, 27 Rabii II—1st Jumada I, 1410H 27-30 November 1989.

35. Final report for the Executive Council of the Islamic Educational, Scientific and Cultural Organization (ISESCO) held its 21st Session in Rabat, capital of the Kingdom of Morocco, on 19-23 Shaaban 1421 A.H., corresponding to 16-20 November 2000 A.D.

36. Final Report, Twenty-Second Session in the Emirate of Sharjah, State of the United Arab Emirates, on 7-11 Shawal, 1422A.H., corresponding to 22-26 December 2001 A.D.

37. Eugene Rogen, *The Arabs: A History* (New York: Basic Books, 2011), 361.

38. Loring Allen, "OPEC Speaks Out," *Worldview* 22, no. 3 (March 1979): 41-46.

39. United States Office of International Energy Affairs, and United States Federal Energy Administration, *The Relationship of Oil Companies and Foreign Governments* (Washington, DC: US Government Printing Office, 1975), 153.

40. Qatar, General Policies, County Policy Paper, 9 February 1984. UNESCO Archives, file reference QTR/680/12.

41. British Council Activities in Qatar, 11 September 1971, UK National Archives, file reference FCO 13/593 and PC16/470/1.

42. Teacher Training College, Doha. 8 April 1974. UK National Archives, file reference BW 90/1827.

43. Letter from R. B. Sergeant to the Inter-University Council for Higher Education Overseas, 4 May 1971. UK National Archives, file reference BW 90/1827.

44. Letter from Sir James Cook to ICM Maxwell, 7 June 1971. UK National Archives, file reference BW 90/1827.

45. Letter from EF Henderson to JAL Morgan Esq., Visit of Dr. and Drs. Llewellyn: 25-26 January 1974, 28 January 1974. UK National Archives, file reference FCO 13/741 1974; see also Sheikha Abdulla Al-Misned, *The Development of Modern Education in Bahrain, Kuwait and Qatar with Special Reference to the Education of Women and Their Position in Modern Gulf Society*, PhD thesis, Durham University, Durham, UK (1984). http://etheses.dur.ac.uk/10485.

46. Letter from EF Henderson to JAL Morgan Esq.

47. Standing Interdepartmental Coordinating Committee on Paid Educational Services, Inter-University Council for Higher Education Overseas, 19 June 1975, UK National Archives, file reference BW 90/1827.

48. Al-Misned, *The Development of Modern Education*, 369.

49. University in Qatar, December 1974, UK National Archives, file reference FCO 13/741, PC 16/470/1.

50. British Council recruiting for faculty of education, Doha, 29 April 1974, UK National Archives, file reference FCO 13/741.

51. Al-Misned, *The Development of Modern Education* (emphasis added).

52. Abdulla Juma Kobaisi, *The Development of Education in Qatar, 1950–1977 with an Analysis of Some Educational Problems*, PhD thesis, Durham University, Durham, UK (1979), 31. http://etheses.dur.ac.uk/1856/.

53. Rogen, *The Arabs*, 393.

54. Memo by R. C. Griffiths. Inter-University Council for Higher Education Overseas, 30 April 1975. UK National Archives, file reference BW 90/1827; IUC 626/4.

55. Ove Arup, "Key Speech," 9 July 1970, Winchester, UK, 17. https://www.arup.com/perspectives/publications/speeches-and-lectures/section/ove-arup-key-speech.

56. General Policy Quatar [sic], Issa G. Al-Kawari, Director of the Amir's Office and Minister of Information. Telegram 04/02/85. Priority, from Beniston. UK National Archives, file reference QTR/680/1.

57. Anie Montigny, "Le Turâth comme Construction de l'Identité Nationale au Qatar" [Turath as Construction of National Identity in Qatar], *Cahiers de Recherche Monde Arabe Contemporain, Maison de l'Orient et de la Méditerranée* 6 (1998): 23–29.

58. Montigny, "Le Turâth."

59. Aga Khan Award for Architecture, *Architecture and Community: Building in the Islamic World Today* (Millerton, NY: Aperture, 1983), 82.

60. Evans was a painter and mural decorator born in London, who studied at the Kingston School of Art and the Royal College of Art from 1941-1943.

61. Education in Qatar, 26 February 1985. UK National Archives, file reference QTR/601/6. Qtr/680/1.

62. Memo from William S. Beniston, 10 December 1985. UK National Archives, file reference QTR/696/2.

63. This was "Youssuf Al Qaratawi" in the archival source.

64. Qatar, General Policies, 9 February 1984. UK National Archives, file reference QTR/680/12.

65. UNESCO, "QATAR. Assistance to Member States for Preservation and Presentation of the Cultural and Natural Heritage. A General Survey and Plan for the Preservation and Presentation of Sites and Monuments. Project Findings and Recommendations." Report prepared for the Government of Qatar by F. A. Khan, Consultant to the United Nations Educational, Scientific and Cultural Organization (UNESCO). Paris, 1 March 1976. UNESCO Archives, file reference RP/1975-76/3.411.6.

66. UNESCO, "QATAR. Assistance to Member States," 10.

67. UNESCO, "QATAR. Assistance to Member States," 17. Note that the author appears to utilize the word "unveiled" incorrectly in this passage, which reads, "But, except for the collection of some surface potsherds, this field has remained neglected and the glorious Islamic traditions, which are so pre-dominant in Arab life today, remain unveiled. Needless to say, the inactivity in this direction was due to the whims of the previous archaeologists who attached greater importance to the pre-Islamic research work. It appears that Islamic sites lie buried under the debris and sand deposits. These should be explored and excavated on a priority basis."

68. Flemming Højlund, ed., *Danish Archaeological Investigations in Qatar 1956–1974* (Aarhus, Denmark: Aarhus University Press, 2017); cf. Holger Kapel, *Atlas of the Stone-Age Cultures of Qatar* (Aarhus, Denmark: Aarhus Universitetsforlag, 1967).

69. Eigil Knuth, "An Early Islamic Fort and Settlement at Murwab," in *Danish Archaeological Investigations in Qatar 1956–1974*, ed. Flemming Højlund (Aarhus, Denmark: Aarhus University Press, 2017), 83–89.

70. Beatrice De Cardi, ed., "Introduction," in *Qatar Archaeological Report: Excavations 1973*, ed. Beatrice De Cardi (Doha and Oxford: Qatar National Museum and Oxford University Press, 1978), 3.

71. Robert Bertram Serjeant, "Historical Sketch of the Gulf in the Islamic Era," in *Qatar Archaeological Report: Excavations 1973*, ed. Beatrice De Cardi (Doha and Oxford: Qatar National Museum and Oxford University Press, 1978), 147–163.

72. Jacques Tixier, *Mission archéologique française à Qatar 1976–1977, 1977–1978*, Tome 1 (Paris: CNRS, 1980); Marie-Louise Inizan, *Mission archéologique française à Qatar*, Tome 2 (Paris: Recherche sur les civilisations, 1988).

73. Masatoshi A. Konishi, Takeshi Gotoh, and Yoshihiko Akashi, "Archaeological Researches in the Gulf: A Preliminary Report of the Excavations in Bahrain and Qatar, 1987/8 Season," *Orient* (January 1988): 18–46.

74. Robert Carter, personal communication, 25 December 2016.

75. Al Meezan, Qatar Legal Portal, "Law No. 2 of 1980 on Antiquities," https://www.almeezan.qa/LawView.aspx?opt&LawID=3976&language=en, accessed 3 June 2019.

76. Daniel T. Potts, "The Gulf Arab States and Their Archaeology," in *Archaeology under Fire: Nationalism, Politics and Heritage in the Eastern Mediterranean and Middle East*, ed. Lynn Meskell (London: Routledge, 1998), 195.

77. Luis Fernandez-Galiano, "Próximo Oriente: Del Golfo a la Meca, construcciones en la arena," *Arquitectura Viva* 111 (2006): 48–49.

78. Neha Vora, *Teach for Arabia: American Universities, Liberalism, and Transnational Qatar* (Stanford, CA: Stanford University Press, 2018).

79. Hanne Nymann, "Archival Material Related to Later Islamic Al Zubarah: Qatar Islamic Archaeology and Heritage Project," in *Qatar Islamic Archaeology and Heritage Project: End of Season Report: 2011–2012*, ed. Stephen McPhillips, Sandra Rosendahl, Alan Walmsley, Paul Wordsworth, and Hanne Nymann (2012), 103–109.

80. Anie Montigny, "Les représentations du changement dans la société qatarie, d'un émir à l'autre (1972–2013)," *Arabian Humanities: Revue internationale*

d'archéologie et de sciences sociales sur la péninsule Arabique/International Journal of Archaeology and Social Sciences in the Arabian Peninsula 2 (2014), https://doi .org/10.4000/cy.2728.

81. Potts, "The Gulf Arab States," 195.

82. Montigny, "Les représentations du changement."

83. Daniel Camara and Mitra Khoubrou, "Qatar 2009: Weathering the Crisis," *Al Manakh* 2, no. 23 (2010): 151.

84. Montigny, "Les représentations du changement," 4.

85. Qatar National Vision 2030 (QNV), General Secretariat for Development Planning, Emiri Decree 44/2008. First published July 2008. https://www .qu.edu.qa/static_file/qu/students/documents/special-needs-qatar-national -vision-en.docx.

86. QNV 2030, General Secretariat for Development Planning, 1.

87. QNV 2030, General Secretariat for Development Planning, 22.

88. QNV 2030, General Secretariat for Development Planning, 20.

89. Richard Cuttler, Tobias Tonner, Faisal Abdulla Al-Naimi, Lucie Dingwall, and N. Al-Hemaidi, "The Qatar National Historic Environment Record: A Platform for the Development of a Fully-Integrated Cultural Heritage Management Application," *ISPRS Annals of the Photogrammetry, Remote Sensing and Spatial Information Sciences* Volume II-5/W1 (2013): 85–90.

90. Tammi Moe and James Onley, "The Qatar Unified Imaging Project: Revealing Qatar's Past," *Journal of Arabian Studies* 3 (2013): 278–279.

2. Modernism versus Modernization

1. Helga Graham, *Arabian Time Machine: Self-Portrait of an Oil State* (London: William Heinemann, 1978), 24.

2. This is as documented in anonymous comments in social media, online newspaper articles, and during research supporting the student-led exhibition "Heritage, Research and Art" in Education City, Doha, in September 2013.

3. Jumanah Abbas, "The Corniche: The Representation of Doha's Waterfront and Its Institutional Buildings," in *Urban Modernity in the Contemporary Gulf: Obsolescence and Opportunities*, ed. Roberto Fabbri and Sultan Sooud Al-Qassemi (London: Routledge, 2022), 138–155. Also see Sharon Nagy, "Dressing up Downtown: Urban Development and Government Public Image in Qatar," *City and Society* 12, no. 1 (2008): 142.

4. Ian Simpson, "Concern amid the Oysters as Pearling Is Honored: Nature and the Environment in Heritage Practice," in *Cultural Heritage in the Arabian Peninsula: Debates, Discourses and Practices*, ed. Karen Exell and Trinidad Rico (Farnham, UK: Ashgate, 2014), 33–49.

5. Kishwar Rizvi, "Forms of Engagement: Architectural Modernism and Heritage in the Arab Gulf States," in *Urban Modernity in the Contemporary Gulf*, ed. Roberto Fabbri and Sultan Sooud Al-Qassemi (London: Routledge, 2021), 1.

6. Doğan Kuban, "Conservation of the Historic Environment for Cultural Survival," in *Architecture and Community*, ed. Renata Holod and Darl Rastorfer (New York: Aperture, 1983), 35.

7. Klas Grinell, "Framing Islam at the World of Islam Festival, London, 1976," *Journal of Muslims in Europe* 7 (2018): 74.

8. Cf. Nasser Rabbat, "Why Is Contemporary Islamic Architecture Risking Banality?," in *Homogenisation of Representations*, ed. Modjtaba Sadria (Geneva, Switzerland: Aga Khan Award for Architecture, 2012), 113–124.

9. Graham, *Arabian Time Machine*, 19.

10. Janet Abu-Lughod, "The Islamic City—Historic Myth, Islamic Essence, and Contemporary Relevance," *International Journal of Middle East Studies* 19, no. 2 (May 1987): 172.

11. Paul Goldberger, "Architecture, Sacred Space and the Challenge of the Modern," lecture at the Chautauqua Institution, 12 August 2010. https://www.paulgoldberger.com/lectures/architecture-sacred-space-and-the-challenge-of-the-modern/.

12. Mohamed Elshahed, "Udo Kultermann's History of Arab Contemporary Architecture," in *Urban Modernity in the Contemporary Gulf: Obsolescence and Opportunities*, ed. Roberto Fabbri and Sultan Sooud Al-Qassemi (Abingdon: Routledge, 2022), 28.

13. Roberto Fabbri and Iain Jackson, "Modernity Reloaded: Architectural Practice and the Gulf Cities," *Histories of Postwar Architecture* 8, no. 5 (2021): 6.

14. Fabbri and Jackson, "Modernity Reloaded," 6.

15. See Khaled Adham, "Rediscovering the Island: Doha's Urbanity from Pearls to Spectacle," in *The Evolving Arab City: Tradition, Modernity, and Urban Development*, ed. Yasser El Sheshtaway (London: Routledge, 2008), 218–257.

16. Aminah H. Alkanderi, "The Emergence of the Arab Engineer: Saba George Shiber, Arab Consulting Engineers (ACE) and Dar al-Handasah," *Histories of Postwar Architecture* 8, no. 5 (2021): 43–68.

17. Mohammad al-Asad, *Contemporary Architecture and Urbanism in the Middle East* (Gainesville: University Press of Florida, 2012).

18. With lead architect Antony Irving.

19. Michael Rice, "National Museum of Qatar, Doha," *Museum International* 29, no. 2–3 (January/December 1977): 7. After the withdrawal of the Turks in 1916, the complex was enlarged, but by 1923, the seat of the government had moved back to the central part of Doha. The complex was already abandoned and deteriorated by the 1970s.

20. Rice, "National Museum."

21. National Museum Drawings, courtesy of architect (submitted for the Aga Khan Award for Architecture), 1980.

22. Renata Holod, *Architecture and Community: Building in the Islamic World Today. The Aga Khan Award for Architecture* (Millerton, NY: Aperture, 1983), 170.

23. National Museum (Qatar), Aga Khan Trust for Culture, Archnet. https://www.archnet.org/sites/6345#.

24. His Highness the Aga Khan, "Preface," in *Architecture and Community: Building in the Islamic World Today. The Aga Khan Award for Architecture* (Millerton, NY: Aperture, 1983), 11–13. See also Kishwar Rizvi, *The Transnational Mosque: Architecture and Historical Memory in the Contemporary Middle East* (Chapel Hill: University of North Carolina Press, 2015), 25–26.

25. Kuban, "Conservation of the Historic Environment," 33.

26. Rice, "National Museum," 81.

27. Rice, "National Museum," 83.

28. Flemming Højlund, ed., *Danish Archaeological Investigations in Qatar 1956–1974* (Aarhus, Denmark: Aarhus University Press, 2017).

29. In 2017, the Qatar Museums Authority received a digitized archive and database of the Qatar collection from the Moesgaard Museum in Denmark.

30. Jonathan Raban, *Arabia through the Looking Glass* (London: Fontana, 1980), 83.

31. Raban, *Arabia*, 90.

32. Fabbri and Jackson, "Modernity Reloaded," 7.

33. Fabbri and Jackson, "Modernity Reloaded," 7. See also Peter Chomowicz, "The Urban Imaginary in Doha, Qatar," *Histories of Postwar Architecture* 8, no. 5 (2021): 120–146.

34. Raban, *Arabia*, 95.

35. Fabbri and Jackson, "Modernity Reloaded," 4–5.

36. Rosanna Law, "The Paradox of Msheireb," *UCL Pamphleteer*, no. 4 (2014): 8.

37. Atlas Bookstore, https://www.atlasbookstore.org.

38. *Time* 82, no. 10 (6 September 1963), cover.

39. *Time* 113, no. 2 (8 January 1979), cover.

40. However, by the 1980s, historians in the United States and European Union were already speaking of postmodern architecture.

41. Architectural Record, "Interview with Philip Johnson," *Architectural Record*, 2 July 2001. https://www.architecturalrecord.com/articles/12621-interview-with -philip-johnson; also see Russell Boniface, "DC's Kreeger Museum Showcases Philip Johnson's Later Works," *AIA Architect* 15 (16 May 2008), https://info.aia .org/aiarchitect/thisweek08/0516/0516d_johnson.htm.

42. 1972 Report from the British Embassy in Qatar to the Foreign Office UK National Archives, August 1891; Chomowicz, "The Urban Imaginary," 124.

43. As in Kuwait, see Farah al-Nakib, *Kuwait Transformed: A History of Oil and Urban Life* (Stanford, CA: Stanford University Press, 2016).

44. Lewelyn-Davies, Weeks, Forestier-Walker, and Bor, State of Qatar Planning Study (London, 1972–1974); Chomowicz, "The Urban Imaginary," 122–123.

45. Chomowicz, "The Urban Imaginary," 125.

46. Chomowicz, "The Urban Imaginary," 126–127.

47. William L. Pereira & Associates, "University Road Cooperative Market-place, New District of Doha," William L. Pereira & Associates records, USC Special Collections #0326 Box 86.

48. William L. Pereira, "Thoughts on Design of Doha Hotel and Conference Center, the Doha Sheraton Hotel and Conference Center," William L. Pereira & Associates records, USC Special Collections #0326 Box 86.

49. Abbas, "The Corniche."

50. Interview with Hans Ulrich, Shumon Basar, Hisham Qaddumi, and Sophia Al Maria, "1972–1982: Spaceship Sheraton and the Making of Doha's Materplans," Global Art Forum 08 (Art Dubai, 2014), 15 March 2014. https:// www.artdubai.ae/global-art-forum-08/.

51. Raban, *Arabia*, 97.

52. Raban, *Arabia*, 96.

53. Raban, *Arabia*, 96.

54. Al-Nakib, *Kuwait Transformed*, 17.

55. Sandy Isenstadt and Kishwar Rizvi, "Modern Architecture and the Middle East: The Burden of Representation," in *Modernism and the Middle East: Architecture and Politics in the Twentieth Century*, ed. Sandy Isenstadt and Kishwar Rizvi (Seattle: University of Washington Press, 2008), 3.

56. Quoted in Fabbri and Jackson, "Modernity Reloaded," 11, referring to *Middle East Construction* (December 1984), 33.

57. Mehran Kamrava, *The Modern Middle East: A Political History since the First World War* (Berkeley: University of California Press, 2009), 402.

58. Rosanna Law and Kevin Underwood, "Msheireb Heart of Doha: An Alternative Approach to Urbanism in the Gulf Region," *International Journal of Islamic Architecture* 1, no. 1 (2012): 131–147.

59. Chomowicz, "The Urban Imaginary," 133–134.

60. Chomowicz, "The Urban Imaginary," 135.

61. Interview with I. M. Pei by Philip Jodidio, Architectour: International Contemporary Architectural Database, https://www.architectour.net/opere /opera.php?id_opera=6075&nome_opera=Museum%20of%20Islamic%20 Art%20-%20MIA&architetto=I.M.%20Pei.

62. Roberto Fabbri, "The Contextual Linkage: Visual Metaphors and Analogies in Recent Gulf Museums' Architecture," *Journal of Architecture* 27, no. 2–3 (2022): 372–397.

63. Interview with I. M. Pei.

64. Gülru Necipoğlu and Alina Payne, "Introduction," in *Histories of Ornament: From Global to Local*, ed. Gülru Necipoğlu and Alina Payne (Princeton, NJ: Princeton University Press, 2016), 3.

65. Description of the Museum of Islamic Art (MIA) in Architectour: International Contemporary Architectural Database, https://www.architectour .net/opere/opera.php?id_opera=6075&nome_opera=Museum%20of%20 Islamic%20Art%20-%20MIA&architetto=I.M.%20Pei.

66. "Qatar Creates," Qatar National Library, 27 March 2019.

67. Rem Koolhaas, "Preservation Is Overtaking Us," *Future Anterior: Journal of Historic Preservation, History, Theory, and Criticism* 1, no. 2 (2004): 1–3.

68. Jean Nouvel, National Museum of Qatar, http://www.jeannouvel.com/en /projects/musee-national-du-qatar/.

69. Chomowicz, "The Urban Imaginary," 137, 139.

70. Ibrahim Mohamed Jaidah, Transitions in Qatar's Architectural Identity, CIRS Monthly Dialogue, Center for International and Regional Studies, Georgetown School of Foreign Service in Qatar, 26 September 2016.

71. *Making Doha, 1950–1950*, National Museum of Qatar, 31 March 2019.

72. Ibrahim Mohamed Jaidah, *Qatari Style: Unexpected Interiors* (Munich: Hirmer, 2019).

73. This term is also spelled *denchel*. See Daniel Eddisford and Kirk Roberts, *Historic Building Survey Report, Origins of Doha Project: Season 2* (June 2014), 14, https://originsofdoha.wordpress.com/wp-content/uploads/2015/03/origins -of-doha-and-qatar-season-2-building-survey-report.pdf.

74. Aga Khan Development Network, Souq Waqif, 2008–2010 Cycle.

75. Mohammad Ali Abdullah (interviewed by Todd Reisz), "Making Souk Waqif: Doha, Qatar," *Al Manakh* 2, no. 23 (2010): 427–429.

76. Abdullah, "Making Souk Waqif," 427.

77. Abdullah, "Making Souk Waqif," 429.

78. Rachel Morris, "Souq Waqif, Doha's Resilient, Labyrinthine Market," BBC Travel, 3 August 2011, https://www.bbc.com/travel/article/20110802-souq -waqif-dohas-resilient-labyrinthine-market.

79. Adham, "Rediscovering the Island," 228; Sharon Nagy, *Social and Spatial Process: An Ethnographic Study of Housing in Qatar*, PhD dissertation, University of Pennsylvania, 1997, 105–115.

80. Alice Bianchi and Ferhan Sakal, "Between Heritage and Urban Development: Challenges for the Management of Cultural Heritage in Qatar," *World Heritage* 72 (June 2014): 70–75.

81. Personal communication, 17 March 2019.

82. General Secretariat for Development Planning (GSDP), *Qatar National Vision 2030* (Doha: GSDP, 2008), 3. https://www.psa.gov.qa/en/qnv1/Documents /QNV2030_English_v2.pdf. See also discussions in Karen Exell and Trinidad Rico, "'There Is No Heritage in Qatar': Orientalism, Colonialism and Other Problematic Histories," *World Archaeology* 45, no. 4 (2013): 678.

83. Msheireb Properties, "Mandate," https://www.msheirebproperties.com /msheireb-downtown-doha/about-msheireb-downtown-doha/mandate/.

84. Msheireb Properties, "Regeneration," https://www.msheirebproperties .com/msheireb-downtown-doha/about-msheireb-downtown-doha/distinction /regeneration/.

85. Ashraf M. Salama, "Intervention Urbanism: The Delicacy of Aspirational Change in the Old Centre of Doha," *UCL Pamphleteer*, no. 4 (2014): 1–2, 5.

86. Bin Jelmood House, https://msheirebmuseums.com/en/about/bin-jelmood -house/.

87. Andrew M. Gardner, *City of Strangers: Gulf Migration and the Indian Community in Bahrain* (Ithaca, NY: Cornell University Press, 2010); and Andrew M. Gardner, Silvia Pessoa, and Laura Harkness, "Migrants and Justice in Qatar: Time, Mobility, Language, and Ethnography," in *The Immigrant Other: Lived Experiences in a Transnational World*, ed. Rich Furman, Greg Lamphear, and Douglas Epps (New York: Columbia University Press, 2016), 253–265.

88. Msheireb Properties, "New Architectural Language," https://www .msheireb.com/msheireb-downtown-doha-about/the-heritage/new-architectural -language/.

89. An example of how design and marketing processes are wrongly conflated, as discussed with the design team of Msheireb: Claire Melhuish, Monica Degen, and Gillian Rose, "'The Real Modernity That Is Here': Understanding the Role of Digital Visualisations in the Production of a New Urban Imaginary at Msheireb Downtown, Doha," *City & Society* 28 (2016): 222–245.

90. William Pereira & Associates, Yanbu, William L. Pereira & Associates records, USC Special Collections #0326 Box 86.

91. *Fortune*, 13 December 1993, 39; however, the interior of the Sheraton Hotel features Islamic design prolifically in its fabrics and finishes.

3. From Mosques to Mangroves

1. Trinidad Rico, "Islam, Heritage, and Preservation: An Untidy Tradition," *Material Religion: The Journal of Objects, Art and Belief* 15, no. 2 (June 2019): 148–163.

2. Mohammed I. Ansari, "Islamic Perspectives on Sustainable Development," *American Journal of Islam and Society* 11, no. 3 (1994): 394–402.

3. Badi al-Abed, "Theory and Philosophy of Architectural Conservation and Preservation in Islamic Civilization," *Historical Kan Periodical* 3, no. 8 (2010), https://www.oalib.com/paper/2265682.

4. Fazlun M. Khalid, "Islam and the Environment," in *Encyclopedia of Global Environment Change*, ed. Peter Timmerman (Chichester, UK: John Wiley, 2002), 335.

5. Rodney Wilson, "Islam and Sustainable Economic Development," in *Sustainable Development: An Appraisal from the Gulf Region*, ed. Paul Sillitoe (New York: Berghahn, 2014), 178–194.

6. Paul Sillitoe, "Introduction: Sustainable Development in the Gulf: Some Introductory Remarks," in *Sustainable Development: An Appraisal from the Gulf Region*, ed. Paul Sillitoe (New York: Berghahn, 2014), 1.

7. Technical Report FIT/9712/QAT/90 Faculty of Science, University of Qatar, Paris, 1978.

8. Technical Report FIT/9712/QAT/90, 2.

9. John Moorehead, *In Defiance of the Elements: A Personal View of Qatar* (London: Quartet, 1977), 89.

10. Eugene Rogen, *The Arabs: A History* (New York: Basic Books, 2011), 453; Olof Linden, Arne Jernelöv, and Johanna Egerup, *The Environmental Impacts of the Gulf War 1991*, IIASA Interim Report April 2004.

11. For example, see Aylin Orbaşlı, "The Conservation of Coral Buildings on Saudi Arabia's Northern Red Sea Coast," *Journal of Architectural Conservation* 15, no. 1 (2009): 49–64.

12. Roberto Fabbri and Iain Jackson, "Modernity Reloaded: Architectural Practice and the Gulf Cities," *Histories of Postwar Architecture* 8, no. 5 (2021): 6–7.

13. Renee Richer, *Conservation in Qatar: Impacts of Increasing Industrialization*, CIRS Center for International and Regional Studies, Georgetown University School of Foreign Service in Qatar, Occasional Paper No. 2 (2008, 2009), 15.

14. "The World's Biggest Art Collector," *Forbes*, 11 May 2004, https://www.forbes.com/2004/05/11/cx_0511conn.html?sh=1d67c15a20a2 and https://www.nytimes.com/2014/11/17/arts/design/saud-bin-mohammed-al-thani-art-collector-for-qatar-is-dead.html.

15. Qatar Museums Authority, "'Adopting a Mosque' Campaign," *Restoration Newsletter* 1, no. 3, 4 (March/April 2013).

16. Qatar Museums Authority, "Heritage Maps," *Restoration Newsletter* 1, no. 2 (February 2013).

17. Qatar Museums Authority, "Heritage Maps."

18. Ashraf M. Salama and Florian Wiedmann, *Demystifying Doha: On Architecture and Urbanism in an Emerging City* (London: Routledge, 2013).

19. Mohammed Jassim al-Kholaifi, ed., *Traditional Architecture in Qatar* (Doha: Museums & Antiquities Department, National Council for Culture, Arts and Heritage, 2006).

20. Al-Kholaifi, *Traditional Architecture*, 42 (figure 7), 44 (figure 9), 43 (figure 8), 47 (plate 2).

21. Al-Kholaifi, *Traditional Architecture*, 52 (plate 3), 57, 59.

22. Qatar Museums Authority, "Progress of Abdullah Shamsan 'Al-Ruwais' Mosque Rescue Project," *Restoration Newsletter* 1, no. 2 (February 2013).

23. Qur'an (9:18) and (2:114), respectively. I am using the translation chosen by the Architectural Conservation section of Qatar Museums in their documentation, but different translations put different emphases on the relationship between a people and their mosque. For example, Arthur Arberry's translation of *Surat al-tawbah* (The Repentance) is "Only he shall inhabit God's places of worship who believes in God and the Last Day, and performs the prayer, and pays the alms, and fears none but God alone; it may be that those will be among the guided"; and for *Surat l-baqarah* (The Cow), "And who does greater evil than he who bars God's places of worship, so that His Name be not rehearsed in them, and strives to destroy them? Such men might never enter them, save in fear; for them is degradation in the present world, and in the world to come a mighty chastisement." Arthur J. Arberry, trans., *The Koran Interpreted*, 2 vols. (London: Allen & Unwin; New York: Macmillan, 1955).

24. Reyhan Sabri, "Transitions in the Ottoman Waqf's Traditional Building Upkeep and Maintenance System in Cyprus during the British Colonial Era (1878-1960) and the Emergence of Selective Architectural Conservation Practices," *International Journal of Heritage Studies* 21, no. 5 (2015): 512-527; Omnia Aboukorah, "Between a Secular Management System and International Standards of Protection: The Heritage of Cairo's Old Quarter," *Museum International* 57, no. 1-2 (May 2005): 120-128.

25. Aboukorah, "Between a Secular Management System," 123.

26. Aboukorah, "Between a Secular Management System," 126.

27. Traditional Gulf Architecture Week (22-25 April 2018, Qatar National Library).

28. Mosque across MDD Project, n.d.

29. Pamela Buxton, *Metric Handbook of Planning and Design Data* (London: Routledge, 2018), Section 27-19.

30. Velina Mirincheva, "John McAslan and Partners' Jumaa Mosque Imparts a Cultural Authenticity," *Architectural Review*, 5 April 2016, https://www.architectural-review.com/buildings/john-mcaslan-and-partners-jumaa-mosque-imparts-a-cultural-authenticity.

31. For example, Allah created seven heavens, the Qur'an is revealed in seven letters or dialects, and there are seven doors to paradise.

32. Mirincheva, "John McAslan and Partners' Jumaa Mosque."

33. US Green Building Council, *Msheireb Mosque LEED Scorecard*, 29 September 2016, https://www.usgbc.org/projects/msheireb-mosque?view=scorecard.

34. Gareth Doherty, "If It's Not Green It Will Become Invisible: A Sociological Account of a Color in Bahrain," *AlManakh* 2 (2010): 342.

35. William Gifford Palgrave, *Narrative of a Year's Journey through Central and Eastern Arabia (1862–63)* (London: Macmillan, 1866), 386.

36. John Gordon Lorimer, *Gazetteer of the Persian Gulf, 'Omān and Central Arabia, Volume I* (Calcutta: Superintendent Government Printing India, 1915), 787-835.

37. Klaus Ferdinand, *Bedouins of Qatar* (London: Thames & Hudson, 1993 [1959]), 45.

38. Jonathan Raban, *Arabia through the Looking Glass* (London: Fontana, 1980), 95.

39. Helga Graham, *Arabian Time Machine: Self-Portrait of an Oil State* (London: William Heinemann, 1978), 26.

40. Anie Montigny, "Les représentations du changement dans la société qatarie, d'un émir à l'autre (1972–2013)," *Arabian Humanities: Revue internationale d'archéologie et de sciences sociales sur la péninsule Arabique/International Journal of Archaeology and Social Sciences in the Arabian Peninsula* 2 (2014), https://doi.org/10.4000/cy.2728.

41. Syed Ahmad Iskandar Syed Ariffin, *Architectural Conservation in Islam: Case Study of the Prophet's Mosque* (Johor Bahru, Malaysia: Penerbit Universiti Teknologi Malaysia, 2005), 27.

42. Diana K. Davis, "Imperialism, Orientalism, and the Environment in the Middle East: History, Politics, Power, and Practice," in *Environmental Imaginaries of the Middle East and North Africa*, ed. Diana K. Davis and Edmund Burke III (Athens: Ohio University Press, 2011), 1–22.

43. Mari Luomi, Muhammad Bilal Shakir, John T. Crist, Bushra Alam, and Dana Qarout, "Environmental Sustainability in Education City: Green Beacon or Green Islands?," *Qatar Foundation Annual Research Forum Proceedings Volume 2012:1* (Doha: HBKU Press), https://doi.org/10.5339/qfarf.2012.EEPS9; Kristian Coates Ulrichsen, *The Gulf States in International Political Economy* (Basingstoke, UK: Palgrave Macmillan, 2016), 92.

44. Pearl-Qatar, *Earth Resources Observation and Science (EROS) Center—Earthshots*, US Geological Survey (USGS), https://eros.usgs.gov/earthshots/pearl-qatar#:˜:text=The%20Pearl%2DQatar%20is%20built,country's%20historical%20pearl%20diving%20sites.

45. UK National Archives, Qatar file 1961–1986 and file 1973–1987.

46. Richer, *Conservation in Qatar*, 2.

47. Ministry of Environment, "Initial National Communication to the United Nations Framework Convention on Climate Change," United Nations Framework Convention on Climate Change, March 2011; accessed 12 July 2016, http://unfccc.int/files/national_reports/non-annex_i_natcom/application/pdf/final_climate_change.pdf, 1, 2.

48. General Secretariat for Development Planning (GSDP), *Qatar National Vision 2030* (Doha: GSDP, 2008), https://www.psa.gov.qa/en/qnv1/Documents/QNV2030_English_v2.pdf.

49. GDSP, *Qatar National Vision 2030*, 8, 32.

50. Colin Michael Hall, Michael James, and Tim Baird, "Forests and Trees as Charismatic Mega-flora: Implications for Heritage Tourism and Conservation," *Journal of Heritage Tourism* 6, no. 4 (2011): 309–323.

51. Vernon Hilton Heywood, *Global Biodiversity Assessment* (Cambridge: Cambridge University Press, 1995), 491, 1109.

52. United Nations Framework Convention on Climate Change (UNFCCC), Subsidiary Body for Scientific and Technological Advice, "Report of the Subsidiary Body for Scientific and Technological Advice on Its Thirty-Seventh Session, Held in Doha from 26 November to 2 December 2012," in FCCC/

SBSTA/2012/5/ (Doha: United Nations Framework Convention on Climate Change, 2013).

53. Quoted on Qatar Foundation's website, The Foundation, https://www .qf.org.qa/content/20th/the-foundation-20th.

54. United Nations Framework Convention on Climate Change (UNFCCC), "Directory of Participants," Conference of the Parties First Session. 6 April 1995, accessed July 2016 http://unfccc.int/cop5/ resource/docs/cop1/inf05r02 .pdf; Sillitoe, "Introduction: Sustainable Development in the Gulf," 15.

55. Qatar General Development Secretariat for Development Planning (QGSDP), "Qatar National Development Strategy 2011–2016," Qatar General Development Secretariat for Development Planning, June 2011, accessed 14 July 2016, http://www.mdps.gov.qa/en/nds/ Documents/Qatar_NDS_reprint _complete_lowres_16May.pdf, 22.

56. QGSDP, "Qatar National Development Strategy," 229; Mari Luomi, *Qatar's Natural Sustainability: Plans, Perceptions and Pitfalls*, CIRS Occasional Paper (Doha: Center for International and Regional Studies, 2012); Wilson, "Islam and Sustainable Economic Development."

57. Gareth Doherty, *Paradoxes of Green: Landscapes of a City-State* (Oakland: University of California Press, 2017), 1.

58. Bassam T. Yasseen, "Urban Development Threatening Wild Plants in Doha City—Qatar: Ecophysiology Is a Prerequisite for Ecological Restoration," *Journal of Plant Sciences* 6 (2011): 113–123; United Nations Food and Agricultural Organization, "Qatar Country Profile," 2013, accessed 1 August 2016, http://www.fao.org/countryprofiles/index/en/?iso3=QAT.

59. *The Peninsula Qatar*, "Green Areas to Be Rehabilitated," 18 August 2016, https://thepeninsulaqatar.com/article/18/08/2016/Green-areas-to-be -rehabilitated.

60. The COMTRADE Database on International Trade reports Qatar imports of live trees, plants, bulbs, roots, and cut flowers worth around $40 million during 2021.

61. *Doha News*, "Official: Aspire Park's Funkiest Trees a Challenge to Import," 26 June 2011, https://dohanews.co/official-aspire-parks-funkiest-trees-a-challenge -to/.

62. Ibrahim Mohamed Jaidah, *Qatari Style: Unexpected Interiors* (Munich: Hirmer, 2019), 21.

63. John Norton, Sara Abdul Majid, Debbie Allan, Mohammed al-Safran, Benno Böer, and Renee Richer, *An Illustrated Checklist of the Flora of Qatar* (Gosport, UK: Browndown, 2009).

64. Second International Forum of the Qur'anic Botanic Garden, "Islamic Perspectives on Ecosystem Management: Qur'anic Botanic Garden, Member of Qatar Foundation for Education, Science and Community Development, in Collaboration with Commission on Ecosystem Management of International Union for Conservation of Nature," 22–24 April 2014. Doha, Qatar.

65. BREEAM has been the world's longest-established method of assessing, rating, and certifying the sustainability of buildings since 1990.

66. Estidama (whose name means "sustainability" in Arabic) is a green building certification system by the Abu Dhabi government.

67. Khondker Rahman, "The Qatar National Master Plan," in *Sustainable Development: An Appraisal from the Gulf Region*, ed. Paul Sillitoe (New York: Berghahn, 2014), 94.

68. The Tarsheed campaign launched on 22 April 2012 (Earth Day).

69. Wesam al-Othman and Sarah F. Clarke, "Charting the Emergence of Environmental Legislation in Qatar: A Step in the Right Direction or Too Little Too Late?," in *Sustainable Development: An Appraisal from the Gulf Region*, ed. Paul Sillitoe (New York: Berghahn, 2014), 116–132.

70. Ali A. Alraouf and Sarah F. Clarke, "From Pearling to Skyscrapers: The Predicament of Sustainable Architecture and Urbanism in Contemporary Gulf Cities," in *Sustainable Development: An Appraisal from the Gulf Region*, ed. Paul Sillitoe (New York: Berghahn, 2014), 313–342.

71. Tim Winter, "Urban Sustainability in the Arabian Gulf: Air Conditioning and Its Alternatives," *Urban Studies* 53, no. 15 (2016): 3270.

72. Traditional Gulf Architecture Week, 22–25 April 2018, Qatar National Library, Education City, Qatar.

73. For its use in Jaidah's designs, see Jochen Sokoly, *Contemporary Architectural Development in Qatar: The Work and Vision of Ibrahim Jaidah and His Design Studio* (Doha: Virginia Commonwealth University Qatar), an exhibition developed and presented by Virginia Commonwealth University School of the Arts in Qatar, 31 August–21 September 2005.

74. For example, see Winter, "Urban Sustainability in the Arabian Gulf."

75. Moorehead, *In Defiance of the Elements*, 84.

4. The Art of *Mal Lawal*

1. Jill Crystal, *Oil and Politics in the Gulf: Rulers and Merchants in Kuwait and Qatar* (Cambridge: Cambridge University Press, 1990).

2. Neha Vora, *Teach for Arabia: American Universities, Liberalism, and Transnational Qatar* (Stanford, CA: Stanford University Press, 2018), 57.

3. Crystal, *Oil and Politics*, 161.

4. Qatar, Ministry of Information, 1976, 29, quoted in Crystal, *Oil and Politics*, 162; Qatar, Ministry of Information, 1976, speeches and statements by His Highness Sheikh Khalifa Bin Hamad al-Thani.

5. Crystal, *Oil and Politics*, 163.

6. Miriam Cooke, *Tribal Modern: Branding New Nations in the Arab Gulf* (Oakland: University of California Press, 2014), 9, 172.

7. Anie Montigny, "Les représentations du changement dans la société qatarie, d'un émir à l'autre (1972–2013)," *Arabian Humanities: Revue internationale d'archéologie et de sciences sociales sur la péninsule Arabique/International Journal of Archaeology and Social Sciences in the Arabian Peninsula* 2 (2014): 12, https://doi.org/10.4000/cy.2728.

8. Sarina Wakefield, "Falconry as Heritage in the United Arab Emirates," *World Archaeology* 44, no. 2 (2012): 281.

9. Natalie Koch, "Gulf Nationalism and Invented Traditions," LSE Middle East Centre Blog, 13 August 2018, https://blogs.lse.ac.uk/mec/2018/08/03/gulf-nationalism-and-invented-traditions/; see also Natalie Koch, "Gulf Nationalism

and the Geopolitics of Constructing Falconry as a 'Heritage Sport,'" *Studies in Ethnicity and Nationalism* 15, no. 3 (2015): 522–539.

10. Montigny, "Les représentations du changement," 12.

11. UK National Archives QTR/680/12 Qatar General Policies 9 February 1984 County Policy Paper.

12. Jonathan Raban, *Arabia through the Looking Glass* (London: Fontana, 1980), 73–74, 81.

13. UK National Archives, QTR/680/13 General Policies, Narrative Review Qatar 1988/1989.

14. John Moorehead, *In Defiance of the Elements: A Personal View of Qatar* (London: Quartet, 1977).

15. Andrew Gardner, "Cosmopolitanism and Urban Space in Doha, Qatar," *Journal of Arabian Studies* 2, no. 11 (2021): 210–222.

16. *Qatar Culture Club: A Blog about Sociology, Written by Students in Doha, Qatar*, http://qatarcultureclub.blogspot.com.

17. *Catnaps: A Collection of Notes on Areas of Personal Interest*, https://catnaps.org.

18. See this discussion unfold in Farah al-Nakib, *Kuwait Transformed: A History of Oil and Urban Life* (Stanford, CA: Stanford University Press, 2016).

19. Moorehead, *In Defiance of the Elements*, 85.

20. Tim Makower, ed., *Drawing from Msheireb: Twelve Artists on a Changing Neighborhood* (London: Bloomsbury and Qatar Foundation Publishing, 2012).

21. Gardner, "Cosmopolitanism and Urban Space."

22. Makower, *Drawing from Msheireb*.

23. Makower, *Drawing from Msheireb*, 14.

24. Makower, *Drawing from Msheireb*, 15; and see Rami El Samahy and Kelly Hutzell, "In Search of Doha's Public Realm," *UCL Pamphleteer* 4 (2014): 10–12.

25. Issa M. al-Mohannadi, "Foreword," in *Drawing from Msheireb: Twelve Artists on a Changing Neighborhood*, ed. Tim Makower (London: Bloomsbury and Qatar Foundation Publishing, 2012).

26. Bonnie James, "Zubarah's Heritage List Hopes Get a Lift," *Gulf Times*, 24 March 2012.

27. *UCL Qatar: Empowering the Present, Unlocking Our Futures* (Edinburgh: UCL Qatar and Akkadia Press, 2020), 78.

28. A fourth Mal Lawal is currently being planned at the National Museum of Qatar, with a focus on the topic of gaming in the 1990s.

29. Michael Rice, "National Museum of Qatar, Doha," *Museum International* 29, no. 2–3 (January/December 1977): 81.

30. See discussions in Karen Exell, *Modernity and the Museum in the Arabian Peninsula* (Abingdon: Routledge, 2016).

31. Qatar Museums Authority, *Mal Lawal* (Doha: Bloomsbury Qatar Foundation Publishing, 2012), 9.

32. Qatar Museums Authority, *Mal Lawal*, 13.

33. Qatar Museums Authority, *Mal Lawal*, 13.

34. Peggy Loar, "Vision for Culture in the Arabian Gulf: National Identities and Emergence," in *Museums in a Global Context: National Identity, International Understanding*, ed. Jennifer W. Dickey, Samir El Azhar, and Catherine M. Lewis (Washington, DC: AAM Press, 2013), 198.

35. Helga Graham, *Arabian Time Machine: Self-Portrait of an Oil State* (London: William Heinemann, 1978), 35.

36. Louis Ibsen al-Faruqi, "Music, Musicians and Muslim Law," *Asian Music* 17, no. 1 (1985): 3–36.

37. Lisa Urkevich, *Music and Tradition of the Arabian Peninsula: Saudi Arabia, Kuwait, Bahrain, and Qatar* (New York: Routledge, 2015).

38. Qatari Songs Night Festival, 11 October 2022, https://www.moc.gov.qa /en/mcs_events/qatari-songs-night-festival-2/.

39. Colleen L. Morgan, Robert Carter, Fatma Abdel Aziz, and Mariam al-Thani, "Public Archaeology and Engagement in the Origins of Doha and Qatar Project," in *Community Heritage in the Arab Region*, ed. Arwa Badran, Shatha Abu-Khafajah, and Sarah Elliott (London: Springer, 2022), 91–108.

40. Uzma Z. Rizvi, "On Refusal (to Record)," in *Methods and Methodologies in Heritage Studies*, ed. Rachel King and Trinidad Rico (London: University College London Press, 2024), 31–34.

41. Kathryn M. Dudley, "In the Archive, in the Field: What Kind of Document Is an 'Oral History'?," in *Narrative and Genre*, ed. Mary Chamberlain and Paul Thompson (London: Routledge, 1998), 163.

42. John Arlidge, "Forget about the Price Tag: Qatar's Shekha Mayassa Is Outbidding the Art World," *London Evening Standard*, 4 October 2013, https:// www.standard.co.uk/esmagazine/forget-about-the-price-tag-qatar-s-sheikha -mayassa-is-outbidding-the-art-world-8856384.html.

43. "Hajj: Journey to the Heart of Islam" was held from 26 January to 15 April 2012; "Hajj: Journey through Art" was held from 9 October 2013 to 5 January 2014.

44. Klas Grinell, "Framing Islam at the World of Islam Festival, London, 1976," *Journal of Muslims in Europe* 7 (2018): 73–93.

45. Karen Exell, "Locating Qatar on the World Stage: Museums, Foreign Expertise and the Construction of Qatar's Contemporary Identity," in *Representing the Nation: Heritage, Museums, National Narratives, and Identity in the Arab Gulf States*, ed. Pamela Erskine-Loftus, Mariam Ibrahim al-Mulla, and Victoria Hightower (London: Routledge, 2016), 37.

46. Exell, "Locating Qatar on the World Stage," 32.

47. "Damien Hirst in Doha: They Will Come," *The Economist*, 18 October 2013, https://www.economist.com/books-and-arts/2013/10/18/they-will-come; and discussions in Serena Iervolino, "Curating Contemporary Global Art in Doha, Qatar: Anticipated 'Conversations', Undesirable Controversies and State Self-censorship," in *Curating under Pressure: International Perspectives on Negotiating Conflict and Upholding Integrity*, ed. Janet Marstine and Svetlana Mintcheva (London: Routledge, 2020), 51–71.

48. Held from 28 March to 30 June 2013 in the al-Riwaq Doha exhibition space.

49. Cf. Christiane Gruber, "Images of the Prophet Muhammad in and out of Modernity: The Curious Case of a 2008 Mural in Tehran," in *Visual Culture in the Modern Middle East*, ed. Christiane Gruber and Sune Haugbolle (Bloomington: Indiana University Press, 2013), 3–31; and see also Christine Crane, *Modernity, Wahhabi Islam, and Monarchial Power in Qatar Exhibited in Its Contemporary Art*, MA thesis, California State University, Dominguez Hills, 2017.

50. https://dohahamadairport.com/relax/art-exhibitions/lamp-bear-urs-fischer.

51. Tom Claassen, *Falcon*, Qatar Museums, https://qm.org.qa/en/visit/public-art/tom-claassen-falcon/.

52. "'Falcon' Art Installation Unveiled at HIA," *Gulf Times*, 18 July 2021, https://www.gulf-times.com/story/696795/falcon-art-installation-unveiled-at-hia.

53. "Salwa Graffiti," *FACT Qatar (Fashion, Art, Culture, Technology)* 2, no. 10 (February 2013): 31–35.

54. Fire Station, Doha, 25 March 2019.

55. Jocelyn Sage Mitchell and Scott Curtis, "Old Media, New Narratives: Repurposing Inconvenient Artifacts for the National Museum of Qatar," *Journal of Arabian Studies* 8, no. 2 (December 2018): 208–241.

56. Denis Byrne, "Western Hegemony in Archaeological Heritage Management," *History and Anthropology* 5 (1991): 273.

57. Trinidad Rico, "Heritage Failure and Its Public: Thoughts on the Preservation of Old Doha, Qatar," *Public Historian* 41, no. 1 (2019): 111–120.

58. Fadi Ahmad Yasin al-Khani, *The Important Role of Friday Mosques in Reviving the Urban Identity of Doha, Qatar*, MS thesis, Urban Planning and Design, Qatar University, January 2018, 70–71.

59. Currently, the piece is undergoing structural tests to define a conservation and installation strategy.

60. Marjorie A. Kelly, "Richard Serra, Damien Hirst and Public Art in Qatar," *Public Art Dialogue* 6, no. 2 (July 2016): 231.

61. Kelly, "Richard Serra," 238–239.

62. Mohammed Arkoun, "Present-Day Islam between Its Tradition and Globalisation," in *Intellectual Traditions in Islam*, ed. Farhad Daftary (London: I. B. Tauris, in association with the Institute of Ismaili Studies, 2000), 179–221.

63. Marwa Maziad, "Qatar: Cultivating 'the Citizen' of the Futuristic State," in *Representing the Nation: Heritage, Museum, National Narrative and Identity in the Arab Gulf States*, ed. Pamela Erskine-Loftus, Victoria Penziner Hightower, and Mariam Ibrahim al-Mulla (London: Routledge, 2016), 123–140.

64. Maziad, "Cultivating 'the Citizen,'" 127.

Conclusion

1. This dates from the first century BC to the first century AD.

2. However, see a discussion of these challenges and tensions in Alaa Alrawaibah, "Archaeological Site Management in the Kingdom of Saudi Arabia: Protection or Isolation?," in *Cultural Heritage in the Arabian Peninsula: Debates, Discourses and Practices*, ed. Karen Exell and Trinidad Rico (Farnham, UK: Ashgate, 2014), 143–156.

3. Cf. Clifford Geertz, *Islam Observed: Religious Development in Morocco and Indonesia* (Chicago: Chicago University Press, 1971), 1.

4. Geertz, *Islam Observed*, 107.

5. Karen Exell, *Modernity and the Museum in the Arabian Peninsula* (Abingdon: Routledge, 2016), 152–153.

6. Qatar Museums, "UCL Qatar to Develop New Cultural Heritage Law," *Gulf Times*, 4 October 2018, https://www.gulf-times.com/story/608233/qm-ucl -qatar-to-develop-new-cultural-heritage-law.

7. Qatar Museums, "UCL Qatar to Develop New Cultural Heritage Law."

8. Kristin A. Eggeling, "Cultural Diplomacy in Qatar: Between 'Virtual Enlargement', National Identity Construction and Elite Legitimation," *International Journal of Cultural Policy* 23, no. 6 (2017): 717.

9. Eggeling, "Cultural Diplomacy in Qatar."

10. Eggeling, "Cultural Diplomacy in Qatar," 725.

11. Eggeling, "Cultural Diplomacy in Qatar," 726.

12. Regency Travel & Tours, a Doha travel company founded in 1987, circulated in the first decade of the 2000s a series of promotional brochures that featured, in English, a selection of local sights, aptly titled "101 Things to Do in Qatar."

13. David Morgan, *The Sacred Gaze: Religious Visual Culture in Theory and Practice* (Oakland: University of California Press, 2005).

Bibliography

Abbas, Jumanah. "The Corniche: The Representation of Doha's Waterfront and Its Institutional Buildings." In *Urban Modernity in the Contemporary Gulf: Obsolescence and Opportunities*. Edited by Roberto Fabbri and Sultan Sooud Al-Qassemi, 138–155. London: Routledge, 2022.

Aboukorah, Omnia. "Between a Secular Management System and International Standards of Protection: The Heritage of Cairo's Old Quarter." *Museum International* 57, no. 1–2 (May 2005): 120–128.

Abu-Lughod, Janet. "The Islamic City—Historic Myth, Islamic Essence, and Contemporary Relevance." *International Journal of Middle East Studies* 19, no. 2 (May 1987): 172.

Adham, Khaled. "Rediscovering the Island: Doha's Urbanity from Pearls to Spectacle." In *The Evolving Arab City: Tradition, Modernity, and Urban Development*. Edited by Yasser El Sheshtaway, 218–257. London: Routledge, 2008.

Aga Khan Award for Architecture. *Architecture and Community: Building in the Islamic World Today*. Millerton, NY: Aperture, 1983.

The Aga Khan, His Highness. "Preface." In *Architecture and Community: Building in the Islamic World Today. The Aga Khan Award for Architecture*, 11–13. Millerton, NY: Aperture, 1983.

Al-Abed, Badi. "Theory and Philosophy of Architectural Conservation and Preservation in Islamic Civilization." *Historical Kan Periodical* 3, no. 8 (2010). https://www.oalib.com/paper/2265682.

Al-Asad, Mohammad. *Contemporary Architecture and Urbanism in the Middle East*. Gainesville: University Press of Florida, 2012.

Al-Faruqi, Louis Ibsen. "Music, Musicians and Muslim Law." *Asian Music* 17, no. 1 (1985): 3–36.

Alkanderi, Aminah H. "The Emergence of the Arab Engineer: Saba George Shiber, Arab Consulting Engineers (ACE) and Dar al-Handasah." *Histories of Postwar Architecture* 8, no. 5 (2021): 43–68.

Al-Khani, Fadi Ahmad Yasin. *The Important Role of Friday Mosques in Reviving the Urban Identity of Doha, Qatar*. MS thesis, Urban Planning and Design, Qatar University, January 2018.

Al-Kholaifi, Mohammed Jassim, ed. *Traditional Architecture in Qatar*. Doha: Museums & Antiquities Department, National Council for Culture, Arts and Heritage, 2006.

Allen, Loring. "OPEC Speaks Out." *Worldview* 22, no. 3 (March 1979): 41–46.

Al-Mohannadi, Issa M. "Foreword." In *Drawing from Msheireb: Twelve Artists on a Changing Neighborhood.* Edited by Tim Makower. London: Bloomsbury and Qatar Foundation Publishing, 2012.

Al-Nakib, Farah. *Kuwait Transformed: A History of Oil and Urban Life.* Stanford, CA: Stanford University Press, 2016.

Al-Othman, Wesam, and Sarah F. Clarke. "Charting the Emergence of Environmental Legislation in Qatar: A Step in the Right Direction or Too Little Too Late?" In *Sustainable Development: An Appraisal from the Gulf Region.* Edited by Paul Sillitoe, 116–132. New York: Berghahn, 2014.

Alraouf, Ali A., and Sarah F. Clarke. "From Pearling to Skyscrapers: The Predicament of Sustainable Architecture and Urbanism in Contemporary Gulf Cities." In *Sustainable Development: An Appraisal from the Gulf Region.* Edited by Paul Sillitoe, 313–342. New York: Berghahn, 2014.

Alrawaibah, Alaa. "Archaeological Site Management in the Kingdom of Saudi Arabia: Protection or Isolation?" In *Cultural Heritage in the Arabian Peninsula: Debates, Discourses and Practices.* Edited by Karen Exell and Trinidad Rico, 143–156. Farnham, UK: Ashgate, 2014.

Ansari, Mohammed I. "Islamic Perspectives on Sustainable Development." *American Journal of Islam and Society* 11, no. 3 (1994): 394–402.

Arberry, Arthur J., trans. *The Koran Interpreted,* 2 vols. London: Allen & Unwin; New York: Macmillan, 1955.

Architectural Record. "Interview with Philip Johnson." *Architectural Record,* 2 July 2001. https://www.architecturalrecord.com/articles/12621-interview-with -philip-johnson.

Ariffin, Syed Ahmad Iskandar Syed. *Architectural Conservation in Islam: Case Study of the Prophet's Mosque.* Johor Bahru, Malaysia: Penerbit Universiti Teknologi Malaysia, 2005.

Arkoun, Mohammed. "Present-Day Islam between Its Tradition and Globalisation." In *Intellectual Traditions in Islam.* Edited by Farhad Daftary, 179–221. London: I. B. Tauris, in association with the Institute of Ismaili Studies, 2000.

Arup, Ove. "Key Speech." 9 July 1970. Winchester, UK. https://www.arup.com /perspectives/publications/speeches-and-lectures/section/ove-arup-key -speech.

Bhabha, Homi K. *The Location of Culture.* London: Routledge, 1994.

Bianchi, Alice, and Ferhan Sakal. "Between Heritage and Urban Development: Challenges for the Management of Cultural Heritage in Qatar." *World Heritage* 72 (June 2014): 70–75.

Boniface, Russell. "DC's Kreeger Museum Showcases Philip Johnson's Later Works." *AIA Architect* 15 (16 May 2008). https://info.aia.org/aiarchitect /thisweek08/0516/0516d_johnson.htm.

Borde Meyer, Agnès. "Safeguarding Iran and Afghanistan: On UNESCO's Efforts in the Field of Archaeology." In *A History of UNESCO: Global Actions and Impacts.* Edited by Poul Duedahl, 300–312. New York: Palgrave Macmillan, 2016.

Bouchenaki, Mounir. "Safeguarding the Buddha Statues in Bamiyan and the Sustainable Protection of Afghan Cultural Heritage." In *The Future of the Bamiyan Buddha Statues: Heritage Reconstruction in Theory and Practice.* Edited by Masanori Nagaoka, 19–30. Paris and Kabul, Afghanistan: UNESCO; Cham, Switzerland: Springer, 2020.

Bowman, Glenn. "Introduction: Sharing the Sacra." In *Sharing the Sacra: The Politics and Pragmatics of Inter-communal Relations around Holy Places.* Edited by Glenn Bowman, 1–9. New York: Berghahn, 2012.

Brusius, Mirjam, and Trinidad Rico. "Counter-archives as Heritage Justice: Photography, Invisible Labor and Peopled Ruins." *Journal of Visual Culture* 21, no. 3 (2023): 64–92.

Buxton, Pamela. *Metric Handbook of Planning and Design Data.* London: Routledge, 2018.

Byrne, Denis. *Counterheritage: Critical Perspectives on Heritage Conservation in Asia.* London: Routledge, 2014.

Byrne, Denis. "Prospects for a Postsecular Heritage Practice: Convergences between Posthumanism and Popular Religious Practice in Asia." *Religions* 10, no. 7 (2019): 436. https://doi.org/10.3390/rel10070436.

Byrne, Denis. "Western Hegemony in Archaeological Heritage Management." *History and Anthropology* 5 (1991): 269–276.

Camara, Daniel, and Mitra Khoubrou. "Qatar 2009: Weathering the Crisis." *Al Manakh* 2, no. 23 (2010): 151.

Cameron, Christina, and Mechtild Rössler. *Many Voices, One Vision: The Early Years of the World Heritage Convention.* London: Routledge, 2013.

Chomowicz, Peter. "The Urban Imaginary in Doha, Qatar." *Histories of Postwar Architecture* 8, no. 5 (2021): 120–146.

Cooke, Miriam. *Tribal Modern: Branding New Nations in the Arab Gulf.* Oakland: University of California Press, 2014.

Crane, Christine. *Modernity, Wahhabi Islam, and Monarchial Power in Qatar Exhibited in Its Contemporary Art.* MA thesis, California State University, Dominguez Hills, 2017.

Crystal, Jill. *Oil and Politics in the Gulf: Rulers and Merchants in Kuwait and Qatar.* Cambridge: Cambridge University Press, 1990.

Cuttler, Richard, Tobias Tonner, Faisal Abdulla Al-Naimi, Lucie Dingwall, and N. Al-Hemaidi. "The Qatar National Historic Environment Record: A Platform for the Development of a Fully-Integrated Cultural Heritage Management Application." *ISPRS Annals of the Photogrammetry, Remote Sensing and Spatial Information Sciences* Volume II-5/W1 (2013): 85–90.

Davis, Diana K. "Imperialism, Orientalism, and the Environment in the Middle East: History, Politics, Power, and Practice." In *Environmental Imaginaries of the Middle East and North Africa.* Edited by Diana K. Davis and Edmund Burke III. Athens: Ohio University Press, 2011), 1–22.

De Cardi, Beatrice, ed. "Introduction." In *Qatar Archaeological Report: Excavations 1973.* Edited by Beatrice De Cardi, 3. Doha and Oxford: Qatar National Museum and Oxford University Press, 1978.

Deep, Lara, and Jessica Winegar. *Disciplining the Middle East.* Stanford, CA: Stanford University Press, 2015.

Doherty, Gareth. "If It's Not Green It Will Become Invisible: A Sociological Account of a Color in Bahrain." *AlManakh* 2 (2010): 342.

Doherty, Gareth. *Paradoxes of Green: Landscapes of a City-State.* Oakland: University of California Press, 2017.

Dudley, Kathryn M. "In the Archive, in the Field: What Kind of Document Is an 'Oral History'?" In *Narrative and Genre.* Edited by Mary Chamberlain and Paul Thompson, 160–166. London: Routledge, 1998.

Eddisford, Daniel, and Robert Carter. "The Vernacular Architecture of Doha, Qatar." *Post-Medieval Archaeology* 51, no. 1 (2017): 107–181.

Eddisford, Daniel, and Kirk Roberts. *Historic Building Survey Report, Origins of Doha Project: Season 2* (June 2014), 14. https://originsofdoha.wordpress.com/wp-content/uploads/2015/03/origins-of-doha-and-qatar-season-2-building-survey-report.pdf.

Eggeling, Kristin A. "Cultural Diplomacy in Qatar: Between 'Virtual Enlargement', National Identity Construction and Elite Legitimation." *International Journal of Cultural Policy* 23, no. 6 (2017): 717–731.

Elias, Jamal. "(Un)making Idolatry: From Mecca to Bamiyan." *Future Anterior: Journal of Historic Preservation, History, Theory and Criticism* 4, no. 2 (2007): 13–29.

El Samahy, Rami, and Kelly Hutzell. "In Search of Doha's Public Realm." *UCL Pamphleteer* 4 (2014): 10–12.

Elshahed, Mohamed. "Udo Kultermann's History of Arab Contemporary Architecture." In *Urban Modernity in the Contemporary Gulf: Obsolescence and Opportunities.* Edited by Roberto Fabbri and Sultan Sooud Al-Qassemi, 18–39. Abingdon: Routledge, 2022.

Exell, Karen. "Locating Qatar on the World Stage: Museums, Foreign Expertise and the Construction of Qatar's Contemporary Identity." In *Representing the Nation: Heritage, Museums, National Narratives, and Identity in the Arab Gulf States.* Edited by Pamela Erskine-Loftus, Mariam Ibrahim al-Mulla, and Victoria Hightower, 27–41. London: Routledge, 2016).

Exell, Karen. *Modernity and the Museum in the Arabian Peninsula.* Abingdon: Routledge, 2016.

Exell, Karen, and Trinidad Rico. "Introduction: (De)constructing Arabian Heritage Debates." In *Cultural Heritage in the Arabian Peninsula: Debates, Discourses and Practices.* Edited by Karen Exell and Trinidad Rico, 1–15. Surrey, UK: Ashgate, 2014.

Fabbri, Roberto. "The Contextual Linkage: Visual Metaphors and Analogies in Recent Gulf Museums' Architecture." *Journal of Architecture* 27, no. 2–3 (2022): 372–397.

Fabbri, Roberto, and Iain Jackson. "Modernity Reloaded: Architectural Practice and the Gulf Cities." *Histories of Postwar Architecture* 8, no. 5 (2021): 4–13.

Ferdinand, Klaus. *Bedouins of Qatar.* London: Thames & Hudson, 1993 (1959).

Fernandez-Galiano, Luis. "Próximo Oriente: Del Golfo a la Meca, construcciones en la arena." *Arquitectura Viva* 111 (2006): 48–49.

Flood, Finbarr Barry. "Between Cult and Culture: Bamiyan, Islamic Iconoclasm, and the Museum." *Art Bulletin* 84, no. 4 (2002): 641–659.

Gardner, Andrew M. *City of Strangers: Gulf Migration and the Indian Community in Bahrain.* Ithaca, NY: Cornell University Press, 2010.

Gardner, Andrew. "Cosmopolitanism and Urban Space in Doha, Qatar." *Journal of Arabian Studies* 2, no. 11 (2021): 210–222.

Gardner, Andrew M., Silvia Pessoa, and Laura Harkness. "Migrants and Justice in Qatar: Time, Mobility, Language, and Ethnography." In *The Immigrant Other: Lived Experiences in a Transnational World*. Edited by Rich Furman, Greg Lamphear, and Douglas Epps, 253–265. New York: Columbia University Press, 2016.

Geertz, Clifford. *Islam Observed: Religious Development in Morocco and Indonesia*. Chicago: Chicago University Press, 1971.

Goldberger, Paul. "Architecture, Sacred Space and the Challenge of the Modern." Lecture at the Chautauqua Institution, 12 August 2010. https://www.paulgoldberger.com/lectures/architecture-sacred-space-and-the-challenge-of-the-modern/.

Graham, Helga. *Arabian Time Machine: Self-Portrait of an Oil State*. London: William Heinemann, 1978.

Grinell, Klas. "Framing Islam at the World of Islam Festival, London, 1976." *Journal of Muslims in Europe* 7 (2018): 73–93.

Gruber, Christiane. "Images of the Prophet Muhammad in and out of Modernity: The Curious Case of a 2008 Mural in Tehran." In *Visual Culture in the Modern Middle East*. Edited by Christiane Gruber and Sune Haugbolle, 3–31. Bloomington: Indiana University Press, 2013.

General Secretariat for Development Planning (GSDP). *Qatar National Vision 2030*. Doha: GSDP, 2008. https://www.psa.gov.qa/en/qnv1/Documents/QNV2030_English_v2.pdf.

Habermas, Jürgen. "Notes on Post-Secular Society." *New Perspectives Quarterly* 25, no. 4 (Fall 2008): 17–29.

Hall, Colin Michael, Michael James, and Tim Baird. "Forests and Trees as Charismatic Mega-flora: Implications for Heritage Tourism and Conservation." *Journal of Heritage Tourism* 6, no. 4 (2011): 309–323.

Harmanşah, Ömür. "ISIS, Heritage, and the Spectacles of Destruction in the Global Media." *Near Eastern Archaeology* 78, no. 3 (2015): 170–177.

Hay, Rupert. "The Impact of the Oil Industry on the Persian Gulf Shaykhdoms." *Middle East Journal* 9, no. 4 (Autumn 1955): 361–372.

Heywood, Vernon Hilton. *Global Biodiversity Assessment*. Cambridge: Cambridge University Press, 1995.

Højlund, Flemming, ed. *Danish Archaeological Investigations in Qatar 1956–1974*. Aarhus, Denmark: Aarhus University Press, 2017.

Holod, Renata. *Architecture and Community: Building in the Islamic World Today. The Aga Khan Award for Architecture*. Millerton, NY: Aperture, 1983.

Iervolino, Serena. "Curating Contemporary Global Art in Doha, Qatar: Anticipated 'Conversations', Undesirable Controversies and State Self-censorship." In *Curating under Pressure: International Perspectives on Negotiating Conflict and Upholding Integrity*. Edited by Janet Marstine and Svetlana Mintcheva, 51–71. London: Routledge, 2020.

Inizan, Marie-Louise. *Mission archéologique française à Qatar*, Tome 2. Paris: Recherche sur les civilisations, 1988.

Irish, John. "UNESCO Chief Says U.S. Funding Cuts 'Crippling' Organization." *Reuters Science News*, 11 October 2012. https://www.reuters.com/article/us-unesco-funding/unesco-chief-says-u-s-funding-cuts-crippling-organization-idUSBRE89A0Q620121011.

Isenstadt, Sandy, and Kishwar Rizvi. "Modern Architecture and the Middle East: The Burden of Representation." In *Modernism and the Middle East: Architecture and Politics in the Twentieth Century*. Edited by Sandy Isenstadt and Kishwar Rizvi, 3–36. Seattle: University of Washington Press, 2008.

Jaidah, Ibrahim Mohamed. *Qatari Style: Unexpected Interiors*. Munich: Hirmer, 2019.

Joy, Charlotte. *The Politics of Heritage Management in Mali: From UNESCO to Djenné*. London: Routledge, 2013.

Joy, Charlotte. "UNESCO Is What? World Heritage, Militant Islam and the Search for a Common Humanity in Mali." In *World Heritage on the Ground: Ethnographic Perspectives*. Edited by Christoph Brumann and David Berliner, 60–77. London: Berghahn, 2016.

Kamrava, Mehran. *The Modern Middle East: A Political History since the First World War*. Berkeley: University of California Press, 2009.

Kapel, Holger. *Atlas of the Stone-Age Cultures of Qatar*. Aarhus, Denmark: Aarhus Universitetsforlag, 1967.

Karlström, Anna. "Spirits and the Ever-Changing Heritage." *Material Religion: The Journal of Objects, Art and Belief* 9, no. 3 (2013): 395–399.

Kelly, Marjorie A. "Richard Serra, Damien Hirst and Public Art in Qatar." *Public Art Dialogue* 6, no. 2 (July 2016): 229–240.

Khalid, Fazlun M. "Islam and the Environment." In *Encyclopedia of Global Environment Change*. Edited by Peter Timmerman. Chichester, UK: John Wiley, 2002.

Knuth, Eigil. "An Early Islamic Fort and Settlement at Murwab." In *Danish Archaeological Investigations in Qatar 1956–1974*. Edited by Flemming Højlund, 83–89. Aarhus, Denmark: Aarhus University Press, 2017.

Kobaisi, Abdulla Juma. *The Development of Education in Qatar, 1950–1977 with an Analysis of Some Educational Problems*. PhD thesis, Durham University, Durham, UK, 1979. http://etheses.dur.ac.uk/1856/.

Koch, Natalie. "Gulf Nationalism and the Geopolitics of Constructing Falconry as a 'Heritage Sport.'" *Studies in Ethnicity and Nationalism* 15, no. 3 (2015): 522–539.

Koch, Natalie. "Gulf Nationalism and Invented Traditions." LSE Middle East Centre Blog, 13 August 2018. https://blogs.lse.ac.uk/mec/2018/08/03/gulf-nationalism-and-invented-traditions/.

Konishi, Masatoshi A., Takeshi Gotoh, and Yoshihiko Akashi. "Archaeological Researches in the Gulf: A Preliminary Report of the Excavations in Bahrain and Qatar, 1987/8 Season." *Orient* (January 1988): 18–46.

Koolhaas, Rem. "Preservation Is Overtaking Us." *Future Anterior: Journal of Historic Preservation, History, Theory, and Criticism* 1, no. 2 (2004): 1–3.

Kuban, Doğan. "Conservation of the Historic Environment for Cultural Survival." In *Architecture and Community*. Edited by Renata Holod and Darl Rastorfer, 32–37. New York: Aperture, 1983.

Law, Rosanna. "The Paradox of Msheireb." *UCL Pamphleteer*, no. 4 (2014): 8–9.

Law, Rosanna, and Kevin Underwood. "Msheireb Heart of Doha: An Alternative Approach to Urbanism in the Gulf Region." *International Journal of Islamic Architecture* 1, no. 1 (2012): 131–147.

Loar, Peggy. "Vision for Culture in the Arabian Gulf: National Identities and Emergence." In *Museums in a Global Context: National Identity, International Understanding*. Edited by Jennifer W. Dickey, Samir El Azhar, and Catherine M. Lewis, 186–205. Washington, DC: AAM Press, 2013.

Lorimer, John Gordon. *Gazetteer of the Persian Gulf, 'Omān and Central Arabia, Volume I*. Calcutta: Superintendent Government Printing India, 1915.

Luomi, Mari. *Qatar's Natural Sustainability: Plans, Perceptions and Pitfalls*. CIRS Occasional Paper. Doha: Center for International and Regional Studies, 2012.

Luomi, Mari, Muhammad Bilal Shakir, John T. Crist, Bushra Alam, and Dana Qarout. "Environmental Sustainability in Education City: Green Beacon or Green Islands?" *Qatar Foundation Annual Research Forum Proceedings Volume 2012:1*. Doha: HBKU Press. https://doi.org/10.5339/qfarf.2012 .EEPS9.

Makower, Tim, ed. *Drawing from Msheireb: Twelve Artists on a Changing Neighborhood*. London: Bloomsbury and Qatar Foundation Publishing, 2012.

Maziad, Marwa. "Qatar: Cultivating 'the Citizen' of the Futuristic State." In *Representing the Nation: Heritage, Museum, National Narrative and Identity in the Arab Gulf States*. Edited by Pamela Erskine-Loftus, Victoria Penziner Hightower, and Mariam Ibrahim al-Mulla, 123–140. London: Routledge, 2016.

Melhuish, Claire, Monica Degen, and Gillian Rose. "'The Real Modernity That Is Here': Understanding the Role of Digital Visualisations in the Production of a New Urban Imaginary at Msheireb Downtown, Doha." *City & Society* 28 (2016): 222–245.

Meskell, Lynn. *A Future in Ruins: UNESCO, World Heritage, and the Dream of Peace*. Oxford: Oxford University Press, 2018.

Meskell, Lynn. "Negative Heritage and Past Mastering in Archaeology." *Anthropological Quarterly* 75, no. 3 (2002): 557–574.

Meskell, Lynn. "UNESCO's World Heritage Convention at 40: Challenging the Economic and Political Order of International Heritage Conservation." *Current Anthropology* 54, no. 4 (2013): 483–494.

Mitchell, Jocelyn Sage, and Scott Curtis. "Old Media, New Narratives: Repurposing Inconvenient Artifacts for the National Museum of Qatar." *Journal of Arabian Studies* 8, no. 2 (December 2018): 208–241.

Mirincheva, Velina. "John McAslan and Partners' Jumaa Mosque Imparts a Cultural Authenticity." *Architectural Review*, 5 April 2016. https://www. architectural-review.com/buildings/john-mcaslan-and-partners-jumaa-mosque-imparts-a-cultural-authenticity.

Moe, Tammi, and James Onley. "The Qatar Unified Imaging Project: Revealing Qatar's Past." *Journal of Arabian Studies* 3 (2013): 278–279.

Montigny, Anie. "Les représentations du changement dans la société qatarie, d'un émir à l'autre (1972–2013)." *Arabian Humanities: Revue internationale d'archéologie et de sciences sociales sur la péninsule Arabique/International Journal of Archaeology and Social Sciences in the Arabian Peninsula* 2 (2014). https://doi.org/10.4000/cy.2728.

Montigny, Anie. "Le Turâth comme Construction de l'Identité Nationale au Qatar" [Turath as Construction of National Identity in Qatar]. *Cahiers de*

Recherche Monde Arabe Contemporain, Maison de l'Orient et de la Méditerranée 6 (1998): 23-29.

Moorehead, John. *In Defiance of the Elements: A Personal View of Qatar.* London: Quartet, 1977.

Morey, Peter, and Amina Yaqin, *Framing Muslims: Stereotyping and Representation after 9/11.* Cambridge, MA: Harvard University Press, 2011.

Morgan, Colleen L., Robert Carter, Fatma Abdel Aziz, and Mariam al-Thani. "Public Archaeology and Engagement in the Origins of Doha and Qatar Project." In *Community Heritage in the Arab Region.* Edited by Arwa Badran, Shatha Abu-Khafajah, and Sarah Elliott, 91-108. London: Springer, 2022.

Morgan, David. *The Sacred Gaze: Religious Visual Culture in Theory and Practice.* Oakland: University of California Press, 2005.

Morris, Rachel. "Souq Waqif, Doha's Resilient, Labyrinthine Market." BBC Travel, 3 August 2011. https://www.bbc.com/travel/article/20110802-souq-waqif -dohas-resilient-labyrinthine-market.

Nagy, Sharon. "Dressing up Downtown: Urban Development and Government Public Image in Qatar." *City and Society* 12, no. 1 (2008): 125-147.

Nagy, Sharon. *Social and Spatial Process: An Ethnographic Study of Housing in Qatar.* PhD dissertation, University of Pennsylvania, 1997.

Necipoğlu, Gülru, and Alina Payne. "Introduction." In *Histories of Ornament: From Global to Local.* Edited by Gülru Necipoğlu and Alina Payne, 1-6. Princeton, NJ: Princeton University Press, 2016.

Norton, John, Sara Abdul Majid, Debbie Allan, Mohammed al-Safran, Benno Böer, and Renee Richer. *An Illustrated Checklist of the Flora of Qatar.* Gosport, UK: Browndown, 2009.

Nymann, Hanne. "Archival Material Related to Later Islamic Al Zubarah: Qatar Islamic Archaeology and Heritage Project." In *Qatar Islamic Archaeology and Heritage Project: End of Season Report: 2011–2012.* Edited by Stephen McPhillips, Sandra Rosendahl, Alan Walmsley, Paul Wordsworth, and Hanne Nymann, 103-109 (2012).

Orbaşlı, Aylin. "The Conservation of Coral Buildings on Saudi Arabia's Northern Red Sea Coast." *Journal of Architectural Conservation* 15, no. 1 (2009): 49-64.

Palgrave, William Gifford. *Narrative of a Year's Journey through Central and Eastern Arabia (1862–63).* London: Macmillan, 1866.

Pollock, Susan, and Reinhard Bernbeck. "Introduction." In *Archaeologies of the Middle East: Critical Perspectives.* Edited by Susan Pollock and Reinhard Bernbeck, 1-10. Malden, MA: Blackwell, 2005).

Potts, Daniel T. "The Gulf Arab States and Their Archaeology." In *Archaeology under Fire: Nationalism, Politics and Heritage in the Eastern Mediterranean and Middle East.* Edited by Lynn Meskell, 189-199. London: Routledge, 1998.

Qatar Museums Authority. *Mal Lawal.* Doha: Bloomsbury Qatar Foundation Publishing, 2012.

Raban, Jonathan. *Arabia through the Looking Glass.* London: Fontana, 1980.

Rabbat, Nasser. "Why Is Contemporary Islamic Architecture Risking Banality?" In *Homogenisation of Representations*. Edited by Modjtaba Sadria, 113–124. Geneva, Switzerland: Aga Khan Award for Architecture, 2012.

Rahman, Khondker. "The Qatar National Master Plan." In *Sustainable Development: An Appraisal from the Gulf Region*. Edited by Paul Sillitoe, 82–96. New York: Berghahn, 2014.

Reisz, Todd. "Making Souk Waqif: Doha, Qatar" (interview of Mohammad Ali Abdullah). *Al Manakh* 2, no. 23 (2010): 427–429.

Rice, Michael. "National Museum of Qatar, Doha." *Museum International* 29, no. 2–3 (January/December 1977): 78–87.

Richer, Renee. *Conservation in Qatar: Impacts of Increasing Industrialization*. CIRS Center for International and Regional Studies, Georgetown University School of Foreign Service in Qatar, Occasional Paper No. 2 (2008, 2009).

Rico, Trinidad. *Constructing Destruction: Heritage Narratives in the Tsunami City*. London: Routledge, 2016.

Rico, Trinidad. *Global Heritage, Religion, and Secularism*. Cambridge: Cambridge University Press, 2021.

Rico, Trinidad. "Heritage Failure and Its Public: Thoughts on the Preservation of Old Doha, Qatar." *Public Historian* 41, no. 1 (2019): 111–120.

Rico, Trinidad. "Heritage Preservation in Religious Landscapes: Disciplinary Challenges for the Middle East and North Africa." *Archaeological Dialogues* 28, no. 2 (2021): 111–120.

Rico, Trinidad. "Islam, Heritage, and Preservation: An Untidy Tradition." *Material Religion: The Journal of Objects, Art and Belief* 15, no. 2 (June 2019): 148–163.

Rico, Trinidad. "Muslim Heritage Preservation Stewardship under UNESCO." Special Issue, "UNESCO World Heritage at 50: What Future for the Past?" *Change over Time* 11, no. 2 (2022): 182–199.

Rico, Trinidad, and Rim Lababidi. "Extremism in Contemporary Heritage Debates about Islam." *Future Anterior: Journal of Historic Preservation History, Theory, and Criticism* 14, no. 1 (Summer 2017): 95–105.

Rizvi, Kishwar. "Forms of Engagement: Architectural Modernism and Heritage in the Arab Gulf States." In *Urban Modernity in the Contemporary Gulf*. Edited by Roberto Fabbri and Sultan Sooud Al-Qassemi, 1–5. London: Routledge, 2021.

Rizvi, Kishwar. "It's Harder Than Ever to Teach Islamic Art—But Never More Important." *Washington Post*, 6 January 2017. https://www.washingtonpost .com/posteverything/wp/2017/01/06/its-harder-than-ever-to-teach-islamic -art-but-never-more-important/.

Rizvi, Kishwar. *The Transnational Mosque: Architecture and Historical Memory in the Contemporary Middle East*. Chapel Hill: University of North Carolina Press, 2015.

Rizvi, Uzma Z. "On Refusal (to Record)." In *Methods and Methodologies in Heritage Studies*. Edited by Rachel King and Trinidad Rico, 31–34. London: University College London Press, 2024.

Rogen, Eugene. *The Arabs: A History*. New York: Basic Books, 2011.

Rosen, Lawrence. "Proceeding of the Doha Conference of 'Ulama on Islam and Cultural Heritage. Doha, Qatar. December 30-31, 2001. Pp 73 in English and Arabic each. New York: UNESCO, 2005." *International Journal of Cultural Property* 15 (2008): 101-103.

Rots, Aike P. "World Heritage, Secularisation, and the New 'Public Sacred' in East Asia." *Journal of Religion in Japan* 8, no. 1/3 (2019): 151-178.

Sabri, Reyhan. "Transitions in the Ottoman Waqf's Traditional Building Upkeep and Maintenance System in Cyprus during the British Colonial Era (1878-1960) and the Emergence of Selective Architectural Conservation Practices." *International Journal of Heritage Studies* 21, no. 5 (2015): 512-527.

Salama, Ashraf M. "Intervention Urbanism: The Delicacy of Aspirational Change in the Old Centre of Doha." *UCL Pamphleteer*, no. 4 (2014): 1-2.

Salama, Ashraf M., and Florian Wiedmann. *Demystifying Doha: On Architecture and Urbanism in an Emerging City*. London: Routledge, 2013.

"Salwa Graffiti." *FACT Qatar (Fashion, Art, Culture, Technology)* 2, no. 10 (February 2013): 31-35.

Schildgen, Brenda D. *Heritage or Heresy: Preservation and Destruction of Religious Art and Architecture in Europe*. New York: Palgrave, 2008.

Serjeant, Robert Bertram. "Historical Sketch of the Gulf in the Islamic Era." In *Qatar Archaeological Report: Excavations 1973*. Edited by Beatrice De Cardi, 147-163. Doha and Oxford: Qatar National Museum and Oxford University Press, 1978.

Shatanawy, Mirjam. "Curating against Dissent: Museums and the Public Debate on Islam." In *Political and Cultural Representations of Muslims: Islam in the Plural*. Edited by Christopher Flood, Stephen Hutchings, Galina Miazhevich, and Henri Nickels, 177-192. Leiden, Netherlands: Brill, 2012.

Sillitoe, Paul. "Introduction: Sustainable Development in the Gulf: Some Introductory Remarks." In *Sustainable Development: An Appraisal from the Gulf Region*. Edited by Paul Sillitoe, 1-37. New York: Berghahn, 2014.

Simpson, Ian. "Concern amid the Oysters as Pearling Is Honored: Nature and the Environment in Heritage Practice." In *Cultural Heritage in the Arabian Peninsula: Debates, Discourses and Practices*. Edited by Karen Exell and Trinidad Rico, 33-49. Farnham, UK: Ashgate, 2014.

Sokoly, Jochen. *Contemporary Architectural Development in Qatar: The Work and Vision of Ibrahim Jaidah and His Design Studio*. Doha: Virginia Commonwealth University Qatar. An exhibition developed and presented by Virginia Commonwealth University School of the Arts in Qatar, 31 August-21 September 2005.

Stein, Deborah. *The Hegemony of Heritage: Ritual and the Record in Stone*. Berkeley: University of California Press, 2018.

Stovel, Herb. "Conserving the Sacred: Special Challenges for World Heritage Sites." *World Heritage Review* 51 (2008): 26-33.

Tanyieri-Erdemir, Tuğba. "Historical Trajectories, Institutional Particularities: The Funding Regime for Religious Heritage in Turkey." In *Funding Religious Heritage*. Edited by Anne Fornerod, 213-226. Farnham, UK: Ashgate, 2015.

Tixier, Jacques. *Mission archéologique française à Qatar 1976-1977, 1977-1978*, Tome 1. Paris: CNRS, 1980.

Tsivolas, Theodosios. "The Legal Foundations of Religious Cultural Heritage Protection." *Religions* 10, no. 283 (2019). https://doi.org/10.3390/rel10040283.

UCL Qatar: Empowering the Present, Unlocking Our Futures. Edinburgh: UCL Qatar and Akkadia Press, 2020.

Ulrichsen, Kristian Coates. *The Gulf States in International Political Economy.* Basingstoke, UK: Palgrave Macmillan, 2016.

United Nations Educational, Scientific, and Cultural Organization (UNESCO). "Conservation Completed on Lion of Al-lāt Statue from Ancient City of Palmyra, Damaged by ISIL." *UNESCO News,* 5 October 2017. https://whc.unesco.org/en/news/1727.

United Nations Educational, Scientific, and Cultural Organization (UNESCO). "Interview with H. E. Sheikha Al Mayassa Bint Hamad Bin Khalifa Al Thani." *World Heritage* 72 (June 2014): 6–7.

United Nations Educational, Scientific, and Cultural Organization (UNESCO). *Proceedings of the Doha Conference of 'Ulama on Islam and Cultural Heritage. Doha, Qatar. December 30–31, 2001.* New York: UNESCO, 2005.

United Nations Educational, Scientific, and Cultural Organization (UNESCO). "Qatar Development Fund Boosts UNESCO Heritage Emergency Fund." *UNESCO News,* 8 December 2015. http://whc.unesco.org/en/news/1403.

United Nations Educational, Scientific, and Cultural Organization (UNESCO), "Reconstruction of World Heritage Mausoleums Starts in Timbuktu (Mali)." *UNESCO News,* 14 March 2014. https://whc.unesco.org/en/news/1112.

United Nations Educational, Scientific, and Cultural Organization (UNESCO). "Statement from the Chairperson of the World Heritage Committee." *UNESCO News,* 31 March 2011. https://whc.unesco.org/en/news/735.

United Nations Educational, Scientific, and Cultural Organization (UNESCO). "UNESCO Announces the Bamiyan Cultural Centre Design Competition." *UNESCO News,* 16 November 2014. https://whc.unesco.org/en/news/1198.

United Nations Educational, Scientific, and Cultural Organization (UNESCO). "UNESCO Director-General Condemns Destruction to the Museum of Islamic Art in Cairo, Egypt." *UNESCO News,* 24 January 2014. https://whc.unesco.org/en/news/1081.

United Nations Educational, Scientific, and Cultural Organization (UNESCO). "UNESCO Hosts First International Coordination Meeting for the Recovery of Aleppo's Heritage." *UNESCO News,* 9 March 2017. https://whc.unesco.org/en/news/1639.

United Nations Educational, Scientific, and Cultural Organization (UNESCO). "World Heritage Committee Meeting Opens in Doha." *UNESCO News,* 15 June 2014. https://whc.unesco.org/en/news/1143.

Urkevich, Lisa. *Music and Tradition of the Arabian Peninsula: Saudi Arabia, Kuwait, Bahrain, and Qatar.* New York: Routledge, 2015.

Vora, Neha. *Teach for Arabia: American Universities, Liberalism, and Transnational Qatar.* Stanford, CA: Stanford University Press, 2018.

Wakefield, Sarina. "Falconry as Heritage in the United Arab Emirates." *World Archaeology* 44, no. 2 (2012): 280–290.

Wild, Robert, Christopher McLeod, and Peter Valentine. *Sacred Natural Sites: Guidelines for Protected Area Managers.* Gland, Switzerland: International Union for Conservation of Nature (IUCN), 2008.

Wilson, Rodney. "Islam and Sustainable Economic Development." In *Sustainable Development: An Appraisal from the Gulf Region.* Edited by Paul Sillitoe, 178–194. New York: Berghahn, 2014.

Winter, Tim. "Urban Sustainability in the Arabian Gulf: Air Conditioning and Its Alternatives." *Urban Studies* 53, no. 15 (2016): 3264–3278.

Wong, Laura E. "Relocating East and West: UNESCO's Major Project on the Mutual Appreciation of Eastern and Western Cultural Values." *Journal of World History* 19, no. 3 (2008): 349–374.

Yasseen, Bassam T. "Urban Development Threatening Wild Plants in Doha City–Qatar: Ecophysiology Is a Prerequisite for Ecological Restoration." *Journal of Plant Sciences* 6 (2011): 113–123.

Index

www.ingramcontent.com/pod-product-compliance
Lightning Source LLC
Chambersburg PA
CBHW020442100426

42812CB00036B/3423/J